unladylike

A FiELD GUiDE TO
SMASHiNG the PATRiARChY
and CLAiMiNG YOUR SPACE

unladylike

CRiSTEN CONGER and CAROLiNE ERViN

illustrated by TYLER FEDER

TEN SPEED PRESS
California | New York

contents

patriarchy says behave

Ladyhood was a real bitch in her heyday. Two centuries ago, white-ladies-only public spaces abounded to protect them from rubbing elbows with working-class women and other deplorables. There were ladies' horses, lounges, boat cabins, railway cars, colleges, and courtroom galleries. They even had their own dessert—lady cakes—made with rose water and a dash of entitlement. Oh, girl.

"Respect for woman, the much lauded chivalry of the Middle Ages, meant what I fear it still means . . . that supercilious caste spirit in America, which cynically assumes, 'A Negro woman cannot be a lady,'" Anna Julia Cooper wrote in her groundbreaking 1892 essay collection, *A Voice From the South*. Born to a black mother and a white slave owner, Cooper was among the vanguard of black feminist organizing of the time, which W. E. B. DuBois described as "at once both the lever and the fulcrum for uplifting the race."[1]

That racist reality of whites-only ladyhood also galvanized activist Ida B. Wells to pursue journalism full time, wielding the power of the pen and her voice to publicize the brutalities of lynchings and sexual violence perpetrated against African Americans in the Jim Crow South. In 1883, Wells had seated

unladylike: (adj.)
1) behaving in a manner that figuratively and/or literally flips off patriarchal subordination, silencing, and sexual double standards
2) foregoing discriminatory privileges while pursuing compassionate, thriving, self-defined lives
3) patriarchy's go-to gender citation for doing womanhood wrong

patriarchy: (noun) men-on-top social hierarchy characterized by fragile masculinity, imposed maternity, and male sexual entitlement

smash the patriarchy: (verb) to flex unladylike persistence for the resistance

herself in a ladies' train car since there wasn't a designated blacks-only car. But when the conductor noticed her, he attempted to physically remove her. Wells later recounted in her autobiography:

> "... the moment he caught hold of my arm I fastened my teeth in the back of his hand. I had braced my feet against the seat in front and was holding to the back, and as he had already been badly bitten he didn't try it again by himself. He went forward and got the baggageman and another man to help him and of course they succeeded in dragging me out."

Afterward, Wells sued the railroad company and won. But when the railroad appealed the decision, the Tennessee Supreme Court overturned the previous ruling on account of Wells' "unladylike persistence." She lived up to the judge's verdict, too, agitating against murderous white supremacy and traveling around the US organizing black women into clubs that could band together to create community and support networks.

Patriarchy's Dreamgirls

By the 1900s, the industrial revolution, capitalism, and urbanism had remodeled the home as husbands' moral refuge from the sinful world where they nobly toiled to provide for wives and children—and pay for occasional brothel visits. Whatever disappointments or venereal diseases befell them, men could return home to a place where *they* always knew best. Ladies got a new, middle-class role model to match, a feminine foil to masculine lust. Idolized in popular ladymags like *Godey's Lady's Book*, the True Woman was expected to want for nothing more than to please and be pleasant, embodying the top-four most desirable traits that turned ordinary gals into wife material.

1. **Piety:** Assigning faith to the fairer sex offered ladies safe intellectual exercise through reading the Bible and gave them another male figure to obey when the man of the house was away. "Religion is exactly what a woman needs," *The Ladies Repository* magazine advised readers circa 1860, "for it gives her that dignity that best suits her dependence."

2. **Purity:** Listen up, ladies. Sex with anyone but husbands and desirous of anything beyond pleasing him and making babies is a one-way ticket to despair, destitution, insanity, and possibly death. So . . . masturbation? Nope. Keep your hands where we can see 'em.

3. **Submissiveness:** Y'all know that tired sitcom trope of the level-headed wife who bites her tongue while her dopey husband does something foolish . . . *again?* That characterization reads like a modern update on Victorian True Womanhood, which urged women to submit to their husbands and always let him think he's right.

4. **Domesticity:** What more could a True Woman ask for than a loving-ish husband and homefires to tend? Children, duh. Being a wife is all right, but fullest expression of womanhood is motherhood.

But as the twentieth century crept closer, headstrong gals were losing interest in patriarchy's prewritten gender scripts. Suffragist and women's historian Matilda Joslyn Gage was one such rebel, and in 1893, she published *Woman, Church and State*, which essentially predicted modern feminism. The system of oppression she called the Patriarchate was a result of organized religion—Christianity specifically—and government working together against women, and it was evident in everything from witch hunts to rape to the denial of property rights and the vote. Together, church and state upheld a misogynistic system, blaming women for sin and using Eve's curse as an excuse to hold all women down—and eventually tax tampons as luxury goods.

MATILDA JOSLYN GAGE

Women's Libbers wanted ladyhood to burn like bras. On March 18, 1970, dozens of feminists marched to the Manhattan office of the *Ladies Home Journal* and demanded the male editor-in-chief resign and promote the female managing editor in his place. The sit-in was largely a publicity stunt to draw attention to how ladymags reduced women to their beauty insecurities, shopping habits, and housewifery. The magazine made the promotion . . . three years later. Even as the gender revolution cooled in the 1980s and 1990s, academics and media outlets deemed *lady* an outdated honorific—until millennial gals later adopted her as slang.

But so long as patriarchy exists, that l-word has staying power; look no further than aspirational lifestyles of "effortless," upscale femininity. As her favored figure, fashions, and baked goods have evolved for better Instagram angles, ladyhood has also lived on through twenty-first century pastimes like slut shaming, skin lightening, body hating, wage skimping, waist nipping, racial profiling, victim blaming, poverty moralizing, motherhood penalizing, non-motherhood double penalizing, sex stigmatizing, and gender policing. In other words, ladies may seem gone, but they're far from forgotten. Constructed from classism, anchored in white supremacy, and reinforced by rape culture, ladyhood was built to last.

Get Unladylike

Regardless of who we are, what we look like, and how many advantages life has dropped in our laps, none of us is immune to patriarchy's ladylike claptrap. Guys get entitlement, gals get objectified, and nonbinary folks get dehumanized and worse. Like a broken record, women are still incentivized to be sexy (but not slutty), beauty-conscious (but not vain), motherly (but not smothering), and presidential (but not mannish). If we don't care to dare those tightropes? How selfish. So shrill. Just sad. Regardless of whether men are literally in charge, we all can internalize sexist preferences and put-downs like a contact high—or low.

Once you spot sexist species, summon patience. It might take more time, headspace, and digging to figure out where it came from and why it won't just die already. That's why this guide exists! The only women patriarchy fears more than unladylike women are *persistent* unladylike women. We're flies in the ointment, harpies at the frat house, and pussies grabbing back. Likeability, attractiveness, and class aren't our currencies, but we're far from bankrupt. So long as we're gutsy enough to get loud, loose, and livid, unladylike witches do what it takes to smash the patriarchy that stands in our way.

At its core, this is a field guide to the patriarchal creepy crawlies that stand between you and the autonomous, safe, compassionate person you were put on this planet to be. To be clear, this isn't about magical makeovers (though we love a good makeover montage). Our unladylike feminism in action applies to all major facets of our lives: brains, bodies, besties, wardrobes, work goals, wife roles, hookups, and f*ckups. No space is exempt, or topic taboo.

We'll reveal modern patriarchy's many disguises and what to do when its influencing, privileging, and profiteering slithers into your home, school, work, and even your mirror. You'll pick up some practical feminist life hacks as well as tips for detoxing from the sexist myths, mindsets, and stereotypes culture constantly force-feeds us. Exactly what that means will be different for everyone. Maybe you'll smash a stiletto through glass ceilings, cure Silicon Valley sexism, or volunteer for a rape crisis hotline—who knows? By the time we've arrived on the last page, we'll have mapped out a ready-to-go battle plan for finding your tribe, rising up, and pushing back *together*.

That includes us, your authors, Cristen and Caroline. We've likewise found ourselves in all sorts of anxious quicksand, booby traps, and oops-I-did-it-again mudslides. We've been bad feminists, catty coworkers, and crazy ex-girlfriends. It happens. We also understand firsthand how easy it is to feel decidedly *un*exceptional, *un*worthy, and *un*hopeful about our potential to make the inside-out change we want to see in ourselves the environments around us. That's why it's our mission to present social justice self-help as intersectionally as possible, make clear the limits of our firsthand perspectives, and stay grounded in the truth that we're all works in progress.

We've been obsessively researching and podcasting about all things gender and feminism for the better part of a decade, and despite witnessing all sorts of rapid progress, there's been no handy guide that holistically addresses what top-to-bottom, brains-to-butt-hair, inclusive feminist living can look like regardless of who you are. *Unladylike* is the hell-raising how-to y'all deserve—the one we wish we'd had while learning to crawl as baby feminists years ago, fresh out of college and sideswiped by professional sexism. We've packed it with judgment-free, age-unrestricted, gender-creative perspectives and pro-tips for adventurous, compassionate, and inclusive womaning and non-binary-ing. Let's go.

21st-century patriarchy & you: a flowchart

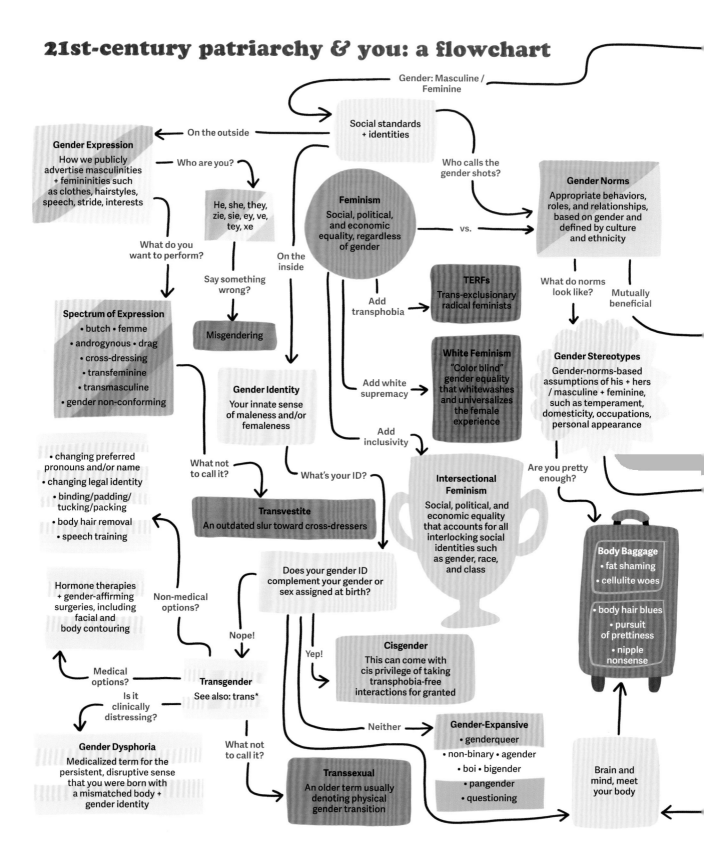

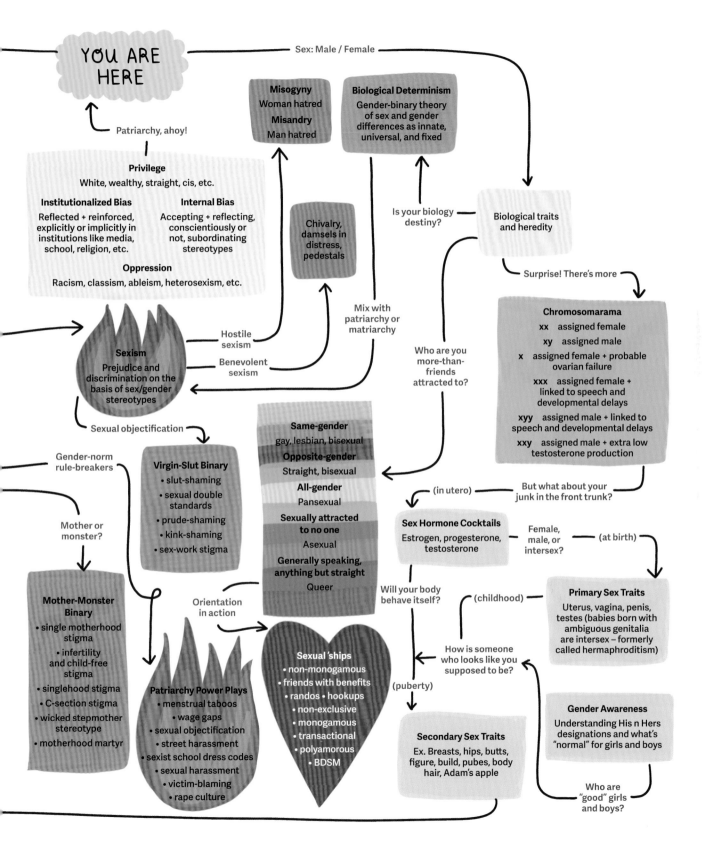

unladylike field kit packing list

Like any good choose-your-own-adventure plot, patriarchy comes with all sorts of booby traps, obstacles, and swamp monsters. So, before we shove off, here are some travel essentials we will need in our feminist fanny packs. Keep an eye out: Throughout this field guide, you'll find corresponding markers that serve as shorthand reminders for when to break out your tools.

 ## Intersectional Binoculars

As we step out on our journeys, it's imperative we toss out our binary bifocals and put an **intersectionality framework** in our sightlines. All of us, from all walks of life, have multiple layers of identity: race, ethnicity, gender, sexual orientation, professional and socioeconomic status, age, ability, religion, political affiliations, and so on. Some layers, like whiteness and ability, come with social benefits, or **privileges**. Others, like poverty and transgender identity, come with the additional challenge of social discrimination.

For a glimpse of how intersectionality works, imagine our overlapping identities—like gender, race, class, and sexuality—as Instagram filters that color and contour how we perceive the status quo, and how it perceives us right back. Now envision swiping through those individual filters to see which of your features and traits sharpen or fade with each one. Then overlay them, one on top of the other. What picture of you emerges? What identities do others see first, versus what you see first? You might be surprised how much has been hiding in plain sight all along.

In her groundbreaking scholarship on intersectionality, UCLA law professor and leading race theorist Kimberlé Williams Crenshaw underscores how "the goal . . . should be to facilitate the inclusion of marginalized groups for whom it can be said: 'When they enter, we all enter.'"[2]

It would take stacks of field guides to cover every square inch of how our smorgasbord of identities can bend and buckle with our circumstances at any given time. Families, finances, learning disabilities, athleticism, Wi-Fi connectivity—so many variables can shape our personal definitions of an unladylike life that's guided by social consciousness, not status consciousness.

up close and intersectional

To understand how intersectionality works, take a stroll through the social prisms that shape your own personhood. Whether we notice it or not, our identities come with stereotypes, respectability standards, and constant surveillance of whether we make or break the ladylike mold. How would your class affect you differently if your gender identity was different? How does your sexual orientation collide with gender rules? Asking yourself these kinds of questions can reveal deeper truths about yourself and also bulk up your empathy.

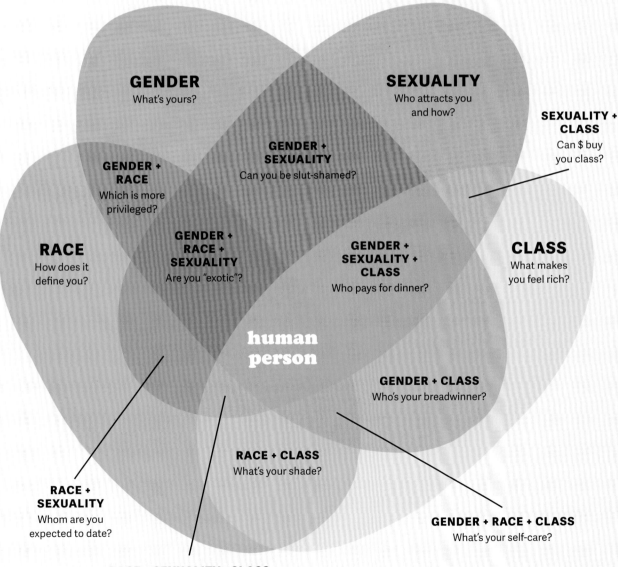

GENDER
What's yours?

SEXUALITY
Who attracts you and how?

SEXUALITY + CLASS
Can $ buy you class?

GENDER + SEXUALITY
Can you be slut-shamed?

GENDER + RACE
Which is more privileged?

RACE
How does it define you?

GENDER + RACE + SEXUALITY
Are you "exotic"?

GENDER + SEXUALITY + CLASS
Who pays for dinner?

CLASS
What makes you feel rich?

human person

GENDER + CLASS
Who's your breadwinner?

RACE + CLASS
What's your shade?

RACE + SEXUALITY
Whom are you expected to date?

GENDER + RACE + CLASS
What's your self-care?

RACE + SEXUALITY + CLASS
Trophy wife or gold digger?

The bottom line is that we, as humans, can no longer be understood as simply one-dimensional "women" and "men," but as individuals with myriad layers of identity, some attached to privilege and others to persecution. And in order to champion equality for the privileged and oppressed alike, our feminisms *must* be intersectional. Full stop. For as civil rights rabble-rouser Fannie Lou Hamer put it, "Nobody's free until everybody's free."

Spectrum-o-Meter

Ladylike compasses point in only two directions: boy or girl. Ho-hum. Male-identified men are expected to look recognizably masculine, and female-identified women are taught to act and doll up in a feminine way. Patriarchy only dignifies cisgender, hetero, monogamous—and preferably married—relationships as family. It defines sex as exclusively penis-in-vagina intercourse. We call bullsh*t. Spectrums of gender and sexuality await if we look beyond these binaries to the dazzling, full scope of human expression. To live unladylike, we've gotta buck the binary and make space for the spectrum to shine.

Pocket Privilege Checker

To activate it, ask yourself this: What do you have that you didn't earn? That simple question led white Wellesley professor Peggy McIntosh to coin the theory of **white privilege** in a groundbreaking 1988 paper. Even McIntosh started out on the defensive, not fully convinced she was part of the problem. If she was "nice" to black women, she thought, how could she be oppressive? "I came to this dawning realization," McIntosh told the *New Yorker* in 2014, "niceness has nothing to do with it."[3]

It's impossible to live a completely bias-free life. But if you find yourself advocating for folks who look just like you at the expense of those who don't, pump the brakes and ask yourself why. It could be racism, classism, ageism, ableism, colorism, and so on—inequalities come in all sorts of disguises. Become aware of your privileges and check them before they wreck your good intentions.

Checking your privilege isn't a single step like marking a box; rather, it's the focal point for realigning your thoughts and actions. Sure, being aware of the privileges you carry—and those the people around you might not—might make you more sensitive and less likely to stick your foot in your mouth when it comes to recognizing and discussing your differences. But awareness also promotes allyship. It takes you on the path of thinking beyond your own circumstances and educating yourself about others' realities so you can find ways to use your position to boost the voices and concerns of your marginalized peers rather than talking over them.

Self-Worth Swiss Army Knife

What *can't* a solid sense of self-worth do for you on your feminist journey? Owning our personal value, dignity, and worth is a cornerstone of the entire feminist movement. It takes self-worth, after all, to name and claim what we're due. Toned-up self-worth mentally buffers us from depression, sustains our focus, and emboldens us to shut out the haters, hear beyond the bullies, and give a giant middle finger to sexists who try to silence us.

Accessing your Self-Worth Swiss Army Knife requires separating the truth of who you are from the projections others put on you. When your self-worth is based on your internal strengths, virtues, and values rather than on fleeting forces like popularity, good hair days, and Instagram likes, it leaves less room for other people to try to define you. Even the ancient Greeks argued that knowing yourself is caring for yourself—it's part of your development as an ethical human. Granted, they also "diagnosed" unladylike women with hysteria, but we'll get to that later.

Comfy Shoes

Firsts are fun to celebrate, but genuine progress takes time—we need to be in it for the long haul. Fact is, there's no silver bullet for smashing the patriarchy. We've marched across Washington and Warsaw, Bangkok and Buenos Aires, Christchurch and Cape Town, and while we've scored some victories and brought our message and enthusiasm back to our neighborhoods, major battles still lie ahead. Come for the feminist marches through the streets and stay for the day-to-day activism and camaraderie.

Language Log

Speech and expression are the greatest powers we possess against self-doubt, sexism, and stigma. But there's more to it than mouthing off. Choose your words responsibly, communicate with compassion, and don't be afraid to innovate. Before the 1970s, for instance, sexual harassment and domestic violence went virtually unpunished because feminist lawyers hadn't invented those terms to name the problems. In the 1980s, not only did LGBTQ activists start reclaiming *queer*, but the 1990s group Queer Nation also imbued it with the positive rallying cry of, "We're here! We're queer! Get used to it!" Likewise, if you hear folks' identities described in ways that are unfamiliar, don't make them do the work of explaining—do *them* the unladylike solid of Googling it first.

Backlash Umbrella

Here's the rain on our liberation parades: Social advancement always promotes backlash. Some people won't want to hear what we have to say. Some will call us terrible names, insult our looks, and possibly threaten harm. That's when it's most important to keep on keeping on, and not let the backlash beat us down. One thing to note, though: If the criticism is coming from our own communities or coalitions, don't get defensive. Doing better relies on asking questions and actively listening.

Finally, whenever we start feeling adrift, uncertain, or anxious, mind our mantra:

stay curious.
build empathy.
raise hell.

ladylike matrix

Before we shove off, take a birds-eye view of how ladylike standards slice and dice us into the likeability haves and have nots. Since by definition, ladies are objects of affection, their most valuable currency is other people's approval. Like Russian nesting dolls, patriarchy contains more rigged systems within it based on those intersectional qualities like ability, skin color, and gender. We call it the Ladylike Matrix.

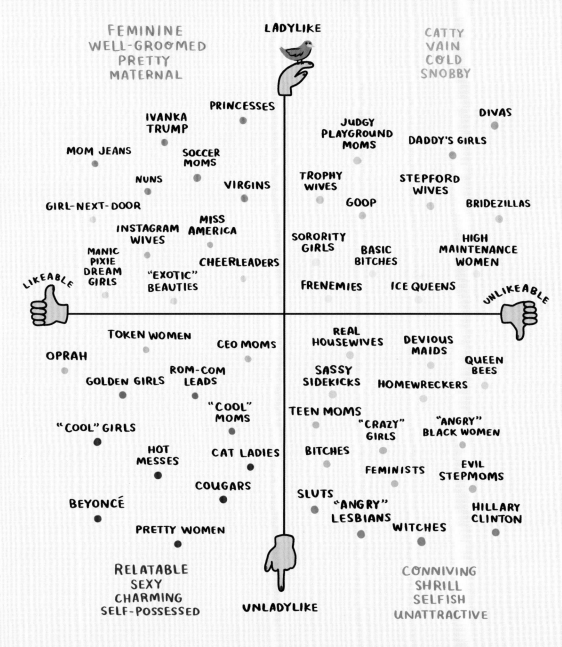

FEMININE
WELL-GROOMED
PRETTY
MATERNAL

LADYLIKE

CATTY
VAIN
COLD
SNOBBY

PRINCESSES

IVANKA TRUMP

DIVAS

JUDGY PLAYGROUND MOMS

DADDY'S GIRLS

MOM JEANS

SOCCER MOMS

NUNS

VIRGINS

TROPHY WIVES

STEPFORD WIVES

GIRL-NEXT-DOOR

GOOP

BRIDEZILLAS

INSTAGRAM WIVES

MISS AMERICA

MANIC PIXIE DREAM GIRLS

"EXOTIC" BEAUTIES

CHEERLEADERS

SORORITY GIRLS

BASIC BITCHES

HIGH MAINTENANCE WOMEN

FRENEMIES

ICE QUEENS

LIKEABLE

UNLIKEABLE

TOKEN WOMEN

CEO MOMS

REAL HOUSEWIVES

DEVIOUS MAIDS

OPRAH

GOLDEN GIRLS

ROM-COM LEADS

SASSY SIDEKICKS

QUEEN BEES

HOMEWRECKERS

"COOL" MOMS

TEEN MOMS

"COOL" GIRLS

"CRAZY" GIRLS

"ANGRY" BLACK WOMEN

HOT MESSES

CAT LADIES

BITCHES

FEMINISTS

EVIL STEPMOMS

COUGARS

SLUTS

BEYONCÉ

"ANGRY" LESBIANS

HILLARY CLINTON

PRETTY WOMEN

WITCHES

RELATABLE
SEXY
CHARMING
SELF-POSSESSED

UNLADYLIKE

CONNIVING
SHRILL
SELFISH
UNATTRACTIVE

gender trouble

WITCHES, BITCHES, AND WIVES

Today's is the most unladylike generation. The successors to Gloria Steinem's outspokenness, Frida Kahlo's self-reflection, and Angela Davis's defiance, Generation Z—which includes anyone born from roughly 1995 to 2005—is also the most gender-norm ambivalent, multiculturally tolerant, and ethnically diverse generation. While talking with Steinem in 2016 for a *Teen Vogue* feature, Gen-Z actress and activist Amandla Stenberg said, "A lot of people are rejecting the binary—that's the future of feminism."

Rejecting the binary. Smashing the patriarchy. The future is female. Feminists deserve all the props for excellent catchphrases, but what are we really talking about? What's the backstory to our pithy platforms?

Until startlingly recently, the (male) scientific consensus insisted that what we now call the **gender binary** didn't stem from nurture, but from nature. From that point of view, femininity and masculinity are biological by-products: Vaginas equaled girly skills and dispositions, and penises equaled dudely ones. As in, literally: our bodies, ourselves. Even suffragists in the mid- to late 1800s, aka the **first wave** of American feminists, bought into this logic, arguing that because women were "naturally" the more sensitive sex,

"[Man] thinks of his body as a direct and normal connection with the world, which he believes he apprehends objectively, whereas he regards the body of a woman as a hindrance, a prison, weighted down by everything peculiar to it."

SIMONE DE BEAUVOIR
feminist philosopher
and writer

they would bring a much-needed moral compass to politics and governance. This brand of appealing for equality by relying on positive gender stereotypes— e.g., women are better communicators, detail-oriented, and nurturing—is called **maternal feminism**.

By the time **second-wave** feminists got riled up in the 1970s, they were out to bust up the binary, proper. From the gender-role-approved traits of submission, nurturance, and sensitivity to the uniforms of high heels, skirts, and bras, the rules seemed decidedly rigged in dudes' favor. A psychologist at Johns Hopkins named John Money, an emerging leader in the fledgling field of sexology, had been making a name for himself with a bold theory that masculinity and femininity were socially conditioned, not biologically ingrained.

Once feminists caught wind of Money's research, they leveraged it as credible evidence from a male scientist that the binary was a bunch of bull and they weren't just making up this whole female oppression thing. Cultural anthropologist and feminist Gayle Rubin was one of the earliest scholars to run with Money's division of gender and sex as a reasoning for what she identified as female oppression for the purpose of heteronormative male sexual pleasure.

a very brief and western timeline of gender

1800s	1900s	1945	1970s
Rigid Victorian-era gender roles establish the "separate spheres" ideology that women's domain is the domestic, and men lord over everything else	A defining struggle of the twentieth century, the "Woman Question" challenges ironclad gender roles as women begin demanding rights to personal and political autonomy, such as being allowed to vote or work after marriage	*Gender* as we know it debuts in the *American Journal of Psychology*, defined as "the social obverse of sex"	Gender becomes *very* groovy in academia and law, giving birth to a litter of familiar terms, including *gender equality* (1971), *gender discrimination* (1973), and *gender politics* (1977)

Money's work provided crucial support for the discriminatory roots of women's societal subordination. In Women's Liberation lingo, gender-related debates over nature and nurture were reframed as essentialist (nature) versus constructivist (nurture). And with that, feminist scholars and lawyers began coining a whole new language of **gender equality**, **gender discrimination**, and **gender politics**—one that we still use today to protest gender typecasting and sexism.

Gen-X feminists who kicked off the feminist **third wave** were as much about making culture as breaking it. In the late 1980s, for instance, the Guerilla Girls collective began disrupting the Manhattan art world by plastering neighborhoods with provocative posters. One of its most iconic asks—"Do women have to be nude to get into the Met. Museum?"—in reference to the collection's bevy of female nudes and scant representation of actual female artists. On the West Coast, riot grrrls were building a feminist punk movement out of zines and all-girl bands like Bikini Kill, Bratmobile, and Sleater-Kinney. "Women were (culturally) under attack but weren't supposed to acknowledge it, weren't supposed to resist it," author Sarah Marcus recounts in *Girls to the Front: The Real Story of the Riot Grrrl Revolution*.

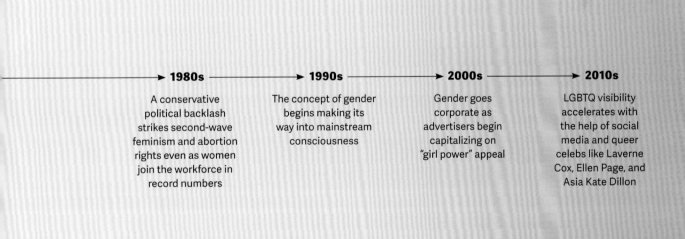

1980s

A conservative political backlash strikes second-wave feminism and abortion rights even as women join the workforce in record numbers

1990s

The concept of gender begins making its way into mainstream consciousness

2000s

Gender goes corporate as advertisers begin capitalizing on "girl power" appeal

2010s

LGBTQ visibility accelerates with the help of social media and queer celebs like Laverne Cox, Ellen Page, and Asia Kate Dillon

Then social media came along in the 2000s, facilitating both a **fourth wave** of feminism and upending how we talk about gender yet again. To be clear, people haven't just made up newfangled gender identities because of the internet; rather, people with atypical gender identities and expressions have been able to find one another online and build communities. Along with the slang abbrevs and hashtags birthed on Twitter and Instagram, online communities have similarly shared, translated, and expanded gender-inclusive terminology into mainstream conversations. Rather than recoiling at what we might not understand at first glance, we can approach unfamiliar language as opportunities to learn.

It tracks, then, that Gen Z, which was raised on social media, would gravitate toward this new lexicon. Today's gender-neutral generation envisions identities as flexible constellations in a dazzlingly infinite universe. Cisgender, bigender, pangender, and demigender are just a few other stops along the spectrum. According to a 2017 global citizenship survey, for instance, roughly 20 percent of teens said they don't consider themselves fully male or female. Meanwhile, most American teens (56 percent) know someone who prefers gender-neutral pronouns such as *they, ze,* or *hir.*

Gender fluidity might seem strikingly modern, but the fact is, Western culture is far behind the global curve. In fact, Europe is the only inhabited continent that's exclusively been all about that boy/girl binary. More than one hundred Native American tribes traditionally recognized more than two genders, and the Blackfoot, Crow, Sioux, and other Great Plains tribes revered Two Spirit people for possessing both masculine and feminine spirits and capabilities. Southern Mexico is the home of *muxe,* people who express an indigenous feminine gender and consider their fluidity a mystical gift. In 2014, India's Supreme Court legally validated *hijra*—a community of transgender women identified since antiquity—as a legal third gender. And more than ten countries, including Canada, Germany, and Pakistan, now offer nonbinary gender designations for passports.

As transgender awareness and acceptance has risen in the past decade, the number of self-identifying trans folks in America has doubled, though they still make up less than 1 percent of the population. And while the binary assumption looks to be loosening its grip a little, it's maddeningly tough to eradicate. Case in point: gender-inclusive bathroom debates. These spaces have always been hotbeds of class privilege and white panic. Nineteenth-century ladies were initially too snobby to use public restrooms for fear of rubbing dirty elbows with working-class women. People of color and disabled people also had to fight for the right to safe, clean restroom access. Today's transphobic handwringing over all-gender bathrooms is just the newest iteration of our prejudicial bullsh*t, but there's hope. According to a 2016 J. Walter Thompson survey, 70 percent of Gen-Z respondents support gender-inclusive loos.

Still, the more we diverge from traditionally "acceptable" masculinity or femininity, the more discrimination awaits in the form of bullying, unemployment, hostile health care, violence, and other forms of intolerance. A study from the National Center for Transgender Equality and the National Gay and Lesbian Task Force found that 71 percent of transgender participants remained closeted as a form of self-protection and preservation.[1] Lesbian, gay, and bisexual tweens and teens are also likelier to experience violence, whether perpetrated by bullies or self-inflicted.

These days, many of us recognize that if we end up wrestling between pressures to conform and deep-seated desires to be our authentic selves, we aren't any less intelligent, capable, or worthy of love and respect. But smashing the binary takes substance, stamina, and support. We've got to stay curious, build empathy, and start more uncomfortable conversations and purposeful confrontations across Gen X to Z and back to the boomers.

Questioning gender rules is just the beginning. Grab your Intersectional Binoculars, friends. There's a sprawling patriarchal ecosystem to weed out.

pronoun pro-tips

Unsure which pronoun to use for someone? First listen for the pronoun that folks who know them use. If that's a no-go, introduce yourself with *your* preferred pronouns, which will invite them to do the same. Oh, and if you use the wrong pronoun, no need to panic. Just apologize as you would for any other mistake. A handy technicality to know: The singular **they** is grammatically polite (and Associated Press-approved) to use. If anyone ever snarks about "newfangled" alternative pronouns, you can inform them that dozens of gender-neutral alternatives, including *hem, nim,* and *shey* have floated in and out of the English language in the past two hundred years alone. In fact, *thon,* an awkward gender-free contraction of "that one" made it into the 1934 edition of *Merriam-Webster*'s dictionary, though it never caught on.

plows up, hoes down

Patriarchy is old, but not organic. Men have been running things practically everywhere throughout recorded history—though not by design, believe it or not. Way back in ancient Mesopotamia, a woman's place was in the fields, not the laundry room. Boys herded animals, and girls hand-tilled, planted, and weeded whatever scraps of land their families could manage. Stone-Age bros weren't huddled in man caves, telling their housewives to get back in the kitchen cave; they worshipped goddesses just like everyone else.

Until around 10,000 BCE, survival had depended on nomadic hunting and foraging, his 'n' hers tasks that held equal importance. In fact, the plants women and kids foraged provided a bulk of their group's CrossFit-worthy paleo diet. Then gender roles got plowed. Once we figured out how to farm and domesticate animals, egalitarianism went to hell in a handbasket.

Not that the agricultural revolution was a bad thing for humankind. It enabled folks to settle down, reliably feed themselves, and have babies. However, with the invention of the plow also came a "premium on male brawn in plowing and other heavy farm work,"sowing beliefs of male superiority and entitlement over time.[2]

A few thousand years later, farming villages had sprung up across modern-day Iraq, Iran, Syria, Israel, Lebanon, and Jordan. Because of the upper-body strength and heft it demanded, the plow shook up the division of labor, leaving men in the fields and women closer to home with the children and animals. There was more than enough caregiving, cooking, and weaving to keep busy, but gender roles had diverged. Even the Mesopotamian goddesses were forced into early retirement. From dirt to deities, the patriarchal harvest had arrived.

Its roots run astonishingly deep, too. In 2011, a trio of Harvard and UCLA economists sifted through mountains of data and found that cultures where plow-based farming was (or remains) the name of the food-supply game have fewer working moms, women-owned businesses, and women in politics. Where those indoor/outdoor gender roles took root, people are likelier to agree that men deserve jobs more than women and that men are natural-born political leaders.

how gender got plowed

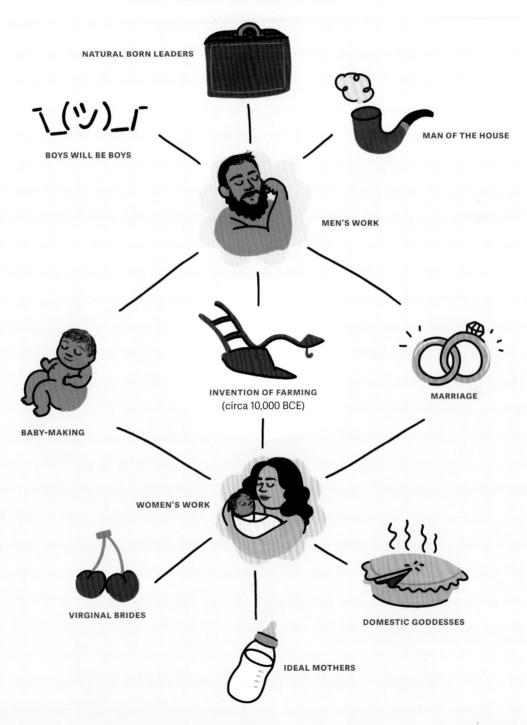

NATURAL BORN LEADERS

MAN OF THE HOUSE

BOYS WILL BE BOYS

¯_(ツ)_/¯

MEN'S WORK

INVENTION OF FARMING
(circa 10,000 BCE)

BABY-MAKING

MARRIAGE

WOMEN'S WORK

VIRGINAL BRIDES

DOMESTIC GODDESSES

IDEAL MOTHERS

How is that possible? Because humans are creatures of habit by default. In the case of binary gender roles, what started out as a practical solution bred **behavioral norms**. Women take care of things at home, and men provide for them. Gradually, those norms calcify into beliefs that ladies should naturally long to be domestic, maternal, and dependent on the man of the house. Within that framework, marriage was the best promotion a woman could get, and healthy male babies were her most valuable asset. But it took another technological breakthrough—the industrial revolution—to begin to dethrone the men's-only manual labor that drove the agrarian economy and crack open extramarital agency for women.

the care and feeding of gender

Our head-to-toe, outside-in, either-or standards of femininity and masculinity are hard to escape. They influence how we're expected to look, dress, walk, talk, sit, smell, think, feel, desire, and aspire. Biologically, in utero exposure to the sex hormones estrogen, progesterone, and androgens may predispose us toward masculine or feminine traits, but the socialization of girlishness usually starts before we're out of the womb, too.

Gender filters our selfies and societal snapshots with shades of femininity and manliness, contouring features and making stereotypes pop. And that's not inherently a bad thing. Feminist sociologist Lisa Wade explains how, on the flip side, androgyny and gender neutrality render us "culturally unintelligible," or unrecognizable as him, her, or they.[3] It's human-animal instinct to split-second determine whether the people we see are familiar, sorting friends from possible foes. But patriarchy weaponizes that bias to play gender favorites with who gets seen, heard, and constantly told to smile.

For a sense of how patriarchy circulates gender and off-gases toxins like toxic masculinity, picture a terrarium. Nothing fancy—a simple one with a few succulents will suffice. Now imagine patriarchy as a social terrarium, or ecosystem, circulating gender in all its iterations through both the visible landscape and seeping unnoticed into the surrounding soil, water, and air.

Here's how the gender cycle goes 'round.

1. We Normalize It

Femininity **gender imprinting** starts at home. Our families are our primary, everyday role models and instructors of how girls and women ought to act and deserve to be treated, for better or worse. For evidence, look no further than gender-reveal parties, one of the most popular and regressive pastimes ever invented by the internet. These clickbaity fêtes are all about the binary, right down to fan-fave themes like pistols or pearls, rifles or ruffles, guns or glitter, touchdowns or tutus, bows or boots, and wheels or heels.

2. We Reenact It with Gender Roles

We begin learning our ladylike parts before we can tie our shoes. As toddlers, we're diapered detectives, sleuthing out which toys, looks, and behaviors match with what gender. This is when kids' preferences for pink and blue emerge, or don't; there's zero evidence that infants are predisposed to like pink. Instead, feminine kids might adopt pink as their fave color because they identify with its girly associations. More telling, though, is how their boyish classmates don't experience a similar affinity for blue but rather an aversion to pink. And merely tolerating it isn't enough because our androcentric culture wastes no time teaching boys that femininity is for sissies.

3. We Recycle It with Gender Stereotypes

Gender wouldn't be such an omnipresent hot shot without cultural institutions and outlets that recycle **gender stereotypes** into the patriarchal atmosphere, which restarts the cycle. Girls get the messages. Between ages seven and fifteen, beauty awareness, weight monitoring, and popularity concerns tend to spike, while self-esteem and well-being nosedive. A 2010 gender development research review also found that during adolescence, girls experience "a notable increase in . . . beliefs that males are granted more power and respect than females." Smart cookies.

babes in toyland

When stores like Target, Disney, and Harrods began rolling out gender-neutral toy aisles in 2015, it was a marketing milestone. Except for a brief gender-neutral trend in the mid-1970s, most toys had been strictly designated boys' or girls'. But remember, feminist parents, nannies, and eccentric aunts: For toymakers, gender-neutral makeovers aren't about pink or blue, but making the green. As sociologist Elizabeth Sweet observes, the palettes hew more masculine blues and greens, or even grays and blacks like Hasbro's "gender-non-specific" EZ Bake Oven it released in 2012.[4] Pinks and purples meanwhile remain verboten to boys. After all, tomboy girls can still achieve rough and tumble status, whereas there's no social upside for boys branded as sissies. Same femmephobia, different shade.

And any gender bending is usually little more than an attempt to make more money. It's straight up foolish to depend on toy companies to be reliably woke babysitters for kids because, by and large, that isn't their goal. To stay in business, they have to sell Bratz dolls and Nerf guns, not political consciousness. Plus, think about which comes first: pink plastic kitchen sets for girls or the stereotypes that girls are naturally drawn to housekeeping. Instead of fretting over whether toys are progressive or regressive, parents should empower themselves to convey gender-positive playtime messages, and no batteries required.

six degrees of misogyny

Older than Medusa and found around the globe, misogyny spins all manner of myths, stereotypes, and conspiracy theories to propagandize female inferiority. Think of it as patriarchy's crooked cop out to punish unladylike gals who swerve outside their sexist lanes. Citations of choice include silencing, shaming, and/or violence. In short, it's an old-fashioned witch hunt.

Trans-Misogyny

Predicated on warped notions that only female-assigned bodies can qualify as "real" women, trans-misogyny dehumanizes, sexualizes, and pathologizes transgender women as deceptive, delusional interlopers. This form of transphobia takes various forms like intentionally misgendering people, slandering trans women as sexual deviants, and kicking them out of the feminist not-so-safe spaces.

Mom-sters

Mother blame is one of misogyny's oldest tricks. What better way to undercut their preggo power than to also hold them accountable for anything that ever happens to their children? Autism, for instance, was initially attributed to "refrigerator moms" who were too cold to nurture, and psychiatrists were similarly convinced that overbearing mothers caused schizophrenia.[5]

Vagina Dentata

As if menstruation didn't provide enough misogynistic entertainment, cultural myths of toothy vaginas are almost as common. These fanged femme fatales speak to the suspicion that women are virility vampires, wielding sexuality to suck away masculine power. The folk-lore also gave Freud ample fodder for diagnosing castration anxiety.

Misogynoir

Gender studies professor Moya Bailey coined this portmanteau to identify the misogyny wrapped in racism projected onto Black women by pop culture and media.[6] Sometimes it's as bald-faced as Bill O'Reilly riffing on Rep. Maxine Waters' hair, and other times it's hidden like the faces we *don't* see on the news, or what journalist Gwen Ifill dubbed "the missing white woman syndrome."[7]

Cyber-Misogyny

Social media (and creepy online message boards) are prime public squares to blow off **aggrieved entitlement**, or man-rage at feeling unjustly manpower-less. Replicating offline harassment, ridicule, and hate speech toward women and girls on the internet, cyber-misogyny's slimy offspring includes online stalking, revenge porn, Twitter rape threats, unsolicited dick pics, and Tinder trolls (see page 135).

Eve-il

Fourth-century philosopher Saint Augustine of Hippo did Biblical Eve wrong, rewriting her as humanity's original sinner, temptress, and poster-gal for why Adams everywhere ought to be in charge. Henceforth, putting her at fault for committing original sin provided a handy excuse to put women in their place. For as Genesis commands as recompense for Eve's apple, "thy desires shall be subject to thy husband, and he shall rule over thee."

pauli

Born in 1910 in North Carolina, **PAULI MURRAY** was the most important queer civil rights agitator and legal mastermind most folks have never heard of. Her intellect, passion, and dogged desire to make sense of her own interlocking identities propelled Pauli along an extraordinary path to helping lay the constitutional foundation for both the civil rights and second-wave feminist movements. As her friend and fellow activist Eleanor Holmes Norton eloquently put it, "she lived on the edge of history seeming to pull it along with her."[8]

Pauli's feminist awakening began at the historically black Howard University law school, where she was one of two female students. Having grown up in the ultra-segregated Jim Crow South—born to the granddaughter of an enslaved woman and her owner—Pauli experienced discrimination and hate as a product of racism. Other colleges had turned her away just because of the color of her skin. But as she later joked in her autobiography, *Proud Shoes*, she earned a "Bachelor in Feminism" at Howard.

True to form, Pauli applied that consciousness into legal theory, coining that double-discrimination of race and gender **Jane Crow.** (Bonus points to Pauli for making a feminist pun.) Thanks to legal scholar Kimberlé Williams Crenshaw's work in the 1980s, we talk about Jane Crow today in terms of **intersectionality**.

Always looking ahead, Pauli knew that challenging sexist laws would take organizing. That gave her the idea for an "NAACP for women," which Betty Friedan spearheaded as the National Organization for Women.[9] Because Pauli's theorizing laid the crucial groundwork to strike down legalized sex discrimination, a pre-Supreme Court Ruth Bader Ginsburg named Pauli as a coauthor in her landmark legal brief.

Guided by her philosophy of social justice as a spiritual pursuit, at age 66, Pauli quit academia and became the first female priest ordained by the Episcopal Church. And in 2004, Saint Pauli was canonized.

WHAT PAULI WOULD DO TODAY: Clap back with facts, speak truth to power, and question everything. When denied grad school acceptance on the basis of race, Pauli called bullsh*t with research, facts, and compelling arguments. She lost her case, but it sparked her game-changing strategy to learn how to rewrite racist policy. In her personal life, as she questioned her attraction to women and intermittent gender dysphoria, bigotry made even less sense less to Pauli. Though she didn't find all the right answers, she trusted herself to seek them out. Pauli was unafraid of ruffling feathers, even if they belonged to progressive women like pen pal Eleanor Roosevelt, or Dr. Martin Luther King Jr. himself. Her secret? Coming with a distinct, considered point of view. Hot takes fizzle fast.

sexism in the wild

How do we disrupt the patriarchal ecosystem and its endless gendering? Tune into your intuition, fire up your senses, and scout out these telltale signs of sexism around you.

- **WATCH WHO GOES FIRST.** Why do we usually say "Mr. and Mrs.," in that order? When the convention developed in the sixteenth century, men came first because they were viewed as the superior sex. And now? A 2010 study from the British Psychological Society combed through online mentions of British and American male-female name pairs and found that ladies went first less than 30 percent of the time.[10]

- **FEEL AROUND FOR DOUBLE TROUBLE.** In later chapters, we'll dig deeper into the sexual double standards that permit guys to sow their wild oats while slut-shaming girls for the doing the same. Contradictory gender roles and stereotypes can also tangle us up in double binds. Boss babes are especially familiar with the professional double bind of female likeability because they have to simultaneously negotiate the stereotype that women are second-rate businessfolks and that women are less aggressive and ambitious than men. Psychologists call this the **superwoman syndrome**.

- **LISTEN UP FOR CODE WORDS.** Especially in the context of describing women and girls, listen for dog whistles like *crazy*, *high maintenance*, *shrill*, *uptight*, *bossy*, and references to unwanted sexual attention as a *compliment*.

- **LOOK FOR THE LANDMARKS.** Sexism haunts us beyond the grave, too, memorializing women's subordinate social status. There are so few public monuments to women that the barrier to access is called the **bronze ceiling**. Ghoulish studies have also found that our headstones are smaller, obituaries fewer and briefer, and that if a photo is printed with a death notice—which is less common for ladies than gents—it's likelier to be a much younger snapshot. Good grief.

- **DON'T TRUST CHIVALRY.** Every so often, though, sexist shots backfire. That's how America got its first female mayor, in fact. In 1887, women were already allowed to run for public office in Argonia, Kansas, so anti-temperance bros nominated prohibitionist Susanna Madora Selter, assuming a woman would sink the anti-booze ballot. Selter's prohibitionist pals spotted the bros' move and voted her into office to spite them.

dressing up gender

"It's not about gender," supermodel Gigi Hadid told *Vogue* in a June 2017 cover story that made much ado about how she and her pop star boyfriend, Zayn Malik, occasionally borrowed each other's clothes. "It's about, like, shapes. And what feels good on you that day."[11] It may sound cute, but it's actually baloney because our clothes aren't our genders, and only a cisgender person is privileged enough to "try on" identities beyond the pink and blue boxes. *Harrumph.*

However, it's easy to think we wear genders like clothes since, whether chosen consciously or not, our closets are capsule collections of **gender expression**. And not only that, our sartorial code-switching—like wearing a more masculine suit to a job interview and then changing into a floral romper to hang out with friends afterward—is **gender fluidity** in action. But when fashion first became a female-gendered interest, it was meant more to repress than express.

Fashion historian Jo Barraclough Paoletti notes in her book *Pink and Blue: Telling the Boys from the Girls in America* that "gender distinctions are among the oldest and most widespread functions of dress."[12] But in fact, the medieval emergence of fashion revolved solely around class. It took another five hundred years for fashion to be gendered as girly.

Prior to the Victorian era, aristocratic fellas were the ones first tiptoeing around in high heels, sporting hairbows, and toting handbags. But nineteenth-century middle class men weren't into finery. Swayed by the **separate spheres** doctrine that coded the private domestic sphere as women's domain and the public professional sphere as men's, these upwardly mobile white guys emphasized their manliness with the so-called Great Masculine Renunciation of overly fussy garments and conspicuous clothing consumption. Out went the tights, hairbows, and fancy hats, which permanently relocated to women's side of the closet. "Real" men were now supposed to be low-key about looking good. Meanwhile, consumer culture and the newfangled activity of shopping for ready-made clothes became thoroughly feminized. After all, men reasoned, fashion and adornment would surely appeal to ladies' inborn vanity. *What gents!*

Kids' closets were exempt the longest from gendered uniforming. Through the late 1800s, all tykes wore plain white dresses, and most parents wouldn't transition boys to pants until they turned seven or eight. In the 1920s, toddlers began wearing gender-specific clothes—though not in the color scheme you'd expect. A 1918 childrenswear trade magazine breaks it down: "The reason is that pink, being a more decided and stronger color, is more suitable for the boy, while blue, which is more delicate and dainty, is prettier for the girl."[13]

It wasn't until after World War II that pink became thoroughly feminized. In the postwar throwback to traditional gender roles, pink was pushed even harder on women than on girls. Kitchens, bathrooms, and vanities in the 1950s were flush with blush appliances, cookware, and furnishings right out of old-school Barbie Dreamhouses.

But pink is no shrinking violet. In her book *Hope in a Jar: The Making of America's Beauty Culture*, Kathy Peiss notes that cosmetics queen Elizabeth Arden wore her trademark shade, "Arden pink"—a more ladylike rendition of her fashion contemporary Elsa Schiaparelli's signature "shocking pink"—as a sort of sinister camouflage. "Pink femininity concealed Arden's acts as an exacting and tough manager who broke a threatened strike, fended off complaints from the Food and Drug Administration, and remained the sole stockholder of her family, despite several marriages and buyout offers," Peiss writes.

Regardless of shades, silhouettes, or status, women's wardrobes still come stitched with an insidiously ladylike lack of pockets. Almost five hundred years ago, men's clothes got pockets, and women's fashion has never caught up. When ladies' style slimmed down in the 1800s, old-school fanny packs previously worn beneath voluminous skirts were replaced with purses, perfectly accessorizing the decorative and caregiving cornerstones of femininity. To this day, loose, masculine pockets provide just enough room for the holy trinity of keys, phone, and wallet, while feminine handbags tote around private *and* publicly shared items, like mints, lip balm, and bedraggled tampons. But that dainty-looking gender baggage is also powerful enough to incite mini-masculinity crises, as evidenced by the horror some dudes exhibit upon hearing the three witchy words "hold my purse."

no more ladylike feminism

Even though feminism has become more fashionable in recent years, cameoing on Chanel runways, Hollywood red carpets, and Beyoncé videos, it's still a risky a look to the ladylike masses, prompting some to keep their gender politics under wraps. Ever heard someone throw down the "I'm not a feminist, but . . ." card? As in, "I'm not a feminist, but I'm all about abortion rights." Social scientists call this rhetorical game the **Feminist Paradox** of agreeing with tenets of feminism but not self-identifying as a feminist.

It's a Cool Girl-ish tactic (see page 209) women use to express an opinion without endangering their likeability and coming off as preachy. Why the bait-and-switch? Because patriarchy likes ladies most when they're easy on the eyes *and* ears, and feminists are still stereotyped as unappealingly enraged. A January 2016 poll conducted by the *Washington Post* and Kaiser Family Foundation found that although a majority of American women and a third of men identify as feminists, 43 percent of respondents agreed that the movement is "angry," and slightly more think feminism amounts to unfair man-blame.

The 2016 poll also reveals a telling divide in how women interpret feminism and its purpose. When asked why gender inequality persists, identical proportions cited "discrimination against women" and "the choices women make themselves." Deeper academic research suggests that bridging that disconnect won't happen by convincing folks they're feminist but by empha-sizing intersectionality and role modeling how, as bell hooks says, feminism is for everybody.

spread the f-word

Sisterhood is powerful *and* powerfully alienating when privileges go unchecked, outcomes overshadow inclusion, and perspectives turn poisonous. We know this because many feminist foremothers fore-*othered*, silenced, and dismissed folks they perceived as too brown, too queer, too disabled, and too uneducated to advance their causes.

After the ratification of the Nineteenth Amendment granted American women voting rights, white suffragists declared victory and shimmied on to their (ill-fated) next cause, the Equal Rights Amendment. But in doing so, they left women of color in the disenfranchised dust. Native American women didn't even qualify as citizens for another four years, and women of Asian descent were excluded from the electoral process until after World War II. Ultimately, it took the Voting Rights Act of 1965 to extend universal suffrage to Chicana, Latinx, Asian American and African American women.

In 1970, *Feminine Mystique* author and second-wave feminist figurehead Betty Friedan mistrusted activist lesbians, labeling them a "lavender menace" to the movement's political cred. Meanwhile, second-wave **trans-exclusionary radical feminists**, or TERFs, disparaged butch and femme gender expressions as parroting patriarchal sex roles and trans women as monstrous men who shouldn't be allowed to access feminist resources like rape crisis centers.[14] Turned off by the cacophony of white nonsense, middle-class women of color forged new intersectional spaces, like the Third World Women's Alliance, which was founded by black and Puerto Rican activists in 1970, and the Combahee River Collective started by queer black feminists in 1974.

Ladylike orthodoxy has worn out her welcome, and it's past time to do better, mess up, fess up, and try again. We can't airbrush away the intolerance feminists have condoned tacitly and from bully pulpits; the point of dredging up unsavory histories isn't to throw luminaries under the bus but to learn from past mistakes in order to create a more vibrant, inclusive present. By better understanding where we've come from, we can more clearly envision the unladylike path ahead and what it takes to stay the course.

Seek a Tribe, Not an Echo Chamber

Being a self-aware ally means venturing out of our personal bubbles and challenging our own beliefs and perspectives. It's time to get comfy with being *un*comfy. If you notice everyone around always looks like you, you might be missing out on opportunities to support and learn from other communities that

don't. Reading, listening to podcasts, and Googling around for voices beyond our "in-groups" are simple ways to start expanding your allyship horizons.

Bust the Hivemind Myth

While the BeyHive is real, the myth of a monolithic female hive mind has been reheated and served up since the suffrage movement to delude and divide women. The first major evidence of this voting bloc myth arrived in 1923, when National Woman's Party founder Alice Paul successfully lobbied her proposed Equal Rights Amendment onto the ballot. Paul thought it was a surefire win with women voters, but she thought wrong. Fifty years later, when the ERA was finally gaining political momentum, arch antifeminist Phyllis Schlafly galvanized a legion of white, conservative fangirls who derailed ratification of the Equal Rights Amendment; launched the pro-life, anti-abortion movement; and reframed gender politics as female self-victimizing.

Don't Underestimate Nonfeminist Women

Here's looking at the 53 percent of American white women who for voted Trump in the 2016 presidential election, which wasn't a statistical shocker judging by white ladies' voting record. In 1984, second-wave feminists and future Hillary diehards were *amped* to support Democratic vice-presidential candidate Geraldine Ferraro, the first female running mate of a major political party . . . then 55 percent of female voters reelected Ronald Reagan much to Phyllis Schlafly's delight.

But nonfeminist women have also supported feminist causes. The 2017 #MeToo movement involved folks across the political spectrum who stood up and spoke out about personal experiences of sexual harassment and assault. Two of the most instrumental public figures leading up to that reckoning were hella conservative former Fox News anchors, Gretchen Carlson and Megyn Kelly, who went public about being sexually harassed by then-network chairman Roger Ailes and pundit Bill O'Reilly, respectively. Neither self-identifies as a feminist, and their politics are far from inclusive, but when majorities of women really, truly unite, it's a force powerful enough to take down patriarchy's most privileged benefactors.

GENDER: IT'S ALL FLUID

Hip-Hop Feminism

Blends feminism, womanism, and hip-hop to challenge misogyny and define space for the unfettered expression of black womanhood. Coined in 1999 by Joan Morgan in her book *When Chickenheads Come Home to Roost: A Hip-Hop Feminist Breaks It Down*.

Womanist

"Womanist is to feminist as purple is to lavender." Alice Walker coined this term to describe black feminism in her 1983 collection *In Search of Our Mothers' Gardens: Womanist Prose*.

Black Feminism

An intersectional theory developed in response to racism and marginalization from white feminists and sexism from men in the Black Liberation Movement. The core philosophy has existed much longer; the 1973 founding of the National Black Feminist Organization is considered its official start.

feminisms of color

Islamic Feminism

A feminist framework that both explores and interprets gender equality through a theological lens. Whereas Western feminism focuses on untangling gendered culture from personal identity, Islamic feminism peels apart gendered culture from belief.

South Asian Feminisms

A blend of feminism and anti-colonialism theory and activism specific to India, Pakistan, Sri Lanka, Bangladesh, Nepal, and Afghanistan.

Indigenous Feminism

A form of transnational feminism that addresses the injustices of colonialism, sexism, and sexual violence that threaten the welfare of American Indian women.

Asian American Feminism

Feminist consciousness and social justice activism organized by and for Asian American cis and trans women, intentionally separate from white feminist groups that had labeled them an invisible "model minority" (see page 72).

Chicana Feminism

Coined in 1971 by Chicana writer and activist Mira Vida to address discrimination at the intersections of gender, race, and working-class politics for Chicana-identified women and American women of Mexican descent.

Pan-American Feminism

A Latin America-US intercontinental feminist movement that began as a peacekeeping response to World War I. Led by Paulina Luisi of Uruguay and Berta Luz of Brazil, it was responsible for getting the fledgling United Nations to recognize that "women's rights are human rights" in 1945.

As we continue holding white feminism accountable, let's broaden our understanding of feminism beyond Western, Euro-centric contexts. Our Intersectional Binoculars can magnify feminisms, too, after all. Think globally and act locally, using that knowledge as a bridge to new initiatives, activists, and communities beyond your backyard.

African + Black Feminisms

An umbrella term for feminisms developed across the African continent—particularly in Egypt, Sierra Leone, and South Africa—over the twentieth century that critique patriarchal customs, racial hierarchies, and Western imperialism. Some activists identify as both African and black feminists.

Aboriginal Feminism

Feminism at the intersection of indigenous rights, race, and gender in Australia both from within and outside Aboriginal communities.

Hawaiian Feminism

Feminism by and for indigenous Hawaiian women (distinct from Native Americans and Asian and Pacific Islanders) that seeks to reclaim and preserve cultural, political, and personal autonomy from colonization.

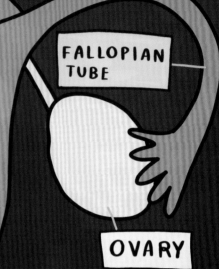

THE
HYSTERICAL UTERUS

HYSTERIA! ANXIETY!

MELANCHOLY! TREMORS!

FALLOPIAN TUBE

FALLOPIAN TUBE

OVARY

OVARY

ENDOMETRIUM

VAGINAL CANAL

CERVIX

STRESSES:
- RIDING IN SPEEDING VEHICLES
- RUNNING AND PLAYING SPORTS
- EXPOSURE TO BUILDUP OF TOXIC BILE

NEEDS:
- SEMEN
- TO HAVE A BABY IN HER
- TO GIVE BIRTH
- TO JUST RELAX
- TO GET SOME GOOD SEXIN'

uterine furies

PMS, IUDs, AND WTFs

How would you like to be the punch line of every period joke, probably bleeding out of your "wherever" like a she-devil? If you've got a uterus, you're 100 percent qualified to be stereotyped as noticeably emotional, moody, and always crying over spilled milk. You're baby crazy and you constantly exaggerate. Ladies, ladies, ladies, the evidence is clear: We're unhinged.

Mary Putnam Jacobi was having none of it in her day. In 1876, the suffragist and medical scientist delivered a clapback for the ages, gathering scores of statistics on women's health, physical strength, schooling, and periods, and published an award-winning Harvard study that shredded claims of brain-induced womb ruin. By fighting sexist science with, well, *non*sexist science, Jacobi kicked the door open for a new generation of eggheads.

Ah, yes. Back to the myth that women are fundamentally impaired by the uterus. Since time immemorial, patriarchy has medically, religiously, and socially perceived uteruses as Pandora's boxes of all those kooky lady-hormones, menstrual curses, and baby-making. Surely no other part of human anatomy has triggered more truly crackpot ideas than what's inside our pelvises. In a stomach-turning twist on two plus two equals four, medieval Jewish philosopher Moses Maimonides

"The notion that women might menstruate in orbit drove the whole place up the wall."

KATHRYN D. SULLIVAN
NASA astronaut

concluded that since women have two breasts, they must also have two uteruses. Hippocrates made it even weirder. The ancient Greek "father of medicine" claimed that during vaginal intercourse, semen travels out the penis, through the vagina, and up the body until it reaches the end of the road in women's hair. Talk about bed head.

Through the lens of **biological determinism**, gender is seen as a product of nature, not nurture. If you're born with a uterus, bio-deet says, you can bend feminine roles only so far because ultimately your body is at the wheel and driving you toward motherhood, like it or not. By that same token, you live up to all the uterus-having stereotypes.

In another sexist lab across town, gynecologists and anatomists put to rest an old theory that the clitoris produced a lady-semen of sorts that was necessary for the baby-making process. That dazzling bundle of eight thousand nerve fibers, they concluded, served no direct reproductive function. So what did the docs do with that info? They ghosted. Women's bodies were too frail to handle the many orgasmic sensations the clitoris offered. And because the uterus was thought to control a lady's nerves, the only way to keep her calm was to get a bun in that oven. Before consumer culture started selling women tinctures, tonics, and personal care products to treat female anxieties, patriarchy sold us history's original cure-all: pregnancy, a force meant to quell our hysteria.

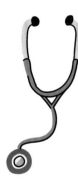

women be crazy at the doctor

According to patriarchal biology, female bodies are baby-making, orgasm-ambivalent, estrogen-pumping, breast-jiggling basket cases. Case in point: the "career woman's disease."

Back in the day, women living with the chronic and severe pelvic pain of endometriosis were thought to be suffering from womb suffocation, hysteria, or a straight-up mental illness. Alleged treatments ran the gamut from icky leeches and bloodletting to torturous hot douches and exorcism.[1] Once women began joining the full-time workforce en masse, physicians pinned the blame on female ambition.

By the 1970s, endometriosis had come to be known as the career woman's disease because of its diagnosis among predominantly white, unmarried, child-free women in their thirties. Furthermore, the typical patient profile was of uptight, anxious perfectionists. The likelier case is that this self-selecting group of women were the only ones wealthy enough to afford medical care for this notoriously difficult-to-diagnose condition.[2]

And what did these shady gynos prescribe? Housewifery, duh. Old-school medical literature commonly recommended homemaking and baby-making as the healthier alternatives to career climbing. In *The Makings of a Modern Epidemic: Endometriosis, Gender and Politics*, Kate Seear also notes the dog-whistling language of women "putting off" pregnancy and breastfeeding, as if anything other than motherhood as a priority is wrong.

"Even if it is too late for our generation, at least we may begin to explain to our daughters the physiological consequences that sometimes accompany certain life decisions," poet-turned-lay-endo-expert Julia Older wrote in an early self-care guide, *Endometriosis*, in 1984. Clearly, the "career woman's disease" myth was so pervasive even endometriosis sufferers sometimes internalized it.

But while it was perfectly acceptable for doctors to attribute the chronic disease to careerism back then, openly discussing chronic medical conditions like endometriosis in the office today remains taboo for fear of coming off as too weak or uncommitted to the bottom line.[3] However, that chilling effect of sexism raises the already steep individual costs of managing the chronic disease—more than $12,000 annually, on average.[4] In a ten-country study, endometriosis patients lost between eight and ten work hours each week from its painful, fatiguing symptoms to the tune of around $200 in weekly lost pay.

the *periodic table*

Menstruation encompasses a heavy flow of information, including everything from hormonal shifts to sexist nonsense, and from side effects to cultural nicknames. That's why we laid it all out on the Periodic Table; no seat-savers necessary.

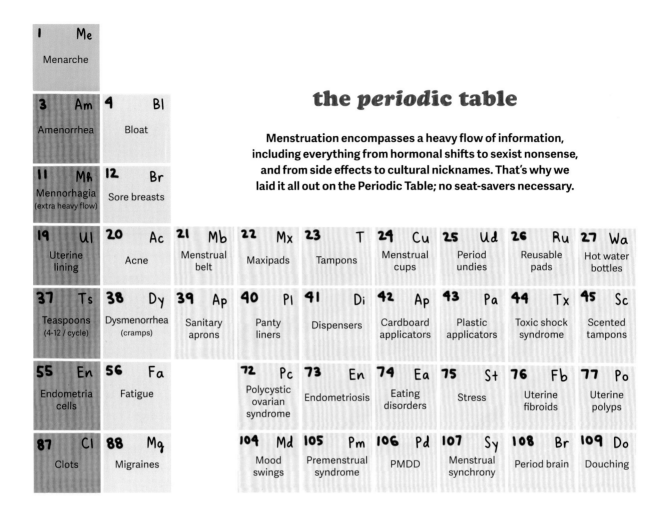

| 1 Me — Menarche |
3 Am — Amenorrhea	4 Bl — Bloat
11 Mr — Mennorhagia (extra heavy flow)	12 Br — Sore breasts
19 Ul — Uterine lining	20 Ac — Acne	21 Mb — Menstrual belt	22 Mx — Maxipads	23 T — Tampons	24 Cu — Menstrual cups	25 Ud — Period undies	26 Ru — Reusable pads	27 Wa — Hot water bottles
37 Ts — Teaspoons (4-12 / cycle)	38 Dy — Dysmenorrhea (cramps)	39 Ap — Sanitary aprons	40 Pl — Panty liners	41 Di — Dispensers	42 Ap — Cardboard applicators	43 Pa — Plastic applicators	44 Tx — Toxic shock syndrome	45 Sc — Scented tampons
55 En — Endometria cells	56 Fa — Fatigue	72 Pc — Polycystic ovarian syndrome	73 En — Endometriosis	74 Ea — Eating disorders	75 St — Stress	76 Fb — Uterine fibroids	77 Po — Uterine polyps
87 Cl — Clots	88 Mg — Migraines	104 Md — Mood swings	105 Pm — Premenstrual syndrome	106 Pd — PMDD	107 Sy — Menstrual synchrony	108 Br — Period brain	109 Do — Douching

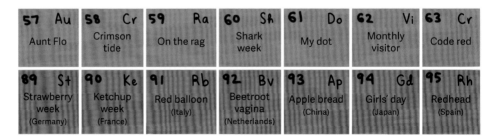

| 57 Au — Aunt Flo | 58 Cr — Crimson tide | 59 Ra — On the rag | 60 Sh — Shark week | 61 Do — My dot | 62 Vi — Monthly visitor | 63 Cr — Code red |
| 89 St — Strawberry week (Germany) | 90 Ke — Ketchup week (France) | 91 Rb — Red balloon (Italy) | 92 Bv — Beetroot vagina (Netherlands) | 93 Ap — Apple bread (China) | 94 Gd — Girls' day (Japan) | 95 Rh — Redhead (Spain) |

Menstrual Milestones

Know the Flow

Menstrual Euphemisms (GLOBAL)

Menstrual Euphemisms (US)

Menstrual Artifacts and Fictions

2 Ms — Menstrual seclusion

| 5 Pu — Puberty | 6 Sp — Spotting | 7 Ov — Ovulation | 8 Es — Estrogen | 9 Ut — Uterus | 10 Hu — Menstrual huts |

| 13 Ar — Menstrala | 14 Th — Thelarche (breast development) | 15 La — Late period | 16 Pr — Progesterone | 17 Cx — Cervix | 18 Ch — Chaupadi |

| 28 Iu — Intrauterine devices | 29 Tr — Period trackers | 30 Cm — Compostable pads | 31 Fr — Free bleeding | 32 Fe — Menstrual feminism | 33 Pr — Pregnancy | 34 Fs — Follicular stimulating hormone | 35 Fp — Fallopian tubes | 36 Mk — Mikvehs |

| 46 Bb — Blue blood | 47 Di — Menstrual disc | 48 Ps — Pessaries | 49 Mj — Menstrual marijuana | 50 Se — Period sex | 51 Tr — Transgender periods | 52 Mn — Menopause | 53 Ed — Endometrium | 54 Mc — Menstrual ceremony |

| 78 Al — Alcoholism | 79 Lb — Weight loss | 80 Pf — Premature ovarian failure | 81 Eq — Menstrual equity | 82 Lv — Period leave | 83 Po — Uterine polyps | 84 Sc — Self-care | 85 Ov — Ovaries | 86 Ma — Menstrual magic |

| 110 Vc — Vaginal cones | 111 Un — Untouchable | 112 Mt — Menstrual taboos | 113 Uc — Unclean stigma | 114 To — No touching | 115 Mn — Monthlies | 116 Mx — Menotoxins | 117 Hy — Hysteria | 118 Ba — Bear & shark bait |

| 64 Bm — Bloody Mary | 65 La — Lady time | 66 Ob — On the blob | 67 Vp — Vampire week | 68 Sa — Satan's waterfall | 69 Vi — Monthly visitor | 70 Rs — Red sea | 71 Cu — The curse |

| 96 Ar — Red army (Russia) | 97 Bk — Broke basin (Portugal) | 98 Un — Uncle chico (Brazil) | 99 En — English have landed (Belgium) | 100 Yo — Got the yolks (Albania) | 101 Ru — The ruler (Chile) | 102 Pi — Painters are in (Australia) | 103 Lw — Lingonberry week (Finland) |

 Symptoms

Menstruation Stations

 Modern Menstruation

Period Parts

the *periodic* table

For more than a century, scientists have puzzled over the link between estrogen and emotions. Though we still don't know precisely how sex hormones estrogen and testosterone work, here's what's clear. Ironically, estrogen is about a thousand times more potent than testosterone, but that doesn't mean hysteria Kool-Aid is surging through our veins. If estrogen were the crazy juice that patriarchy wants us to believe it is, daily life would be a minute-to-minute roller coaster of tears—or at least more than it already is.

Instead, research suggests estrogen is more of a buffer against the blues, correlated to *positive* moods, *lessening* depressive symptoms, and *improved* emotional intelligence. Plus, focusing exclusively on estrogen's complex neuro-chemical interplay with our emotional processing gives this multipurpose cocktail short shrift. It promotes secondary sex characteristics, particularly breast and hip development, along with bolstering bone strength. On the downside, it also predisposes us to breast cancer, endometriosis, and uterine fibroids. Regardless, not sorry, patriarchy: Estrogen doesn't make women irrational nutjobs.

Menstrual Milestones

Around the world, first menstruation—**menarche**—drops at 12.43 years old, on average; from there, Aunt Flo comes a-knocking between four hundred and five hundred more times until menopause.[5] In 1900, menarche happened closer to our fourteenth birthdays, but factors including climate change, industrialization, and nutrition have summoned it sooner. Typically, this happens a couple years after **thelarche**, or breast development, and roughly six months after peak **high velocity**, or growth spurting. No wonder this head-to-toe physiological makeover is associated with spiked social anxiety, body shame, and self-objectification.[6] In developing countries where menstrual aids aren't readily available, period-related fear and shame is even more entrenched and confining.

It wasn't until 1920 that the Girl Scouts became the first organization of its size to formally teach girls about menstruation, which was around the same time that advertisements for menstrual products began appearing in women's magazines.[7]

Know the Flow

Light days. Heavy flows. Breakthrough bleeding. Getting to know our flow isn't just brunch small talk fodder (kidding . . . or are we?), it's a handy health monitor. Texture and flow are the two primary health indicators to watch. "It's good to remember that regular cycles happen because your body is making an egg," Cleveland Clinic gynecology Linda Bradley told *TIME* in 2016. If something is out of whack, our bodies might say, "Yo, let's hold off on the egg this go-round."[8]

Period flukes will happen. Naturally, some months will be more intense than others, as are different shades of red and brown. But recurring extra-long, extra-bloody, and extra-chunky cycles could indicate underlying issues like uterine polyps or fibroids. Except for birth control–induced menstrual cessation, barely there periods could also signal malnourishment or excessive weight loss. The nose knows, too; a distinctively smellier period might be worth a gyno visit to check for vaginal infections or STIs.

Menstrual Euphemisms

Menstruation taboos are so pervasive that humans have come up with literally thousands of ways to avoid direct talk about periods. *Shark week, strawberry fields, the curse*—virtually every culture has its own ladylike ways of saying, "My uterine lining is sloughing off, and it's a bloody mess down there." The linguistic origins of the word *taboo*, BTW, are related to the Polynesian word for menstruation.

Menstrual Artifacts and Fictions

From ancient Egyptian pessaries to modern-day period tracking apps, the history of menstruation is littered with all manner of lady-diapers like menstrual belts and sanitary aprons. Also, shout-out to whoever invented that laundry detergent-blue liquid in maxi pad commercials that serves as a visual euphemism for all that chunky blood coming for white jeans everywhere.

- **1921:** Kotex disposable maxi pads hit the market
- **1933:** Gertrude Tendrich patents a tampon applicator and launches Tampax tampons
- **1936:** Tampons debut at the Chicago World's Fair
- **1937:** Leona Chalmers patents the first usable commercial menstrual cup
- **1972:** The National Association of Broadcasters lifts its ban on television advertising for menstrual products

In the 1970s, feminist self-help books recommended repurposing old diaphragms as menstrual cups, but now we have our pick of all shapes and sizes and of disposable and reusable pads, tampons, menstrual cups, and the newest blood catcher on the block, menstrual discs that fit over the cervix.

Menstrual Symptoms

Bloating, breakouts, and breast tenderness are common period symptoms. Premenstrual syndrome (PMS), however, might be more of a side effect of pathologizing female emotions as hysterics than a biological fact. In recent years, studies comparing the timing of women's mood complaints and menstrual cycles suggest that the presumption of PMS and period-induced grouchiness are a cultural exaggeration. "[The] whole PMS notion serves to keep women non-irritable, sweet, and compliant the rest of the time," University of Toronto menstruation researcher Sarah Romans told the *Atlantic* in 2012. It's fishy that we jump to the PMS conclusion, Romans says, rather than considering how female moodiness might be attributed to the stresses of gender inequality, caregiving, and the host of behavioral and appearance-related pressures patriarchy constantly flings at women.[9]

Menstruation Stations

Historically, periods have freaked everyone the f*ck out, prompting the practice of menstrual seclusion. Because of superstitions that menstruating bods are unclean and even toxic to the touch, people on the rag have been sent away to menstrual huts and other traditionally women-only spaces. These beliefs are especially potent in India and Southeast Asia, where most girls aren't taught about periods until after menarche, menstruating folks aren't allowed inside Hindu temples, and contact with certain foods during menstruation is verboten.[10] Healthier habits are slowly spreading, however. In 2017, the Nepalese government banned the practice of *chaupadi*, or menstrual hut seclusion, after three women died inside the tiny shacks most likely because of poor ventilation.[11]

Modern Menstruation

Contemporary feminism emphasizes destigmatizing menstruation and champions menstrual equity in schools and the workplace by providing free menstrual products, and clean and accessible spaces for students and workers to go with their flows. Some feminist groups and labor activists have also begun lobbying for paid period leave benefits, despite evidence that women might be hesitant to use them to avoid reinforcing stereotypes that female bodies are too delicate and unreliable for paid labor and promotion. But on the other side of the economic spectrum, menstrual dignity can be an unaffordable luxury—food stamps don't cover period supplies, and cost leaves supplies out of reach for people experiencing poverty and homelessness.

Period Parts

One way to literally empower your pelvis at home is to practice **Kegel exercises** up to three times a day. Even though *Sex and the City* sold them to us as sexercise, they're designed to strengthen pelvic floor muscles around the urethra, vagina, and rectum. As we get older and (maybe) give birth, those muscles naturally weaken, sometimes leading to **uterine prolapse**, when the uterus sags into the vagina. Kegels can also reduce everyday **stress incontinence**, or peeing a smidge when you exert sudden physical pressure like sneezing, laughing, and running.

patsy

Hawaii Representative **PATSY MINK** might've never become the first woman of color elected to US Congress in 1964 if overt sexism hadn't stonewalled her teen dream of becoming a doctor. Despite being Maui High School's first-ever female student body president and class valedictorian, Patsy was rejected from a dozen medical schools on the basis of sex.

Patsy's legal interests led her to politics, and she became Hawaii's first female territorial representative (1956) and territorial senator (1958). Once in Washington, Patsy set out to level the white, patriarchal playing fields and championed efforts to improve education access, family assistance, and civil rights.

She also confronted racialized sexism and confounded stereotypes that her Japanese American ethnicity made her naturally deferential and modest, or "a lovely Oriental doll," as one journalist described her. Of course, Patsy was no doll; she was a bulldozer. In 1970, a Democratic old boys' club member insisted that women were fundamentally unfit for the Oval Office on account of our "raging storms of monthly hormonal imbalances."[12] Patsy couldn't abide.

"His use of the menstrual cycle and menopause to ridicule women and to caricature all women as neurotic and emotionally unbalanced was as indefensible and astonishing as those who still believe, let alone dare state, that the Negro is physiologically inferior," she wrote in a letter demanding his Democratic committee dismissal. It made the news, and the Dems complied.

But these thirty-seven words Patsy shepherded into law are the crowning jewel of her political career: "No person in the United States shall, on the basis of sex, be excluded from participation in, be denied benefits of, or be subjected to discrimination under any education program or activity receiving federal financial assistance."

Thanks to **Title IX of the Education Amendments of 1972** sex discrimination at school was outlawed. That same year, Patsy ran for president . . . sort of. Unlike her fellow candidate Shirley Chisholm, who was making a serious bid for the party nomination, Patsy appeared on a few state ballots to send a message. She wanted to show girls—and sexist old boys—that women could try for the top spot. Otherwise, she reasoned, "without a woman contending for the presidency, the concept of absolute equality will continue to be placed on the backburner as warmed-over lip service." Patsy served twelve terms in Congress—one for every med school that rejected her.

WHAT WOULD PATSY DO TODAY: She would run!

hysterical sexism

In 2017, American women occupied leadership roles more than ever before. At first, the extracurricular pipeline looks promising: We're likelier to go to college, graduate, and pursue postgrad academia. Compared to just a third of professional employees and managers fifty years ago, women now make up a slight majority.

Beyond that, the pipeline quickly clogs up. Despite the progress made, the pace of leadership parity has remained approximately glacial. The Ivy League schools didn't appoint a woman president until Judith Rodin took over at University of Pennsylvania in 1994. Only twenty-seven states have ever elected a woman governor—all of them white, as of the 2018 election season. Women's highest and winningest elected office in the land has been US secretary of labor, starting with Social Security inventor Frances Perkins in 1933, and six other women since.

Ready your golf clap for a snapshot of today's tepid leader board. According to data gathered by the Pew Research Center, American women are missing in action the higher up the chain you look.[13]

- 30%: US Supreme Court
- 24.8%: State legislators
- 21.1%: Cabinet members
- 21%: Senators
- 21%: Local mayors[14]
- 19.1%: US Representatives
- 8%: Governors
- 5.4%: Fortune 500 CEOs[15]

Depressing as these stats are, we don't share them to be complainers. Relying on these numbers alone as evidence of sexism probably won't convince anyone who isn't already predisposed to agree with you. But looking at the hard data can help quantify the extent of hysterical sexism and its real-world results. One of the many idiosyncrasies of patriarchy is how it convinces us that the world isn't actually biased or bigoted.

Less hamstrung by gendered expectations of propriety and generally uncomfortable listening to women, men have historically been able to leap past their female counterparts into leadership roles. But that's not news. We have to dig

down deeper to the gender differences of opinion. When the Pew Research Center polled Americans to find out how they felt about hypothetically voting for a woman candidate for president, most people weren't bothered by the prospect. But of those who said no way, 33 percent said they didn't think a woman could pull it off, and 27 percent said a man could do it better. Ouch.

"Men and women have become socialized to internalize a powerful stereotype of females as having legitimate authority only when performing nurturant tasks," Northwestern University psychologist Solomon Cytrynbaum explains. "When women attempt to exercise authority in areas deemed culturally inappropriate to the traditional stereotypic sex-role, and behave in nontraditional 'unfeminine' ways, they run into difficulty because subordinates experience disruptive feelings."[16]

baby machines

The pressure for women to have children is so pervasive that researchers in the 1970s coined the concept of **mandatory motherhood**, and with it still comes the assumption that women without kids are less likely to be fulfilled, happy, and well adjusted. Plus, nearly 40 percent of Americans still agree that the country's declining birth rates are bad for society in general. What gives? In 2017, one researcher uncovered a large degree of anger and disapproval directed at childless women and men, indicating a belief that having children is a "moral imperative."[17]

However, way back in 1916, psychologist and early feminist Leta Hollingworth blew that moral imperative out of the water. She blamed church and state for reinforcing a system that promoted "natural" femininity through motherhood, keeping women house-bound and powerless. These motherly norms and the insistence on maternal instinct, Hollingworth claimed, amounted to social control. But since Hollingworth's day, the mandatory motherhood imperative has mutated into a "femmepowerment" work-life balance ideal wherein we expect moms to "have it all."

Expectations of glowing pregnancies and maternal bliss have historically stifled expecting and new moms' mental health needs as well. In 1892, author and social reformer Charlotte Perkins Gilman penned "The Yellow Wallpaper," a fictional first-person story that traces one woman's mental breakdown after giving birth. A critique of strict gender roles and expectations, the story mirrors Gilman's own experience. At 26, she was prescribed a **rest cure** in a sanatorium, where she was diagnosed with "nervous prostration" before being sent home to "live as domestic a life as possible," according to the doctor's orders. The experience was isolating for Gilman and her character alike. Left locked in a nursery for the summer, the fictional character becomes obsessed with, you guessed it, the room's wallpaper, behind which she's convinced people—including herself—are trapped.

About 15 percent of pregnant women experience **antenatal depression**, or depression during pregnancy. Sometimes this stems from pre-existing depression or from going off antidepressants during pregnancy, but it can also be triggered for the first time when a woman gets pregnant. It's more common to hear about **postpartum depression**, which about 14 percent of mothers develop. In about half of those cases, it's a continuation of depression that started during pregnancy. Pressure put on moms to love pregnancy and always find joy in motherhood can make it hard for women suffering from depression to seek help and is anything but empowering.

tick-tock goes the biological clock

Flamboyant *Cosmopolitan* editor Helen Gurley Brown never intended to tell women they should "have it all"—the kids, the career, the money, and the man. When she penned her famous book *Having It All* in 1982, Brown envisioned a kind of manifesto for "mouseburgers," aka women who came from little, who weren't entirely successful, but who were willing to put in the work to get there. She wanted to dispense her advice on how to multitask as a working woman and call it *The Mouseburger Plan*. Despite Brown's insistence that "having it all" was cliche, the publisher thought otherwise, and the title has haunted us ever since.

In 1978, *Washington Post* reporter Richard Cohen had written about how career women were hearing the ticking of a clock wherever they went, drowning out the sound of their heels clicking on that career-ladder climb. A few months later, according to Moira Weigel in her book *Labor of Love: The Invention of Dating*, a reporter for the *Boston Globe* took a more fatalistic tack. Examining the same women Cohen had written about, Anne Kirchheimer described them as older women who'd missed out, "and suddenly the ticking of the biological clock is getting louder and louder," driving men away with their desperation.

It's true that pregnancy rates peak in our twenties and tend to bottom out in our mid forties. According to the American College of Obstetricians and Gynecologists, fertility decline accelerates at thirty-seven, while chances of miscarriage escalate.[18] But take those general guidelines with an unladylike grain of salt, because fertility research tends to rely on slippery data.

Birth records alone don't account for variables such as contraceptive history, sex frequency, and underlying health issues that might affect conception. Studies asking couples about their conception timelines also rely on our unreliable human memory. Even finding a stable pool of study participants can be tough because there's often a narrow window between when couples start trying and when some will conceive. Besides, getting preggers usually takes about eight months, on average. And all the while, our patriarchal culture's biological imperatives keep on ticking us off with constant threats to our reproductive rights.

choosing childfree choices

Whether you're a confirmed baby avoider or simply don't want to add another human to your world, that decision is usually a conscious choice. Today, nearly one in five American women reach menopause without having had children, a significant increase from one in ten in the 1970s. Not everybody drifted there by chance, of course. According to a major national survey, just as many women rowed there in their childfree-by-choice boats as were pulled there involuntarily by life's tides.

In lengthy interviews with childfree folks, researchers found that all but two subjects had given the concept *a lot* of thought, framing the process as a "working decision" that both women and men considered over long stretches. Those other two? They'd always just sort of known deep down that they didn't want to be parents. The men researchers spoke with were concerned with their personal, everyday lives getting interrupted, and many of the women cited worries regarding overpopulation, the environment, and bringing a kid into this nutty world.

But it's not as if choosy non-moms are only focused on kid-created climate change. A separate study found that childfree women largely felt motherhood's costs outweighed its benefits and were more likely to focus on potential losses of freedom, independence, and mobility over any childrearing rewards. They envisioned motherhood as a burden, forcing them to give up opportunities for travel and self-improvement and losing their own identities under the dominant "mom" identity.

The women who actively chose not to have kids also frequently cited a lack of **maternal instinct**, or whatever other gendered emotions they felt women were *supposed* to have about children. They'd deeply internalized socially constructed messages about the selfishness of childless women and told researchers they didn't feel they could measure up to the June Cleaver role expected of them. Questioning assumptions about how women are supposed to mother could go a long way in relieving the pressure of unrealistic expectations and dismantling fears about what kind of woman—mother or not—we should be.

ABCs: abortions 'n' birth control

Frets over female emotions have historically played a disproportionate role in the evolution of women's health care, yielding bygone eras of the mythical hysterical wombs, menotoxins, and nervous illnesses. Even though the medical community has barely found its way around the uterus, paternalistic assumptions that ladies must be protected from their own medical decision making continue to dominate debates about reproductive rights. Mandatory ultrasounds, waiting periods, and parental consent to obtain abortions are often touted as preventive care to ward off patient regret down the road.

But it turns out, according to a recent *PLOS One* study, there's a greater than 99 percent probability rate that women who terminate pregnancies won't regret their decision down the road. After tracking a diverse participant sample of women who had undergone first-trimester and later term abortions for three years, the researchers found 95 percent didn't regret their decision at any point in time and likewise experienced diminishing emotional impact. Unlike what anti-choice rhetoric warns, abortion doesn't haunt most people who opt for it.

Challenging the myth that abortions are a one-way ticket to the Pits of Despair, the study also spotlights how we tend to process abortion-related emotions.

- **Partner support and social acceptance matters.** It's not terribly surprising that if the biological father is in the picture, his opinion impacts a woman's resolution to seek an abortion. As expected, supportive partners (who were likeliest in cases of first-trimester abortions) shored up confidence, while women "whose partners did not want or were not sure if they wanted to terminate the pregnancy" felt less sure they were doing the right thing. Societal views also strongly sway women's tendencies toward regret. The higher the stigma and the lower the social support, the more negative emotions women deal with.

- **Regret does not correlate to length of pregnancy.** Despite anti-choice assumptions that the longer a person is pregnant, the more emotionally disastrous an abortion, the data suggest nothing of the sort. Women also experienced reduced emotional intensity over time: The feelings of relief and happiness experienced shortly after the abortion tended to subside, as did negative emotions. Notably, the study found no differences in emotional trajectories or decision rightness between women having earlier versus later procedures.

- **Complicated emotions are not unique to abortion.** Safely terminating a pregnancy is far from the only health-care intervention we may worry about. Grappling with regrets has been documented among patients undergoing many medical procedures, including sterilization, breast cancer treatment, and heart surgery, as well as among women making other major nonmedical life decisions (e.g., marriage and employment). There's strong empirical evidence that—surprise!—women have a solid success rate in making their own reproductive decisions and feeling good about it, whether that means carrying a pregnancy to term or not.

Are your uterine furies raging yet? If not, our next step along the hysterical sexism highway should rile them up.

american abobos

Abortion is a fact of life. Always has been, and always will be. Throughout history, women—especially those married with children—have taken pregnancy termination into their own hands, even at the risk of injury or death. From ancient Greece and Rome to colonial America, abortion was generally a nonissue so long as it happened before the **quickening**, or the first time the fetus starts kicking around in the womb. Until the mid-nineteenth century, even the Catholic Church was relatively chill regarding pre-quickening abortions based on the belief that the fetus didn't yet have a soul.

Women often "restored the menses" through miscarriage-inducing recipes and folk remedies—some safer and more effective than others—passed along from other women and even colonial housekeeping guides. While wealthier ladies could eventually get their hands on "female pills" that might do the trick, everyday gals generally went the DIY route, drinking unsavory beverages like castor oil, gin with iron filings, and pennyroyal tea. More active types might also try horseback riding, climbing trees, and heavy lifting to induce miscarriage, while others took more drastic measures like douching with lye or attempting

expensive anti-choice nonsense

Just because American women *technically* have reproductive rights doesn't mean the abortion-access path is clear of confusing, expensive, time-consuming hurdles. The more hurdles there are, the more time and money it takes for women to access this essential care. For instance, while the average first-trimester abortion in the United States costs between $300 and $500, waiting until the second trimester can bump the cost up to an average of $1,500.

- **HYDE AMENDMENT:** The late Representative Henry Hyde gave women a swift kick in the uterus with his eponymous provision passed in 1976, three years after *Roe v. Wade* legalized abortion. His nefarious effort to block abortion access prevents any federal funds from paying for abortion except in extreme cases of rape, incest, or when the woman's life is at risk.

- **CRISIS PREGNANCY CENTERS:** These fake clinics exist to confuse and deter people seeking abortions. Often setting up shop near actual women's health clinics, CPCs are under no obligation to present women with medically accurate information, nor do they have any sort of medical licenses.

- **TRAP LAWS:** Restrictions known as Targeted Regulation of Abortion Providers attempt to make it too expensive to operate. Usual tactics include requiring specific sizes for hallways and procedure rooms, requiring providers to have relationships with hospitals, and mandating clinics be a certain distance from a hospital.

- **MANDATORY WAITING PERIODS:** Based on absolutely zero good science, many states add to the abortion-access burden by requiring women to wait anywhere from eighteen to seventy-two hours after they come in for their pre-abortion counseling appointment to actually get the procedure. The extra time means many women are forced to take time off work and either shell out cash for lodging or make multiple trips.

- **MANDATORY ULTRASOUNDS:** Several states require ultrasounds as part of pre-abortion counseling purely for guilt or shaming purposes as opposed to actual, real medical necessity. Depending on where you are and what your insurance covers, you might end up footing the bill since the procedure isn't medically required.

- **FETAL BURIAL LAWS:** A handful of states (we're looking at you, Texas and Indiana) have attempted to pass laws forcing people to pay to bury or cremate fetal remains post-abortion, rather than having hospitals and clinics dispose of them as medical waste, which would add yet another layer of shame and financial burden.

- **PRIVATE INSURANCE LAWS:** Having private insurance means you don't have to worry about the Hyde Amendment, but you still might have to grapple with state insurance regulations. Eleven states bar all insurers from covering abortion, and nine states don't even have exceptions for pregnancy as a result of rape or incest.

to rupture the cervix with thin, sharp objects like knitting needles, bicycle spokes, and coat hangers.

But by 1900, abortion had been criminalized across the United States. What happened? White fright and patriarchy happened, that's what. At the turn of the twentieth century, abolition, urbanization, and immigration presented a triple threat to American white supremacy, and pale folks were nervous. Even worse, white ladies were having fewer babies. Meanwhile, doctor bros were busy organizing themselves into the American Medical Association, which banded together to put midwives and abortionists—who were sometimes one and the same—out of business. Whereas England's criminalization of abortion at least framed it as an act of desperation, allowing some sympathy for the women who sought it, the puritanical United States cast it as wicked, reckless, and unfit for polite society.

baby blockers

Between 1940 and 1960, douching was the go-to birth control method among American women, and Lysol was the most popular rinse.[19] "One most effective way to safeguard her dainty feminine allure is by practicing *complete feminine hygiene* as provided by vaginal douches with a *scientifically correct* preparation like Lysol," one ad spelled out. Housewives couldn't legally get their hands on birth control until 1965; all the single ladies had to hold out until 1972. In the domestic tradition of DIY abortion, "feminine hygiene" was a euphemism for illicit reproductive freedom. Of course, that "complete feminine hygiene" was also completely unhealthy. In 1911, at least five women died from Lysol douching, and nearly two hundred had to be medically treated for Lysol poisoning.[20]

Lawmakers and social conservatives are always eager to block access to abortion, but that doesn't mean they've ever jumped at the chance to help women access safe, reliable birth control to prevent those pregnancies in the first place. But here's the thing: Just like women have and will always seek abortions (no matter the financial, physical, or emotional costs), they've always sought out ways to keep the stork away.

contraception concerns

So how do you know which birth control path is right for you? Get nosy about it. There's a cornucopia of contraception out there, and you're entitled to research and ask questions; even if a harried nurse sighs at your follow-up questions, you aren't doing anything wrong by advocating for your own well-being. That means requesting however much information you need about whatever contraception options your provider offers. Here are a few ideas to keep in mind when you're on the case:

- **CONSIDER SIDE EFFECTS.** Different bodies respond differently, not only to different types of birth control, but even to different brands in the same category. Changes like more or fewer headaches, and more or less acne are common. Afraid your libido might tank and your waistline expand? Generally, studies don't support those fears.

- **MYTH BUST INFERTILITY.** Hormonal birth control—like the Pill, patches, rings, and some IUDs—does not sterilize you, nor does it have long-term effects on your fertility once you stop taking it. Remove that IUD, and the pregnancy-preventing hormones leave with it. Stop popping the pill, and within a few weeks to months, ovulation will resume.

- **MONITOR MENTAL HEALTH.** Studies are inconsistent, but it does appear that hormonal contraception—perhaps progesterone in particular—can *slightly* boost a small number of women's risk for depression, but many other factors are also at play when it comes to a mental health diagnosis. Do your future wellness a favor and talk to your doctor about managing your moods plus meds.

- **EXAMINE EFFECTIVENESS.** IUDs and implants are the most effective methods of birth control, each with a baby-blocking success rate of more than 99 percent. Not only that, the non-hormonal copper IUD can serve as emergency contraception if it's implanted within five days of having unprotected sex.

- **MIND THE GAP.** If, for whatever reason, you decide to switch contraceptives, holler at your nurse practitioner about the best way to transition. In general, don't leave any time between one method and the next (you might actually need to overlap them) and use backup methods like condoms until the new method has taken effect.

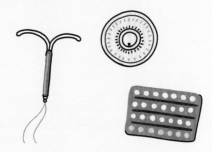

LEGAL EAGLE

BIRTH CONTROL

The first oral contraceptive hit the US market in 1960 thanks to Margaret Sanger and Katharine Dexter McCormick (see page 189), but it took a while for society to expand beyond "womb veils" (aka diaphragms) and vulcanized rubber condoms to figure out who could pop the Pill—and who should pay for it.

- *Griswold v. Connecticut* (1965): Under the Fourteenth Amendment right to privacy, SCOTUS gave married couples the green light to use the Pill.

- *Baird v. Eisenstadt* (1972): SCOTUS moved things along and ruled birth control was legal for everybody, regardless of marital status.

- *Burwell v. Hobby Lobby* (2014): Sure, you can use birth control, but your religious employer doesn't have to pay for it. SCOTUS ruled in favor of craft store Hobby Lobby, meaning that family-owned and closely held companies with religious objections don't have to provide free, sinful contraception under the Affordable Care Act.

When people weren't crossing their fingers and counting on the withdrawal method, they might rely on trusty ol' condoms, which go as far back as 3000 BCE, although it wouldn't be until the nineteenth century that actual rubber became a thing (quite a step up from animal intestines or linen). Today, nearly 65 percent of married or partnered-up women of baby-making age around the world rely on some type of contraception.

It's more than a little ridiculous that birth control is treated as anything other than the public-health investment it is—even mega-rich investor Warren Buffett recognizes the value of betting on it. Through one of his family foundations, Buffett has helped support research into reproductive health and contraception with the idea that "unless women can control their fertility . . . you are sort of wasting more than half of the brainpower in the United States," according to Judith DeSarno, a former director at the Buffett Foundation.

In Colorado, where the foundation invested $50 million from 2008 to 2013 to help the state provide patients with free IUDs and health-care professionals with training, the teen pregnancy rate dropped 40 percent, and their abortion rate fell more than 33 percent. Investing in and supporting family planning—as feminists, midwives, and witches have been preaching forever—allows girls and women more control over the path they choose.

But, chances are, we don't have to convince you how great and potentially liberating birth control can be. According to a 2017 survey of American voters, 85 percent of women consider birth control to be a vital part of preventive health care, and a majority agree with Warren Buffett and believe affordable birth control plays a role in women's financial stability, gender equality, happiness, and sexual freedom. Oh, and gender aside, eight out of ten voters say women should have the freedom to get it on without worrying about getting preggers.

reproductive injustices

For unladylike women, the fight hasn't revolved solely around the right to abortion and birth control. Contraceptives' benefits cut across race and class lines; access doesn't. Today, exercising reproductive rights can feel like a luxury, particularly for women of color, whose fertility has too often been at the mercy of others.

"At the heart of **reproductive justice** is this claim: all fertile persons and persons who reproduce and become parents require a safe and dignified context for these most fundamental human experiences," Loretta Ross and Rickie Solinger write in their 2017 book *Reproductive Justice: An Introduction.* Governments owe their citizens access to that safe and dignified fertility management, the pair writes, because it constitutes a human right.

The reproductive justice struggle encompasses the ability to:

- Fully and safely pursue life, liberty, and happiness through having and raising the healthy family you want

- Freely nurture your well-being on multiple levels, from the physical and spiritual to the political and economic

- Access the health care and living wages that can allow you to build the life you want

There's a violent history of blocking access to reproductive choice and justice. In 1883, Englishman Francis Galton argued for segregation and forced sterilization of the "unfit." His ideas flourished in the early twentieth century among upper-class white people nervous about a changing society who subsequently began funding investigations into weeding out undesirables. Even *Cosmopolitan* (a decidedly less sexy ladymag back then) got in on the action, encouraging its readers to jump on the "inspiring" chance for hereditary betterment and elimination of disability. Ooh-la-la! The eugenics movement decidedly stood in the way of empowering women whose choice whether to bear children traditionally hadn't been up to them.

In 1927, the US Supreme Court upheld sterilization in the case of a young white woman from Virginia named Carrie Buck, who'd gotten pregnant through rape and was declared "feeble-minded." Defending his majority opinion upholding states' rights to forcibly sterilize women and girls on the basis of disability— real or perceived—Supreme Court Justice Oliver Wendell Holmes reasoned that "[t]hree generations of imbeciles is enough." That high court decision flung open the state-level floodgates to institutionalize women and easily argue against their fitness to be mothers as a reason to sterilize them.

Starting in the 1950s, doctors, social workers, and others shifted their focus more exclusively to poor women of color, particularly black women. Motivated by racist and classist desires to reduce black women's claims on public assistance, US officials violated thousands of women's human rights and typically left little paper trail. Often referred to as Mississippi appendectomies, secret sterilizations were routinely performed when women came in for procedures ranging from C-sections to tumor removals to actual appendectomies.

Between 1907 and 1983, an estimated 70,000 women were forcibly sterilized across the United States, although it's virtually impossible to know exactly how many were abused through the eugenics-based protocol. If doctors recorded the procedure at all, they often indicated it was voluntary, hidden among a rising number of actual voluntary, contraceptive sterilizations that women were requesting. Hearing it euphemistically referred to as getting your "tubes tied" also misled some women into thinking it was reversible.

Usually it was impoverished brown mothers who were outright coerced with threats of their financial aid, health care, or custody rights being withheld unless they agreed to a tubal ligation. As part of the War on Poverty declared by President Lyndon B. Johnson in 1964, family planning services pushed sterilization for Mexican American women, whom they stereotyped as "hyper-breeders" and "welfare moms in waiting." By the 1970s, the Indian Health Service had sterilized nearly a quarter of Native American women, while social workers in Puerto Rico pushed sterilization during home visits, and some employers preferentially hired sterilized women.

The stigma, shame, and fear that came along not only with infertility but also with the violation of their bodies kept many women silent, isolated in their pain and assuming they were alone. What recourse did they have in such a racist system? Civil rights leader and voting rights activist Fannie Lou Hamer, herself a victim of forced sterilization in 1961, never once kept quiet about the abuse, nor was she reticent to point out the fear of racial violence women of color faced if they dared seek justice: "Me? Getting a white lawyer to go against a white doctor? I would have been taking my hands and screwing tacks into my own casket."

Compulsory sterilization isn't a uniquely American oddity, nor has it entirely stopped: According to the Center for Investigative Reporting, almost 150 women in California prisons were forcibly sterilized between 2006 and 2010, spurring the state's governor to sign a bill banning the practice in prisons. The fight to ensure reproductive justice for the increasing number of American women behind bars continues. Only a handful of states have laws or prison policies that fully ban the shackling of inmates during labor and delivery, an inhumane and humiliating practice that puts the health and safety of both mother and baby in jeopardy. But without proper enforcement and education for prison workers, many women are still subjected to shackling. Incarcerated women also struggle to access pre- and postnatal medical care and abortion care, endure sexual violence at the hands of correctional officers, and face a high risk of both STIs and unintended pregnancy.

Supporting reproductive justice goes beyond supporting birth control and abortion rights. It means supporting and embracing women's lived experiences, empowering them to organize and push back against inequality, and doing what we can to lift up those most marginalized. It means speaking out against exploitation, exclusion, and barriers to health care access. And it means getting a little loud and a little uncomfortable by stepping outside your own routine into movements from the grassroots level to the national stage.

head games

CRAZY, SHRILL, AND SAD

The cult of intelligence is the oldest old-boy network, flourishing way back in Western antiquity when Plato and Aristotle waxed hyperbolic about the male body's expert engineering and superior, semen-filled brains. That misogynistic mindset also soured Charles Darwin's scientific revolution. Like most of his contemporaries, the distinguished naturalist was straight-up stupid about women. The way he saw it, man simply has "higher eminence, in whatever he takes up, than can woman—whether requiring deep thought, reason, or imagination, or merely the use of the senses and hands." His anecdotal evidence? All those boy geniuses! His cousin and founding eugenicist Francis Galton pulled the same patriarchal parlor trick in defense of his central framework linking brain size and intelligence. If women can be so smart, his retort still echoes, then where were the lady Mozarts, Picassos, and Einsteins?!

The sexism lingers. A 2017 study published in the journal *Science* discovered that girls start doubting their gender is "really, really smart" from age six. Even though they're likelier to predict that girls earn higher grades than boys, the study results suggested they dissociate from the so-called "raw intellectual talent" à la *Good Will Hunting*, Ironman, or Mark Zuckerberg.[1] And these early associations aren't just a phase;

"Assent, and you are sane; / Demur, you're straightaway dangerous, / And handled with a Chain"

EMILY DICKINSON
poet and attic dweller

social science has consistently affirmed how visual role models—or their absence—shape our interests, ambitions, and future career paths.

So where is all this **boy genius bias** coming from? Pretty much everywhere. Pop culture replicates this through default male archetypes like absentminded professors, mad scientists, and whatever those guys do on *The Big Bang Theory*. Classrooms replicate this dichotomy, too. In a 2016 visual analysis of scientists depicted in elementary textbooks, a whopping 75 percent were men. The pattern similarly snakes its way into higher education, with words like "brilliant" and "genius" cameoing significantly more often in professor evaluations and academic letters of recommendation for men, while female profs and postdocs receive more praise for being "knowledgeable" and "productive."[2]

"The vast social project of science is ignored in favor of celebrity scientists mythologized as stubborn individuals—similar to cowboys on the frontier—who strike out on their own and discover unexplored territory," antiquarian Lisa Hix wrote in *Collector's Weekly* about how science culture was invented for boys. There's Carl Sagan in his turtleneck and Steve Jobs in *his* turtleneck. Alan Turing is being cranky again, and don't even think about bothering Thomas Edison. The same can be said for the arts and the canon of lone, male geniuses who skew not-so-respectful to women (fictional and not), like Henry Miller and Pablo Picasso, who treated women so disposably even his daughter refused to go to his funeral.

"Men like Louis C.K. may be creators of art, but they are also destroyers of it," Amanda Hess wrote in the *New York Times* in 2017 about how the male genius shield enables misogyny and abuse. "They have crushed the ambition of women and, in some cases, young men—boys—in the industry, robbing them of their own opportunities."[3] There's still a lot more unlearning and rehumanizing to do toward that figure. Does that mean you can never dance to David Bowie again? No. It means masterpieces, punch lines, and seemingly pure magic don't compensate for treating people like disposable muses.

what to expect when you're expecting neurosexism

The female brain has always been put in its place, just like the body it operates. How has this pink versus blue brain binary gotten so stuck in our heads? Because "science." By the turn of the twentieth century, still the early days of professionalized science, the myth of women's "missing five ounces of brain" had spread across Europe and America, claiming that female intellect is innately inferior because women and their "[delicate] brain fibers" are literally airheads. True, female brains tend to weigh 10 percent less than male brains. Too bad the white science bros of the day were too sexist to consider that brain size develops in proportion to *body* size, not intelligence; otherwise, manbrains wouldn't stand a chance against elephants, whose brains are three to five times larger than humans'.

During the Victorian era, those early anthropologists, anatomists, and medical doctors were hot with brain fever, obsessively sketching, measuring, and weighing all the skulls and brain matter they could collect. That often meant purchasing the anonymous cadavers of indigenous peoples, slaves, convicts, and the impoverished just to dissect and dispose of them like animals. Convinced as ever that size equals prowess, those nineteenth-century skull fanatics manipulated that dirty data into patriarchal, white supremacist scientific theories that educated gents were the biggest-headed and thus the most advanced members of the entire human species.

Male and female brains are structurally indistinguishable to the neuroscientist's naked eye. Rather than pink or blue blobs in our craniums, our supposed male and female brains look more like Jackson Pollock–style pink- *and* blue-splattered masterpieces. These mosaics of neurons rarely look alike; even identical twins don't share a matching set. That means slight brain structural differences across massive populations can't tell us much about how male and female intellects compare. In 2016, the most detailed map of the cerebral cortex underscored that "each individual is unique in terms of the pattern of cortical folds and in the size and shape of areas of the cortical map." In other words, the male/female brain binary is actually more of a spectrum.

Structural sex differences *do* exist. On average, the same regions are slightly bigger, smaller, denser, and more or less connected among men and women's brains. But ironclad mega-studies consistently find that the Venn diagram of neurotypical male and female brains looks far more like a circle than Olympic rings. Same goes for IQs. To the chagrin of mansplaining know-it-alls everywhere, there's no gender gap when it comes to average intelligence.

Yet modern neuroscience hasn't fully advanced beyond the brain binary. Brown University biology and gender studies professor Anne Fausto-Sterling argues that has everything to do with the binary gender beliefs still baked into brain research. "[D]espite the many recent insights," she writes in *Sexing the Body: Gender Politics and the Construction of Sexuality*, "this organ remains a vast unknown, a perfect medium on which to project, even unwittingly, assumptions about gender."

What's *really* happening in our collective heads is that when it comes to "the majority of social, cognitive, and personality variables,"[4] we're all working with pretty much the same stuff in our noggins. Feminist neurobiologists like Cordelia Fine describe this as **overlap**. That phenomenon is also one reason Fine has led the scholarly charge against drawing stark behavioral conclusions from all this newfangled neurological mapping, like male selfishness and female altruism. As she details in *Delusions of Gender*, brain imaging alone can't account for "the influential interactions between genes, brain, social experience, and cultural context." Instead, it promotes more of the same old **neurosexism**, and you don't have to be a rocket scientist to spot it (although America's first female rocket scientist, Mary Sherman Morgan, probably witnessed it everywhere in the lab).

As privileged white women began elbowing their way into higher education, a host of doctors and experts tried to scare them away with fake science that still sounds familiar. Even if a girl was smarter than the average ditz, they insisted a menstruating body couldn't withstand the mental strain of advanced learning. "An American girl, yoked with a dictionary, and laboring with [menstruation], is an exhibition of monstrous brain and aborted ovarian development," Harvard medical professor Edward H. Clarke warned in his 1873 treatise against coeducation. Studying "in the boys' way," as he put it, endangered ladies' uteruses and future baby-making.

And if it sounds like we've been strolling along the binary tightrope, you heard right. Because of learning disabilities' stigma—and unfounded phobias of disability as either hypersexualized or hypervictimized—their intersections with sexual orientation and queer gender identities are actively avoided. But parents, doctors, and teachers ought to pay closer attention since autism and gender nonconformity hang out a noticeable amount. Kids at autism clinics are up to seven times likelier to be gender nonconforming, and on the flip side, kids at gender clinics are up to fifteen times likelier to have an autism spectrum disorder. Yet among transgender people with autism, desires for nonbinary gender expression and hormonal transition are commonly dismissed as cognitive defects.

black girls' not-so-special education

Teachers generally tend to praise girls' gender-appropriate behavior and the appearance of their work, while compliments for competence and creativity are more often doled out to the boys. By far, though, looks-based judgments fall harshest on African American girls in the classroom. Starting as early as preschool, they're more than twice as likely to face school suspension in all fifty states. During the 2011-2012 schoolyear, the US Department of Education found that 12 percent of black female students in elementary and middle schools were suspended compared to 1 percent of their white classmates over the same period. Colorism also gets in the mix, as darker-skinned girls are the likeliest of all to get on a principal's bad side.

Hmm, what could be going on here? What could possibly explain the fact that black girls in the Washington, D.C., public school system are more than seventeen times likelier to be sent home compared to white girls? Are African American girls simply too much to handle? Or are school administrators disproportionately targeting them—whether intentionally or not?

When the National Women's Law Center (NWLC) dug into this issue in 2017, it isolated a host of unfortunately familiar biases pulling the strings: "Stereotypes of black girls and women as 'angry' or aggressive, and 'promiscuous'

 **CLAP BACK WITH FACTS**

the gendering of learning disabilities

The Learning Disabilities Association of America defines LDs as "neurologically based processing problems," and boys' have been analyzed far longer and more robustly than girls' in part because male educational achievement has historically been more prized thanks to—you guessed it!—patriarchy. Today, boys still make up a majority of students with identified LDs, but researchers are increasingly recognizing how girls are also good—*too good*—at hiding theirs.

- **ADHD:** Attention-deficit/hyperactivity disorder amps up in puberty for girls but not boys. Left untreated, adulting with untreated ADHD presents a fresh set of challenges like time management, organization, and stress management, which fosters what's called a "learned helplessness style" of responding to negative situations with a despairing sense of powerlessness.

- **AUTISM:** The foundational diagnostic criteria for autism spectrum disorders were based on boys-only research, and as late as the early 2000s, autism was popularly described as the product of "an extreme male brain." In general, girls' slightly better social skills tend to camouflage autism suspicions as well, a coping mechanism known as "masking." However, a *Scientific American* investigation into the autism gender puzzle warned that "the autistic tendency to be direct and take things literally can make affected girls and women easy prey for sexual exploitation" as well as abusive relationships.

- **DYSLEXIA:** As with ADHD and autism, we used to think dyslexia only messed with boy brains. Now, researchers suspect the dyslexic community is evenly split between girls and boys.

or hyper-sexualized can shape school officials' views of black girls in critically harmful ways." Before they're even old enough to drive, black girls are perceived as seductive Jezebels and berating Sapphires in waiting—and punished as such.

Even positive stereotypes applied to African American women, specifically assertiveness, backfire on younger black women in learning environments as "talking back." Speaking of which, black girls are likelier to end up in more punitive academic settings to begin with, attending schools with fewer counselors and more police officers on hand.

"This uneven discipline is often the result of deeply ingrained racist and sexist stereotypes that push black girls out of school," NWLC education director Neena Chaudhry told *U.S. News & World Report*. Getting kicked out of school may then tip the dominoes into teen pregnancy, criminality, and permanent lack of access to opportunity.

A research-backed intervention offers hope. National Black Women's Justice Institute cofounder Monique W. Morris says teachers can make a world of difference (which, of course, is easier said than done in too many public school classrooms). "[Black] girls express that a caring teacher is most important in their learning environment," Morris told the *Atlantic* in 2016. "When they connect with a teacher and feel a genuine love and appreciation for their promise as scholars, their relationship with school is more positive."

In the early 1800s, free black women responded to racist barriers to schooling and higher education by forming their own book clubs. This spirit rings in the 1831 founding charter of Philadelphia's all-black Female Literary Association: "As daughters of a despised race, it becomes a duty . . . to cultivate the talents entrusted to our keeping, that by doing so, we may break down the strong barrier of prejudice." Famed abolitionist William Lloyd Garrison was so moved by the group's charter, he personally paid them a visit. Founding member Sarah Mapps Douglass was also a rare black, female science lecturer who focused on teaching girls and women about anatomy, reproduction, and hygiene. Her public teaching not only "powerfully embodied performances of black women's humanity and intelligence," but also served a community that was often barred from access to city hospitals and doctors.

Unladylike women have a knack for participatory, or DIY, media. In order to freely express ourselves, swap ideas, and record personal histories, we've often had to go rogue—girls' diaries included. Ever since printing technology became more accessible in the 1800s, American women have been collaborating and creating their own pamphlets, broadsides, and booklets to spread the word about suffrage, labor rights, sexual health, family planning, and cannabis remedies.[5] But they weren't the only gal-made media mavens shaking up patriarchal culture.

After hatching the idea with four feminist girlfriends in 1911, **RAICHŌ HIRATSUKA** began her work as the founding editor of *Seitō,* or *Bluestocking*. It was Japan's first literary magazine "created by brains and hands of Japanese women today," the debut issue declared. Featuring a standard mix of personal essay, haiku, and fiction, *Seitō* revealed the personal feelings and frustrations that resonated with its female readers and provoked more direct explorations of women's rights issues off the page.

In fact, Raichō's poetic, inaugural editorial went down in Japanese history as the country's unofficial declaration of women's rights: "In the beginning, woman was the sun. She was an authentic person. Today she is the moon. She lives by others, shines with the light of others; she is the moon with the pallid face of an invalid . . ."

Raichō and her fellow Seitōsha who helped publish *Bluestocking* didn't go unnoticed, especially once the Japanese press began referring to them as "New Women." Partly a subtweet to Western liberated feminists, the label also referenced the women's open resistance to Japan's state-monitored "good wife, wise mother" femininity standard. Even though the magazine's circulation never topped five thousand, the government banned certain issues lest they wreak havoc on Japanese family values. After all, these reform-minded feminists were known to sample alcohol, dine with geishas, and have same-sex affairs.

In 1915, twenty-nine-year-old Raichō stepped away from *Seitō* around the same time it folded. She had grander ambitions ahead. In 1920, she founded the New Women's Association and launched Japan's first campaign for female suffrage (which was not realized until 1945).

WHAT RAICHŌ WOULD DO TODAY: No doubt, she'd launch a multimedia empire complete with podcast, magazine, book, and live shows to bring more women and nonbinary folks into the feminist fold.

girls of color in american classrooms

In 1837, America's founding women's college, Wesleyan, welcomed its first class. The following year, Oberlin College became the first mixed-sex school, and by the turn of the century, most new universities routinely accepted (white) women. But allowing ladies in the classroom didn't magically free female students from the hyper-gendered roles they were expected to fulfill, which is why Oberlin gals also had to complete laundry, sewing, and dishwashing duties as part of their curriculum.

Confounding administrators' marginal expectations, women excelled at a lot more than ironing. Worse, the prospect of college was getting even more popular among the menstruating masses. "Too many women students were enrolling, and they were doing too well academically," Princeton historian Nancy Weiss Malkiel wrote about elite institutions battening down admissions against women lest their girlbrains sour their scholastic reputations.

But women's colleges weren't universally inclusive, either. In 1900, abolitionist and women's rights ally W. E. B. DuBois publicized his verified finding that it was easier for a black man to get accepted to a predominantly white men's college like Harvard or Yale, than it was for a black woman to get into a predominantly white women's college. Women of color might attend a less-racially-ass-backwards school like Virginia's coed Hampton Institute or Georgia's Spelman College instead.

Judging by a 1914 anecdote, racism hung around for a good while at elite women's colleges. That year, Radcliffe University president LeBaron Russell Briggs went to bat for an African American applicant, Mary Gibson. His pitch to donors? She wasn't like *other* black girls, owing to her light skin and appearance that could pass as "Spanish."

Even when predominantly white women's colleges accepted black applicants, the students would likely be assigned to a segregated dorm, tucked away from campus hubs. International girls of color had an easier, if exoticized, go of it. When Kang Tongbi, a Chinese suffragist and anti-foot-binding activist, became Barnard's first Asian student in 1907, it made news in the *New York Times*, *Harper's Weekly*, and the *New York Tribune*. But as a hugely ambitious young woman from a privileged background, Tongbi negotiated with that exoticism by almost leaning into it. On campus, she rented the most expensive apartment the college offered and threw lavish tea parties. No kidding. Her extracurriculars also included the suffrage club because that was something rad ladies did back then.

counterproductive compliments

Who doesn't like praise? Employees work harder when they feel appreciated, and college students get an extra surge of motivation when their classmates are recognized. And when we're already feeling pretty great about ourselves, we eagerly devour enthusiastic compliments because they match our self-esteem and self-image.

But just like praise can puff us up, it can also collapse us into two-dimensional versions of ourselves, reinforcing harmful gender and racial stereotypes—and revealing way more about the praisers than the praisees in the process.

Take the **skinned-knee effect**: When little girls act shy, anxious, or afraid, parents tend to roll with gender expectations and reward the behavior with kisses and coddling. Meanwhile, boys are more likely to hear, "Suck it up, kid!" It's possible that this message—that helplessness is not only okay, but feminine and praiseworthy—sticks, leaving some of us to wallow in it, consciously or not. Thanks a lot, patriarchal gender expectations!

But those same expectations shift when we dive deeper into the experiences of women of color.

The Amazing Invincible Woman

Look! It's a bird! It's a plane! It's . . . a black woman who's sick of your racist assumptions that she's too tough to ever need a hand or a break.

Resilient, unyielding, and unbreakable, the **strong black woman** is a mama bear figure who's rewarded not for her vulnerability, but for how many burdens she can shoulder. She puts others' needs before her own but is too independent to be suitable wife or girlfriend material. If only she'd let others do for her! Yeah, if only.

The dehumanizing trope is "at odds with African American women's very survival," author Tamara Winfrey Harris wrote in *Bitch* magazine in 2014. Black women are more likely to suffer from chronic health problems that self- and preventive care could alleviate, like diabetes, heart disease, and stress. The stereotype can become a psychological barrier to mental health treatment, reinforcing the notion that black women possess superhuman strength in the face of centuries of slavery, abuse, and discrimination and don't need outside help. Such cultural assumptions contribute to fewer black women seeking or completing treatment for mental health conditions and substance abuse.

And black women are also more likely to be the victims of sexual violence and homicide at the hands of a partner. But we typically don't gather around our televisions for updates when they go missing. Society overlooks them and their needs and assumes they don't require the same type of protection and concern that white women—historically, the vision of true femininity and womanhood—are afforded.

Those twin stereotypes were born out of slavery. Black women were viewed as property capable of performing grueling manual labor, and black children were put to work at the earliest age possible, while helpless white women were sheltered inside the home and white children were given not only the safe time and space to play, but also greater legal protections.

The implications today are heartbreaking, and they reach far beyond adult women not feeling they can ask for help. A 2017 study from Georgetown Law's Center on Poverty and Inequality revealed that in the United States, adults judge black girls as young as five to be more adultlike than their white

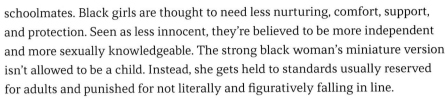

schoolmates. Black girls are thought to need less nurturing, comfort, support, and protection. Seen as less innocent, they're believed to be more independent and more sexually knowledgeable. The strong black woman's miniature version isn't allowed to be a child. Instead, she gets held to standards usually reserved for adults and punished for not literally and figuratively falling in line.

America's Next Top Model Minority

Asian and Pacific Islander girls get called more racial slurs than any other group. But why don't we ever hear about that outstanding stat? Administrators may not be paying close enough attention because **model minority** mythology labels Asian students as a homogenous mass of tailor-made star students. So other kids assume, "You're not *that* oppressed, so racist stereotypes and jokes aren't *really* racist, right?" Wrong. Contemporary studies consistently confirm the mental health toll of an unrealistic pressure to excel and glide past racism as if lubed up with superhuman privilege.

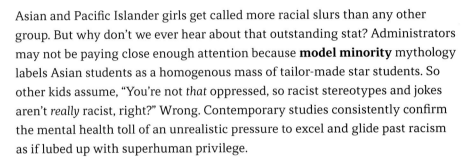

When this stereotype began accruing currency in the 1950s, scholar Emily Wu says it was more about concern over what white students were up to. "That speaks to America's anxieties about juvenile delinquency," Wu told the *Washington Post* in an interview about her 2013 deep dive on the issue, *The Color of Success.* By the 1970s, model minority status had gone mainstream as the wage gap between Asian American men and white American men closed.

That financial leap forward sprouted a Very White Idea that Japanese Americans, for instance, survived the atrocity of World War II internment camps and essentially hacked racism through hard work and family loyalty. Not only that, the *New York Times* glowingly reported in 1966, Japanese Americans accomplished this with "their own almost totally unaided effort."

This backhanded bullsh*t shouldn't get a politeness pass. The financial fetishizing of Asian Americans is a middle finger by proxy to so-called "problem minority" African Americans who clearly just aren't doing enough to help themselves. "It is more than simple chance that the appearance of the 'model minority' term coincided with the rise of the African American

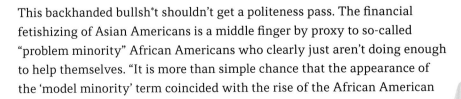

civil rights movement and Chicano civil rights movement," Bernadette N. Lin wrote in a *Harvard Crimson* essay disavowing its dehumanizing effects. She was all too familiar with them as a third-generation Asian American science major at an Ivy League school. "Why don't we acknowledge this?"

Perfection Is Preferred

Perfectionism is the iceberg that can sink your success *Titanic*. On the surface, it hardly looks threatening: It's put together, polished, and professional; it's hardworking, punctual, and driven. Beneath the waves, however, is a mountain-sized fear monster that keeps the perfectionist frantically churning to avoid failing, making mistakes, or looking, well, imperfect.

When perfectionists are floating in low-pressure situations, they're great. But when they get out of their depth and don't have healthy outlets or ways to cope, they wind up crushed by pressure and helplessness, putting them at risk for depression, eating disorders, and even suicidal tendencies—particularly if they think people value them only for that perceived flawlessness.

Perfectionism intersects with gender and race when those stereotypes fuel our need to:

- Consistently have to perform twice as well to be seen as almost equal, often for still less validation or pay

- Answer sexist or racist scrutiny with unquestionable competence

- Fight any voice in our heads that might whisper, "Imposter!"

When you're racked with self-doubt, it's easy to feel like you're deceiving your peers when you pull off a win. This is **imposter syndrome**: the feeling that at any minute, people will see through your veneer and realize you're not nearly as smart or talented or accomplished as they thought. Somewhere along the line, what would otherwise be a healthy, productive drive to do your best becomes twisted into an endless cycle of fear, overwork, accomplishment, and rejection—not from others, but from an internal push against rewards or reassurances you feel are unwarranted.

In the 1970s, as women were riding feminism's second wave right into nine-to-five office jobs and banging on that glass ceiling, psychologist Pauline Clance started to notice a trend among the bright, accomplished female students in her Oberlin College classes. Despite their hard work and success, they were convinced they were going to be found out as frauds who didn't deserve to be there.

Clance and fellow psychologist Suzanne Imes investigated how far this imposter phenomenon went among women. They found that regardless of age, imposter syndrome froze women between a fear of failure and an inability to accept their own success. Clance and Imes linked the women's feelings of phoniness with generalized anxiety, low self-confidence, and depression.

Much of it stemmed from messages the women got as kids. The women who'd been considered the sensitive or social sibling—rather than the bright one—never got over the need to earn validation through brain-busting work. Other women had parents who constantly praised their brilliance and talent. But as they got older and encountered challenges that took *work* to overcome, they felt like frauds for having to work hard in order to keep up the appearance of effortless perfection.

Imposters' and perfectionists' meltdown-level anxiety over the possibility of screwing up can manifest in a few different ways.

- **Avoidance:** The weight of anxiety over expectations can lead to procrastination, flagging motivation, and sometimes even self-sabotage when you feel you're falling short of the unrealistic standards you've set for yourself. In assuming you need to be perfect right off the bat, you leave no room to experiment, learn, grow, and enjoy your achievements.

- **Overcompensating:** The fear of failure can prompt a massive amount of overwork, even if that constant buzzing is full of unproductive busywork meant to disguise your anxiety from yourself. Talk about a recipe for burnout! When you sacrifice your creativity, spontaneity, and *actual* interests for the endless work of proving yourself, you wind up also sacrificing the activities that help you recharge.

dismantle the imposter

It's okay to own your skills and unapologetically go after what you want, even if you're an outsider. Here are some tools to confront the overworked imposter in the mirror:

- **CONFESS YOUR FEARS:** Group therapy is one successful way to interrupt the imposter cycle. Sharing our deep-seated, secret fears and anxieties not only helps dispel the mythology we've built up around ourselves, but it also gets us to think beyond ourselves and fosters empathy with fellow hardworking humans. Allow yourself to be vulnerable, and you'll start to realize you're not the only one who feels this way.

- **GET OUT OF YOUR HEAD:** Volunteering can be another effective coping strategy. If workaholic imposters can drag themselves away from their desks, they might find that refocusing their energy onto a common, greater goal of helping the community eases their anxiety.

- **REFOCUS YOUR ENERGY:** Find outlets that allow you to express the full depth and breadth of your experience. Carving out time for healthy priorities, rather than narrowly focusing on each and every personal misstep, can help reshape the way you structure your days. Rather than spending an hour crafting an email, try limiting yourself to ten minutes and spend the rest of the time calling lawmakers to protest harmful legislation!

- **TALK TO YOURSELF:** Practicing some basic mantras might help shift you to a more realistic perspective. Remind yourself that everyone screws up, there's no such thing as perfection, and there's always a learning curve. Be patient, loving, and kind with yourself, and talk to yourself the way you would to your best friend.

- **EMBRACE CHALLENGES:** Having a growth mindset means you love a challenge and learning new information. You accept that adversity is a part of life and that, with help from others, you can evolve and grow. Your intelligence and skills aren't set in stone, so there's far less reason to fear vulnerability, change, and failure. Embrace your fear, too—it's likely communicating that what's in front of you is important to you and possibly life-changing.

- **FAKE IT TILL YOU MAKE IT:** Humans are terrible judges of their own skill levels, so it's no surprise that confidence often gets conflated with competence. Here's some context: Men and women tend to process success and failure differently, and women tend to have overall lower expectations of their ability to succeed. Men are often overconfident in their abilities, and while they attribute their successes to innate strengths, they blame failures on external factors like bad luck. Women, on the other hand, chalk up our success to those external factors, while blaming ourselves for failure. Seize the power of mediocre men, and stride confidently in the direction of your dreams—even if it takes you a minute to actually believe in yourself.

- **Multitasking:** Women are said to be innately better than men at multitasking, an assumption that stems from women's traditional roles as caregivers and household CEOs. But unless you're among the 2 percent of the population considered to be **supertaskers**, with a genetically inherited predisposition to masterfully juggle to-do lists, your efforts at darting between tasks are actually undermining your concentration and productivity. When we regularly and heavily multitask, we essentially lose the ability to tune out irrelevant information and distractions, allowing the useless stuff to clutter our memories. Chasing an impossibility doesn't make for greater productivity. In fact, heavy multitaskers also tend to be more impulsive. Chill out and check off your to-do list one item at a time.

minding your mental health

Many of our struggles begin when we're kids—issues like ADHD and phobias—but stuff starts to get real when we hit adolescence. That's when genetic disorders like schizophrenia and mood disorders, including major depressive and bipolar disorder, surface.

It helps to keep in mind that while some early mental health struggles fade with age, even moderate problems can echo into adulthood in terms of how you relate to others and cope with difficulty and stress. And as we age, more anxiety issues percolate, including panic, generalized anxiety, and post-traumatic stress disorders, all of which hit women harder and more often than men.

Factors that compound our anxiety and depression spirals include:

- **Lacking agency:** Social and economic rank are perhaps some of the most significant predictive factors of depression. People who have low self-confidence and self-worth, who feel inferior and defeated, are more likely to develop depression. That risk narrows when we have the ability, freedom, and confidence to control our own lives, in addition to the time, money, and resources to guard our health and safety. But in patriarchal cultures that seek to repress or control women's sexuality, reproductive choices, and movement through the world—and considering that women make up the bulk of the world's poor—we don't always have that agency. Gender-, race-, and sexual-orientation-based violence, unequal pay, and discrimination are all social frameworks that leave women feeling powerless, hopeless, humiliated, and trapped—and all contribute to women's disproportionate risk for depression and anxiety.

- **Concealing your true self:** Pretending to be someone you're not is a drag, and the negative effects run deep. Constantly monitoring both your environment and your own speech and actions to prevent anything taboo from slipping out is draining, mentally and physically. For instance, on days when publicly out queer people have felt forced to conceal their sexual orientation, they've reported feeling lower self-esteem and psychological well-being.

- **Not making like Elsa and letting it go:** Rumination is both a symptom of and contributor to our mental health struggles, and it shows up more commonly in women. An intensely repetitive, dysfunctional type of self-focus, rumination can trap you in negativity loops. People with major depressive and generalized anxiety disorders are hypersensitive to stress, which can send them into one of those loops. Being trapped at rumination station not only leaves you feeling powerless, but it also increases aggression and clouds your ability to clearly think through what actually went down. It's a hard cycle to break; ruminating tricks you into withdrawing and avoiding support networks and other things that might otherwise help you feel better.

- **Isolating yourself:** Depression and anxiety can make it incredibly hard to leave the house some days, which compounds all the negative feels. Being alone—and feeling lonely—for extended periods means your powers of resilience and empathy take a hit, and your stress level skyrockets. Feeling supported can go a long way in bolstering your mental health and happiness. Just look at parenting patterns. In countries like Norway and Hungary—places with family policies that help parents balance their work and family lives—parents are happier than those without kids. In the United States, however, there is a massive happiness gap favoring the child-free. To combat the gap regardless of your current kid situation, work to head off isolation by building a network of family, friends, and others you can turn to before the going gets rough. Then actually reach out.

- **Being a stress magnet:** Women's brain chemistry makes us more sensitive to stress—obviously a big anxiety trigger—and we're more likely to feel the physical fallout, such as headaches, upset stomach, and being on the verge of tears. And while more women than dudes say we want to find ways to manage our stress, many of us say we're too tired and lack the willpower to follow through on a major stress buster and self-care tool: exercise.

It helps to know your triggers. Among online communities, **trigger warnings** are recognized as inclusive protocols that give users a heads-up of psychologically sensitive topics ahead, such as self-harm, sexual violence, and eating disorders. Forensic psychologists have found that the distress they intend to ward off aren't chain reactions from "triggers" but psychological **stressors**.

"[Post-traumatic stress disorder] triggers may be far less obvious and seemingly arbitrary: colors, objects and odors are common triggers that simply could not be predicted or forewarned against," noted a 2015 review of research on PTSD and the use of trigger warnings in classrooms. That offers a tip to survivors and allies alike. Because everyday traumas can be relived through so many sensory avenues, mindfulness—and compassion toward the complexity of how triggers work—is an essential healing balm.

coping mechanisms

It turns out that as women make equality inroads in society—as we enter the workforce full time, earn closer-to-equal pay, and have access to birth control at greater rates—we also close the heavy-drinking gender gap. And Western women have, on average, caught up with the guys in terms of how much we're imbibing. Drinking patterns are tied to gender roles and expectations, and in cultures that highly value male superiority and traditional femininity, heavy drinking is simply not an activity that's normalized for women. It's a culturally approved habit that exhibits power and risk-taking—hello, traditional masculinity—and in the United States, regardless of gender, it's associated with higher status among our peers.

Our workplace culture of catching happy hour with coworkers and handshaking our way through boozy networking events—and relying on those cocktails

to calm our social anxiety—further strengthens the link and normalizes the habit. It's probably fine if you're using that time to solidify coworker or client relationships; less beneficial if you don't know your limits.

Closing the gender gap does draw attention to the need for more gender-sensitive and appropriate treatment across the board. Men are more likely to tell their doctor about alcohol abuse problems and seek help from a specialist, but they're not as forthcoming about feeling depressed. Women are far more likely to discuss their depression with a primary care physician and receive a prescription. Even when men and women show up at the doctor's office with the same symptoms, women are still likelier to get a depression diagnosis. But women traditionally have *not* been as likely to disclose troublesome drinking habits.

Pouring a glass or five of chardonnay has become a hyper-normalized way to cope with the stresses and strains of modern womanhood, and with tongue-in-cheek names like Mommy's Time Out and Mad Housewife, wine brands are capitalizing on the trend. Mommies or not, women are leading the wine-drinking charge, making up 60 percent of US imbibers. Playing up the housewife trope is part of an age-old stereotype of women excessively and irresponsibly self-medicating with **mother's little helper**.

That's a pop-culturally catchy name for Miltown, which arrived on the postwar medical-boom scene in 1955. The first psychopharmaceutical (in human speak, a drug that wouldn't knock you out like morphine, laudanum, and other nineteenth-century-asylum favorites) was a hit. By 1956, doctors had written 36 million prescriptions to ease patients' nerves, and while several male celebrities were open about taking it, Miltown quickly became associated with housewives. Cue the hand-wringing.

Political conservatives and feminists alike took issue with the tranquilizer boom, which had expanded to include benzodiazepines Librium and Valium. Many saw it as indicative of larger, unaddressed problems: an addiction-fueled counterculture apathetic to politics and, even scarier, suburban mothers trying to mentally escape systemic sexism. In her 1963 book *The Feminine Mystique*, Betty Friedan described middle-class housewives who "blotted out" feelings of emptiness and pointlessness with tranquilizers, and studies revealed middle-class moms were indeed the most likely to use tranquilizers. The media freaked out: Who was holding down the home front? Who was lovingly and lucidly baking pie and pressing shirts?

On top of everything, one researcher warned in 1972, many of those same housewives might have experimented with the dreaded marijuana, a sure sign suburbia was no Norman Rockwell safe haven. Talk about unladylike! Today, more women are coming out of the cannabis closet, including celeb faves like Rihanna and the *Broad City* gals. Famous or not, plenty of women are busting the dude-bro stereotypes surrounding weed and opting for a little THC over

 **CLAP BACK WITH FACTS**

mental health

Few of us are strangers to depression and anxiety. About 322 million people worldwide live with depression, and 264 million are dealing with anxiety.

- **GENETICS ARE A BITCH.** If your immediate family members have mental health conditions like major depression or panic disorder, you're *two to three times* likelier to develop that condition yourself.

- **WOMEN ARE MENTAL HEALTH MULTITASKERS.** Women are about *twice* as likely as men to experience major depression, and they're more prone to dealing with a cluster of mental health conditions.

- **MEN ARE INCLINED TO STRUGGLE WITH IMPULSE CONTROL.** They have higher rates of antisocial personality, ADHD, and intermittent explosive disorders, and they're more likely to struggle with alcohol dependence.

- **PLENTY OF AMERICANS TAKE MEDS.** About 12 percent take an antidepressant, while just over 8 percent take a sedative, hypnotic, or antianxiety drug.

- **IT'S GENDERED, NATCH.** Twenty-one percent of women say they take antidepressants, compared to 12 percent of men.

- **THERE'S A RACIAL ELEMENT.** Nearly 21 percent of white Americans take a psychiatric drug, compared to about 9 percent of Hispanic, Asian, and black Americans.

tippling, arguing it's a safer option. In fact, middle-aged moms today are more likely to smoke pot than their teenagers are.

Should Friedan's ghost be concerned? Cannabis does interfere with emotional processing and empathizing to a degree, but that could be good news for clinically anxious or depressed people for whom everyday interactions are more of a painful slog through negativity. And while high doses of THC have been shown to drain serotonin stores, low doses seem to boost them. In other words, proceed with caution, just as you would with booze or pharmaceuticals.

Feminist criticism in the 1970s that doctors might be writing prescriptions while ignoring women's actual concerns and mental health might be fair, but slamming meds across the board came with a downside: stigmatizing mental-health treatments that could benefit women as just an indulgent escape for bored, spoiled housewives and people who couldn't face reality.

meds and wellness

Let's get one thing straight: It's totally and completely okay to feel your feelings and get moody, vulnerable, or emotional. After all, women's brains have extra overhead compartment room for packing things like memory, language, and picking up on others' emotions. You don't have to medicate away the fact that you cry when you're happy or sad or stressed, or that you angrily break out in hives when a gross dude catcalls you, or that politics and misogyny have you despairing a little.

"Women's emotionality is a sign of health, not disease," psychiatrist and author Julie Holland wrote in a 2015 *New York Times* column. "It is a source of power."[6] Yeah, girl!

Tools like antidepressants and antianxiety medication come in when our power has been stripped *away*, when our mental health and emotional realities interfere with our ability to function in our daily lives. Just as it's okay to feel feelings, there's also nothing weak, shameful, or shortcutty about taking meds.

Taking control of your care and prioritizing your health, wellness, and well-being are part of that depression-buffering sense of agency. No matter your age, if you start noticing signs and symptoms that something is shifting mentally or emotionally, reach out and remember that you're not alone. Approach friends who've been there and find online communities where people are open about their own struggles and solutions. If you can access a therapist, make talk therapy a regular part of your routine so you can work through hurdles and unhealthy patterns that have been tripping you up. Through cognitive behavioral therapy, mental health professionals can help you shift your thought patterns and reactions, steering you toward achieving healthy, empowering goals and developing assertiveness.

But health care systems can be a convoluted, expensive mess to navigate, and women often struggle to get doctors to take their complaints seriously. Getting help for mental illness or addiction can be a process littered with stigma and complications for many women, who are more likely than men to experience barriers to care such as:

- Depression and anxiety symptoms that might prevent them from reaching out or sticking with treatment

- Embarrassment and shame over seeking addiction treatment in particular, which can fuel even more self-medicating behavior

- Financial and transportation barriers to treatment

- Time restrictions because of family caregiving responsibilities

Considering this mountain of BS, it makes sense that some of us would go the DIY route in trying to take charge of our health. The ballooning, $3.7 *trillion* global wellness economy—which encompasses everything from alternative medicine and spas to fitness and public health—reflects that. You can practice wellness in accessible, beneficial ways like eating healthier, seeking preventive care, exercising, and sleeping more, but an Instagram-ready wellness wave

barriers to care

Diving a little deeper into different communities' experiences with mental health and access issues it can get even more complicated:

- Child-related concerns are often heightened among black women, who are more likely than their white counterparts to lose custody of their kids when going through mental health or addiction-related treatment.

- LGBTQ folks are at three times the risk of experiencing a mental health issue, and LGBTQ youth are four times more likely to attempt suicide. When seeking treatment, they deal with double the stigma: against mental-health problems in general and against their sexual orientation, gender identity, and/or gender expression in particular.

- Mood disorders and other conditions go underdiagnosed in the deaf community because of obstacles to communication like a lack of interpreters, misreading emotions and expressions, and difficulty translating some abstract concepts. Deaf girls in particular struggle with embarrassment over asking questions through an interpreter.

(complete with "detoxing" and vagina-steaming) has swept in. Women are shelling out loads of cash to pick up an assortment of crystals, wellness powders and potions, and astronomically priced juice-cleanse kits.

Some of these purchases and pursuits might have no ill effects other than leaving your wallet a little lighter, but crossing your fingers that your crystals will do anything other than look lovely sparkling under your desk lamp leaves your very real brain chemistry unaddressed. We want to feel like we're empowered and in control, with clean chakras to boot, but we also want quick, efficient solutions. Unfortunately, you can't pop Echinacea for major depression. While the hope those crystals and juice concoctions afford you is nothing to sneeze at and establishing the intention to take care of yourself is crucial, mental health is complicated, and addressing it requires long-term work.

One tactic that's *not* a bunch of woo-woo dipped in fairy dust: mindfulness and getting still. It's no surprise that the practice of focusing on the present, rather than fretting over the past or anxiously anticipating the future, has migrated from yoga classes and meditation sessions to offices, schools, and advice columns. Contemplating and observing your own experience, feelings, and state of mind through peaceful self-awareness rather than anxiety-ridden self-focus and rumination is a useful tool to help deal with depression, anxiety, and even obsessive-compulsive disorder. Researchers even link mindfulness with an uptick in autonomy, optimism, and sexual satisfaction. It's true: Being present and engaged equates to fewer distractingly negative thoughts bouncing around inside your brain and even promotes more orgasms.

However you choose to do it (the mindfulness, not the orgasms), whether through dedicated meditation or just sitting quietly, spend some quiet time with yourself at least a few times a week to practice stillness, focus on your breathing, reflect on what you're grateful for, and generally decompress.

Paying closer attention to our gut reactions and feelings can tell us as much as any tarot reading, too. Male philosophers, psychoanalysts, and other "thinkers" of the eighteenth and nineteenth centuries dismissed intuition as part of women's emotional, feelings-heavy realm, subordinate to the power of masculine reason, but the unnecessary gendering of thought is their problem, not ours. Intuition is essentially a lifetime of memories, experiences, and patterns that have piled up in our psyches to help us make sense of our worlds faster and more efficiently. It's part logic, part emotion, and it's what gives us that feeling in our guts when something is so right or so, so wrong—an indispensable tool for unladylike living.

dare to self-care

For a group of people stereotyped as gentle and caring, we women sure can fall on the job when it comes to directing those energies toward ourselves. To strengthen, propel, and maintain a movement, there must be mechanisms in place that stoke the fires of the people fighting for change. Honest communication among allies and emotional support from empathetic peers are all positive external forces that help keep you going, but you have some powerful emotional muscles you can flex as well.

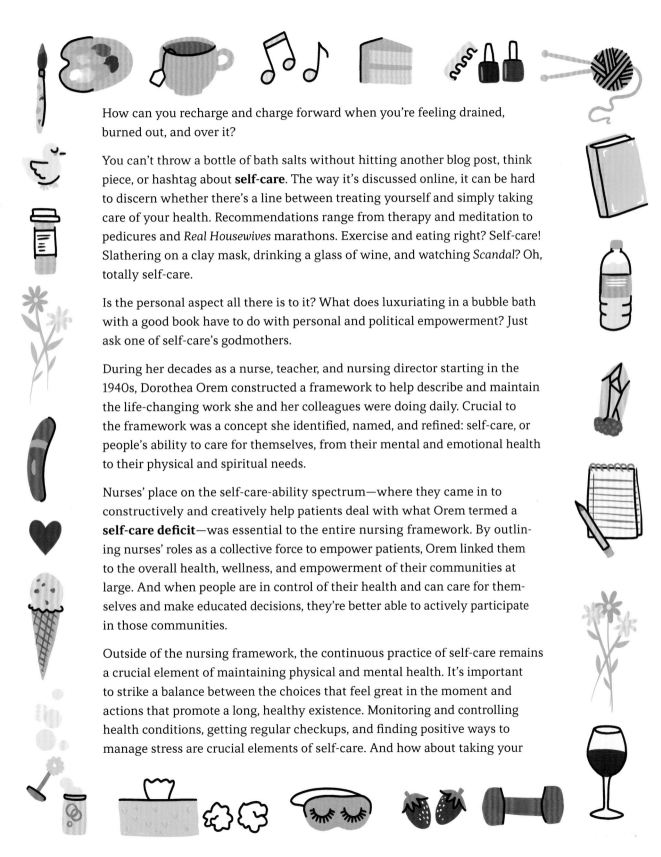

How can you recharge and charge forward when you're feeling drained, burned out, and over it?

You can't throw a bottle of bath salts without hitting another blog post, think piece, or hashtag about **self-care**. The way it's discussed online, it can be hard to discern whether there's a line between treating yourself and simply taking care of your health. Recommendations range from therapy and meditation to pedicures and *Real Housewives* marathons. Exercise and eating right? Self-care! Slathering on a clay mask, drinking a glass of wine, and watching *Scandal*? Oh, totally self-care.

Is the personal aspect all there is to it? What does luxuriating in a bubble bath with a good book have to do with personal and political empowerment? Just ask one of self-care's godmothers.

During her decades as a nurse, teacher, and nursing director starting in the 1940s, Dorothea Orem constructed a framework to help describe and maintain the life-changing work she and her colleagues were doing daily. Crucial to the framework was a concept she identified, named, and refined: self-care, or people's ability to care for themselves, from their mental and emotional health to their physical and spiritual needs.

Nurses' place on the self-care-ability spectrum—where they came in to constructively and creatively help patients deal with what Orem termed a **self-care deficit**—was essential to the entire nursing framework. By outlining nurses' roles as a collective force to empower patients, Orem linked them to the overall health, wellness, and empowerment of their communities at large. And when people are in control of their health and can care for themselves and make educated decisions, they're better able to actively participate in those communities.

Outside of the nursing framework, the continuous practice of self-care remains a crucial element of maintaining physical and mental health. It's important to strike a balance between the choices that feel great in the moment and actions that promote a long, healthy existence. Monitoring and controlling health conditions, getting regular checkups, and finding positive ways to manage stress are crucial elements of self-care. And how about taking your medicine, drinking enough water, surrounding yourself with badass babes, and slipping into a meditative state as you practice your eyeliner technique? Yup, all can qualify if they're part of an ongoing and well-rounded approach to bolstering and maintaining your mental, physical, and spiritual health. Care for yourself and your health, and turn inward when you need to, so you're better prepared to fight on.

What self-care means will be different for everyone, but here are a few core tactics to keep in mind to get yourself centered.

- **Rest when your body tells you to.** When you're facing stress or crisis, your sympathetic nervous system switches on your fight-or-flight stress response, giving you lots of energy (and lots of the stress hormone cortisol) to assess the danger and either defend yourself or flee to safety. Once you're no longer in immediate danger, your parasympathetic nervous system works to quiet things down, telling your body to **rest and digest**.[7] Obey the orders.

- **Breathe.** Taking shallow, rapid breaths can progress to hyperventilation, putting you at risk for a panic attack. Try to slow down. Breathe in deeply through your nose and exhale through your mouth for four to six seconds each until you feel your heart rate begin to slow.

- **Take breaks and stretch.** Your muscles tighten in response to stress. It's part of that preparation for a potential fight. Remember to rest, stretch, and perform self-massage.

- **Drink water.** Hydrate to prevent fatigue and dizziness, not to mention electrolyte imbalances and urinary problems.

- **Eat something.** People's stomachs respond differently to stress; some overeat while others lose their appetites altogether. If you forget to eat during a crisis, you'll put yourself at risk of running out of steam quickly and wind up dizzy, weak, and nauseated.

- **Clean up.** Taking a shower and tidying up your space won't save the world, but it can help set the right tone for the day. They're small, basic steps to help you relax and signal to yourself, "I've accomplished something."

audre

When **AUDRE LORDE** found out shortly before her fiftieth birthday in February 1984 that a tumor was growing in her liver, she opted not to undergo the standard biopsy. The poet had already survived breast cancer and was in no rush to throw her body back into the tailspin of surgery and radiation. Doctors told Audre she needed treatment immediately, which would give her four or five months to live; without, she'd have three or four. With a to-do list full of traveling, loving, writing, learning, and speaking, and presumably a short timeline either way, Audre decided against traditional, recommended treatments that she believed would interfere with enjoying the ride.

Instead, she literally and figuratively traveled her own path—one that worked for her but certainly isn't right for everyone—and went on to live eight more years. In Germany, she sought homeopathic treatments, taught, and wrote about how black feminists might best combat racism. In Switzerland, she sought more alternative therapies, meditated, and painted, ultimately realizing that her isolation from loved ones wouldn't help her heal. In the Caribbean, she immersed herself in sun and song before returning to New York, where she surrounded herself with "the positive energies of so many women who carry the breath of my loving like firelight in their strong hair."

In her journal entries, which eventually became the 1988 essay "A Burst of Light," Audre contemplated the empowerment she felt through writing, listening to her body, and staying true to her own treatment and self-care wishes. Choosing to exercise agency over her health care decisions was "physical resistance," she wrote—a way to maintain as much power, control, and normality as possible.

"I respect the time I spend each day treating my body, and I consider it part of my political work," she wrote. "It is possible to have some conscious input into our physical processes . . . a kind of training in self-love and physical resistance."

Audre considered living the remainder of her life as a black, lesbian, activist poet to the fullest to be a revolutionary act in the framework of "this fucked-up whiteboys' world." As she wrote, "Caring for myself is not self-indulgence, it is self-preservation, and that is an act of political warfare."[8]

WHAT AUDRE WOULD DO TODAY: She would encourage the women who have been overlooked and pushed aside to unapologetically and unflinchingly claim the space they want on this life journey. No one else will give it to you.

body baggage

TOO FAT, TOO HAIRY, TOO YOU

Even if we can flawlessly distinguish between airbrushed and IRL figures and can list a refrigerator full of food that tastes better than skinny feels, societal body baggage comes in all shapes and sizes. Take science fiction icon Octavia Butler. Long before she reached the height of literary acclaim, a six-foot-tall teenaged Octavia just wished she could make herself less obvious instead of standing head and shoulders above the rest of her peers.

That body baggage weighs us down with hourglass expectations and myths that we're crazy and dirty; conditions us to police ourselves through celebrity weight-watching and cellulite lies; and demands we stay as smooth as possible through body-hair shaming. It suggests we should shrug off the side effects of conditions like endometriosis, which 10 percent[1] of women around the world deal with; polycystic ovarian syndrome (PCOS), which up to 20 percent of women experience[2]; and chronic fatigue syndrome, a diagnosis women are four times likelier than men to receive.[3]

"Women are not just men with boobs and tubes," says Janice Werbinski, a gynecologist and executive director of the Sex and Gender Women's Health Collaborative. "We can actually harm women by not researching them correctly and knowing the differences."

"Physical force seems to be the only thing in which women have not demonstrated their equality to men, and whilst we are waiting for the evolution which is slowly taking place and bringing about that equality, we might just as well take time by the forelock and use jiu jitsu."

EDITH GARRUD
suffragist and female self-defense evangelist

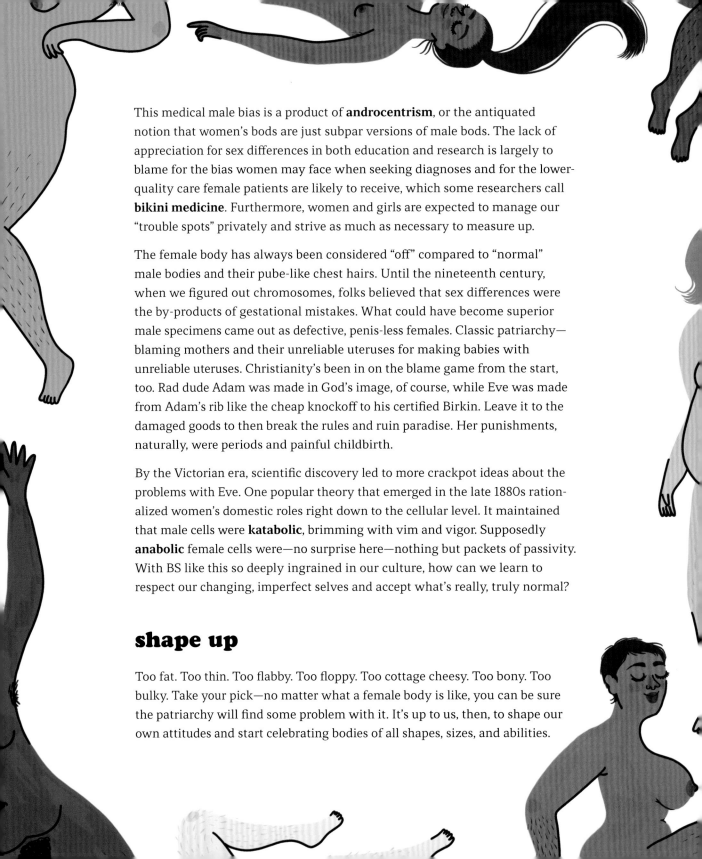

This medical male bias is a product of **androcentrism**, or the antiquated notion that women's bods are just subpar versions of male bods. The lack of appreciation for sex differences in both education and research is largely to blame for the bias women may face when seeking diagnoses and for the lower-quality care female patients are likely to receive, which some researchers call **bikini medicine**. Furthermore, women and girls are expected to manage our "trouble spots" privately and strive as much as necessary to measure up.

The female body has always been considered "off" compared to "normal" male bodies and their pube-like chest hairs. Until the nineteenth century, when we figured out chromosomes, folks believed that sex differences were the by-products of gestational mistakes. What could have become superior male specimens came out as defective, penis-less females. Classic patriarchy—blaming mothers and their unreliable uteruses for making babies with unreliable uteruses. Christianity's been in on the blame game from the start, too. Rad dude Adam was made in God's image, of course, while Eve was made from Adam's rib like the cheap knockoff to his certified Birkin. Leave it to the damaged goods to then break the rules and ruin paradise. Her punishments, naturally, were periods and painful childbirth.

By the Victorian era, scientific discovery led to more crackpot ideas about the problems with Eve. One popular theory that emerged in the late 1880s rationalized women's domestic roles right down to the cellular level. It maintained that male cells were **katabolic**, brimming with vim and vigor. Supposedly **anabolic** female cells were—no surprise here—nothing but packets of passivity. With BS like this so deeply ingrained in our culture, how can we learn to respect our changing, imperfect selves and accept what's really, truly normal?

shape up

Too fat. Too thin. Too flabby. Too floppy. Too cottage cheesy. Too bony. Too bulky. Take your pick—no matter what a female body is like, you can be sure the patriarchy will find some problem with it. It's up to us, then, to shape our own attitudes and start celebrating bodies of all shapes, sizes, and abilities.

because genetics

There are innumerable products like bogus cellulite creams, underarm smoothers, and stretch mark erasers designed to dupe us into spending money to change physical traits that are purely genetic and largely can't be altered. Rather than cave to patriarchal pressure, flip it the bird by embracing that the following features—not flaws—are normal AF.

- **CELLULITE:** Lumps and bumps show up thanks to fat pushing up against fibrous tissue. Women are more likely than men to experience it, and it becomes more visible as we age and our skin loses elasticity.

- **NOTICEABLY DIFFERENTLY SIZED BEWBS:** Humans aren't symmetrical in general, so it follows that our boobs wouldn't be, either. Boob shapes also change with hormones and menstrual cycles, and early injuries can affect how they shape up.

- **INNER THIGHS THAT RUB TOGETHER:** Your skeleton, muscles, fat, and skin are programmed to take a certain shape. Congratulations, you're human! A gap doesn't necessarily equal fitness, health—or happiness.

- **VISIBLY PERT NIPPLES:** Your nips are home to a bazillion nerve endings, which are super sensitive to cold and touch, and they sit above some muscles. And while, yes, they perk up when you're turned on, they're essentially two giant goosebumps. That's right: The same type of unconscious nervous system response that prompts goosebumpy flesh when you're cold also nudges neurons to tighten those under-nip muscles and get them to stand at attention.

- **STRETCH MARKS:** Our tiger stripes are a type of scarring we get when weight gain prompts hormones to take a chisel to collagen and elastin fibers in our skin.

- **MALE-PATTERN BODY HAIR:** We all have facial hair, whether it's an errant chin hair or a lustrous mustache. Suddenly seeing a growth spurt likely means you're experiencing normal hormone fluctuations. Genetic conditions can be responsible for coarse hair sprouting in areas we'd normally associate with men or body-hair patches showing up in seemingly random spots. Other culprits include polycystic ovarian syndrome, adrenal gland disorders, and certain meds.

Granted, we've taken baby steps in the right direction as evidenced by the mainstreaming of plus-size fashion. From upstarts like blogger-turned-swimsuit-designer Gabi Gregg to full-figured model Ashley Graham on the cover of a *Sports Illustrated* swimsuit edition, women are speaking up, and retailers and tastemakers are increasingly respecting and reflecting body-size diversity. But it's worth questioning how far those commodified images and wardrobe offerings can go toward redressing our tireless—and tiring—pursuit of shapeliness. After all, why should penises be the only anatomy we subjectively judge with the caveat that size isn't everything?

The go-to example of the potential unhealthy side effects of body-size standards is corsetry, which is somehow still a thing in the twenty-first century. Although women having ribs removed to facilitate corset tight-lacing is mostly fearmongering myth, maternity corsets were definitely a thing in the 1880s, and long-term corset use was known to damage the spine. Today's Kardashian-promoted workout corsets, more delicately marketed as "waist trainers," aren't much better for bods.

Learning to sort what beauty standards expect of us versus what genetics gave us—like it or not—is a handy way to hone a healthier body image.

ableist body politics

Of all the body baggage patriarchy dumps on our psyches, it's often heaviest for people with disabilities. The gender binary doesn't merely discriminate against people with disabilities and chronic illness. It actively threatens the perceived wholeness of their humanity in proportion to noticeable differences in mobility, mannerisms, speech, and/or appearance. That constant surveillance of "normalcy" makes navigating the tightropes of masculinity and femininity extra precarious, taxing, and sometimes impossible.

"Bodies operate socially as canvases on which gender is displayed and kinesthetically as the mechanisms by which it is physically enacted," observed disability theorist Thomas Gerschick. "Thus, the bodies of people with disabilities make them vulnerable to being denied recognition as men and women."[4]

Integration into our ableist society therefore depends on "passing," or publicly disguising or hiding as much disability as possible, as well as privately bartering with gender norms. According to our social scripts, diminished male physical assertiveness demands a hypermasculine gender performance, while barriers to achieve female attractiveness standards spark what sociologists call **emphasized femininity**.

"Half a man" disability-shaming can be tough to negotiate, since patriarchy centers on the embodiment of dominant manliness, while prettiness pressure leaves more room for negotiation. Women may conscientiously emphasize their femininity through unmistakably girly outfits, accessories, and interests, while others liberate themselves entirely from beauty standards and like it that way.

 CLAP BACK WITH FACTS

disability terminology

Regardless of your abilities, taking time to learn and use inclusive language—and avoiding terms that aren't yours to reclaim—demonstrates a commitment to allyship.

- **CRIP:** A disability- and queer-inclusive self-identifier that promotes disability as a dynamic culture. Because of the derogatory baggage "cripple" still carries, not all disability activists are down with this term, and it's definitely off-limits to able-bodied folks.

- **DISCEGENATION:** Sexual relationships between disabled and nondisabled partners, historically considered taboo.

- **IDENTITY-FIRST VERSUS PEOPLE-FIRST:** Two primary models of disability language. Identity-first opts for describing disabled people in that order: *disabled* in front of *people*, to redefine disability as independent from personhood. In a switcheroo, people-first language literally puts *people* first, as in *people with disabilities*, to reflect how disability is relative to environment, not solely biological functioning. Many prefer people-first language, but it's better not to presume a universal preference among the large disability population.

- **INSPIRATION PORN:** Disabled people aren't here to provide magic moments of inspiration that reinforce the ableist hierarchy of "normalcy."

barbie boobs

Dressed in a fetching striped swimsuit and Ariana Grande–worthy ponytail, Barbara Millicent Roberts's career as a full-time femininity role model began at the 1959 American Toy Fair. "Barbie You're Beautiful," proclaimed her original tagline, and millions of girls agreed. But lovely dolls had been around for ages. What was it about Barbie that made her so special?

Her bustline, of course. Her womanly figure could've been disastrously inappropriate, but Mattel got away with selling the first kids' doll with breasts by designing her with all-over adolescent smoothness. Barbie has no nipples, labia, or below-the-neck body hair, desexualizing her just enough to pass parental muster while retaining her aspirational edge.

Gender scholar Catherine Driscoll has described this balancing act of Barbie's public profile as culturally situated "simultaneously between images of sexy womanhood, images of adolescent experimentation with gender and identity, and the open-endedness of child's play."[5]

Indeed, while kiddos loved Barbie, mid-century moms initially hated her. One woman informed a Mattel marketer that she'd "call them 'Daddy Dolls'—they are so sexy. They could be a cute decoration for a man's bar."[6]

Keeping Barbie out of the bar meant selling her to mothers as a well-groomed, dainty lady who, despite her broad shoulders, mile-long legs, humongous boobs, and waspy waist, could potentially influence little girls to be little ladies as well. And with her smooth, hairless figure, she was the perfect receptacle for white girls' projections about their potential future selves rather than their baby-doll–mothering tendencies.

Her looks—and countless changes to them over the years—have been Barbie's greatest marketing tool. But until 2016, when Mattel launched curvy, petite, and tall versions of their iconic career girl to boost slumping sales, her measurements were anything but relatable. An IRL Barb would stand 5'9" tall, with a 21-inch waist and a 30-inch bust.[7] What a pain in the back.

But there are tradeoffs to these tradeoffs. Take street harassment, for instance. The feminist theory that all female-identified folks are sexualized overlooks the cultural desexualization and infantilization of disabled girls and women. For one example, at one of the first feminist conferences on women and disability, activist Judy Heumann noted, "You know, I use a wheelchair, and when I go down the street I do not get to be sexually harassed. I hear nondisabled women complaining about it, but I don't ever get treated as a sexual object."

Invisibility to catcallers might sound empowering. But as always, consider the source. It's not coming from Heumann's personal agency or sidewalk harassers' elevated respect for women in wheelchairs. It's rooted in ableist culture, and if feminism is serious about leveling the equality playing fields, it must be inclusive for *every* body.

nip slips

Boobs are like snowflakes. No two are exactly the same, regardless of whether they're on the same body. That's one of boobs' many quirks that mesmerize us human animals. Of all our collective body parts, everyone stares the most at breasts. Eye-tracking research confirms it—watch out![8]

But despite our collective obsession with boobs, they don't always get the right kind of attention. This is especially true when it comes to how breasts affect casual exercise and professional sports. We still need to figure out how to vault over boob barriers: Breast size, discomfort, and straight-up embarrassment dissuade girls and women from exercising. This matters for a variety of important reasons.

- **Bodies with boobs need exercise.** By age fourteen, girls drop out of sports at twice the rate of boys. According to the US Centers for Disease Control and Statistics, fewer than 20 percent of high school girls get daily physical activity, which is almost half as much as boys; at least thirty minutes of daily physical activity is the benchmark.

- **Exercise is good for breast, general, and mental health.** Breasts benefit in all sorts of ways from sweating to the oldies. Research links exercise to a lowered breast cancer risk, improved immune function, and healthier insulin levels. And friendly shout-out to exercise for also strengthening

bobbi

Kicking off high heels doesn't make it easier to run away from sexism. Just ask **BOBBI GIBB**, who in 1966 became the first woman to complete the Boston Marathon, albeit unofficially. Men had flown to the moon and back, yet women weren't allowed to race farther than four kilometers (2.4 miles) at a stretch because "experts" presumed uteruses couldn't withstand that much exertion and that marathoning endangered women's fertility and femininity.[9] In fact, the American College of Sports Medicine didn't declare long-distance running safe for women until 1980.

"We were expected to be housewives, that's all," Bobbi told the *New York Times* in 2015. "We weren't expected to have minds, and we weren't expected to have bodies that ran." That's why when Bobbi attempted to register for a Boston Marathon bib number, organizers refused. Outraged, Bobbi trained anyway, lacing up a pair of nursing oxfords and hitting the pavement. On April 19, 1966, she snuck onto the Boston Marathon route fueled up from a roast beef dinner and wearing a one-piece swimsuit, hoodie, shorts, and a fresh pair of men's Adidas sneakers. She finished with a third of her all-male competitors trailing, but the press treated her as a cute novelty, with *Sports Illustrated* describing her as a "shapely blonde housewife."

The following year, Bobbi darted into the marathon again, but all eyes were on another interloper, Kathrine Switzer. Using her initials to not give away her gender, Kathrine had successfully registered for the marathon. But when a race official tried to physically throw Kathrine off the course, photographs of the visibly irate man grabbing at Kathrine's sweatshirt instantly attracted more rebellious female runners and "physical activists" to follow their lead.

"It was the first time in my life I did something completely for myself," Bobbi told *Runner's World* in 2016. "It wasn't my teachers telling me to finish my homework, or my parents begging me to be more like the other kids. The running was only for me. That made it exhilarating and so much more meaningful."

WHAT BOBBI WOULD DO TODAY: She'd follow her feminist anger to the finish line. When life gave Bobbi lemons, she made anger-ade. Initially, she wanted to run the marathon because it seemed fun, but when she was turned away on the basis of sex, she got mad. Real mad. The following year she was determined to get in the race just to prove sexism wrong. And *that* is the beneficial power of getting pissed off.

our bones and hearts, improving body image, and managing depression and anxiety.

- **When bodies move, boobs move.** A lot. And there are no muscles dedicated to holding those funbags in place. Nipples on a C- or D-cup breast can accelerate up to 45 mph in one second of sprinting—faster than a Ferrari! In an hour of jogging, a pair of breasts will bounce several thousand times, oscillating up to eight inches in a figure-eight pattern. Because of all that motion, breasts can pose an impediment to exercising pretty much as soon as we begin developing them. As with menstruation, girls need a more supportive bra-ducation to help find the chest harnesses that enable us to move freely.[10]

- **Boob-bounce-phobia is real.** Not only can breasts in motion cause physical pain, but also our self-objectification ramps up as if our chest jiggle beams out from us like sonar straight to bro brains. In a 2016 study of middle-school girls in the United Kingdom, 73 percent cited at least one boob-related worry about exercising in front of boys at school as well as being naked around other girls in locker rooms.[11]

smooth down

The curation of armpit, leg, and pubic hair, as well as arm, upper lip, and eyebrow fuzz for some bodies, is a feminine beauty norm, and it isn't exclusive to the West. Wealthy Late-Period Egyptians employed personal body shavers to get rid of everything except their eyelashes and brows. In ancient Islamic cultures, ritual head-to-toe hair removal was a religiously motivated custom for married women; men were also directed to keep their mustaches trimmed and pit thickets at bay.

As for American gals, our culture's female body-hair hang-ups can be blamed on doctors and business dudes. First, the American Dermatological Society invented **hypertrichosis**, or excess body hair, as a lady affliction in the 1870s. Then in the 1910s, sleeveless dresses came into vogue, and magazines like *Harper's Bazaar* began advertising depilatory powders—including one called Ashes of Roses!—to remove any "objectionable" hair. In 1915, Gillette capitalized on pit hair panic and debuted the Milady Decollette. Selling the first blade designed for women required careful word choice, though. "Shaving" sounded too masculine, so they opted for "smoothing." Also, "underarm" was obviously too risqué because of its boob proximity, so it couldn't appear in ad copy.

Circa World War II, nylon went to the war effort, which meant bare legs were a common sight. Presto! Cactus legs became pegged as unsightly. And as the new millennium approached, the bare-down-there beauty norm crept up our thighs and camped out on our vulvas like an ingrown hair. Trendsetting porn led the way in the 1980s, and it wasn't long before pubes had practically disappeared from *Playboy* centerfolds.

But porn didn't invent the look. Cleanliness culture did. The idea that groomed pubes are more hygienic has persisted across ages and cultures. For roughly two hundred years leading up to the nineteenth century, Turkish women would frequent special rooms in bathhouses designated solely for down-there depilation. Today in the US, a nationally representative study from 2016 found an "overwhelming majority" of the many women of all ages who groom their pubic hair do so because they think it's more hygienic. It's a total myth, though. Mid-grooming nicks and tears can increase risk of infection. The researchers also talked to gynecologists mystified at how many patients regularly apologize if their pubic hair is untrimmed when they're in stirrups, or intentionally tidy up before appointments.

Our unladylike take? There's no right or wrong way to maintain your hair anywhere. Different folks are comfortable with different razor strokes, and whether that means a smooth-all-over approach or luxurious rainbow-dyed pit hair, you do you. As long as it really is *for* you, that is. One thing to consider about the Perennial Pubes Issue is this: If you suspect or know that someone won't wanna get intimate with you because of the presence of pubic hair, beware. Don't let someone else's follicular hang-ups send you sprinting for the wax just to please them.

If you're ever feeling unsure, remember a badass named Harnaam Kaur. Endocrine disruption caused by polycystic ovarian syndrome means that this British activist grows a thick, lustrous beard, and after agonizing teen years marked by endless depilating and being bullied nonetheless, Kaur finally got sick of taming it. Now, she joyfully rocks her facial hair and has become an international role model—and sometimes fashion model—for body positivity.

nettie stevens's mealworms

At the turn of the nineteenth century, we had no clue about the social facets of gender, let alone the scientific under-pinnings of biological sex. The prevailing theory insisted that a mother's first trimester diet determined whether she had a boy or girl.

In the early 1900s, geneticist Nettie Stevens began unraveling the answer. Born and raised in Vermont, Stevens didn't come from money, but after years of saving up, the 39-year-old completed grad school at Bryn Mawr and jumped into full-time research on sex determinism with a focus on . . . mealworms. Stevens discovered what she called hetero chromosomes, or what would later be named X and Y chromosomes. She realized that biological sex is genetically inherited through our chromosomes.

True to sexist form, Stevens's fellow scientists didn't buy her theory and gave her no credit at the time. But she is now recognized for making major contributions to science.

fragile phallus fallacies

Why is masculinity so fragile? Because penises. Those fleshy members pose massive (and micro 0.6 percent of the time) liabilities for patriarchies. They're as aesthetically and functionally unpredictable as they are pop-culturally undignified and vulnerable to frat-boy humor. Of all humanity's anatomical quirks, the cis male life force dangling out on its own is our closest approximation of biological slapstick. Little wonder, then, that the hiccups, hang-ups, and horrors our societies have produced—like codpieces, American football, and President Donald Trump—are fundamentally preoccupied with the perennial anxiety of What Your Penis Says About You.

To navigate sex in a patriarchy, we have to first familiarize ourselves with **penis primacy**. Going back to the Egyptian god Osiris, phallic imagery has represented pretty much the most respected traits society has to offer: strength, endurance, smarts, know-how, male privilege, class privilege, domination, and lust. So revered was male virility and intellect that Greek physician and philosopher Galen and other ancient intellectuals were convinced that men's brains produced their semen. To put it in marketing speak, penises are the "core brand identity" of patriarchy's masculine product.

But with great penile power comes a lot of preoccupation with size. Indian Sadhus use weights to increase their penis length, while the Topamina of Brazil allegedly let venomous snakes bite their penises to get a size boost that lasts six months. Just as feminine beauty standards encourage us to pay closer attention to our facial pores than anyone else ever could, penis primacy insists that size matters, despite mounting evidence that a vast majority of the time, it doesn't. Research consistently finds that straight and bi women are generally size-ambivalent. Global data debunking racialized penis stereotypes don't soften insecurities, either.

Characterized by a fixation on size and appearance, small penis syndrome is associated with body dysmorphic psychological patterns. Even though micropenises (under 2.5 inches soft) are extremely rare, one study on the syndrome found that 12 percent of men thought theirs were smaller than they should be. But big wasn't always the ideal. In Greek antiquity, Vienna sausages were deemed superior to bratwurst. Ivy League classics professor Andrew Lear explained to the online magazine *Quartz*, "Greeks associated small and non-erect penises with moderation, which was one of the key virtues that formed their view of ideal masculinity."

But as manhood modernized, phallic imagery became harder and larger. Penises became measuring sticks of dudes' sexual prowess, brute strength, and dominance. Just look at the Lady Chatterley Syndrome literary trope. Named for D.H. Lawrence's 1928 softcore classic, *Lady Chatterley's Lover*, it's all about repressed, aristocratic ladies falling in lust with working-class men who teach them what sexual pleasure really feels like. Kind of like *The Notebook*, but with cheating. After Lady C.'s husband sustains a World War I injury that leaves him disabled from the waist down and impotent, she becomes gradually overcome with sexual frustration. Emotionally lost and horny, our girl Chatterley ends up getting hers from the groundskeeper instead. But the connection Lawrence drew between the husband's complete emasculation and his physical disability more troublingly reflects the ableism embedded in our body mythologies.

vagina anxiety

Uncertainty, embarrassment, and shame over how vaginas look, smell, and queef have provoked all manner of unhealthy, bummer behaviors like douching, using chemical-soaked scented menstrual products, and enduring sexual self-consciousness.

But chances are, whatever's going on in your undies is totally normal, and thankfully, with little more than healthy curiosity and some lube, we can teach ourselves to literally come as we are. Not only that, getting up close and understanding our genitalia and how to care for it is a radical act of self-education—and probably not what you'll learn in a classroom. Diagrams of biologically female reproductive systems in anatomy textbooks often illustrate only the external, visible tip of the clitoris called the **glans**, whereas its internal structure extends as much as five inches. Talk about burying the lede!

The vaginal truth is fairly simple. Asymmetrical labia, unkempt hair, discharge, and signature odor are all perfectly normal features of perfectly normal vulvas (what's on the outside) and vaginas (what's on the inside). If this is news to you, you're not alone. Whereas population-wide penis dimensions were available by 1899, the first comparable survey on labia length was published more than a century later in 2005. And it turns out that, just like penises, their lengths vary, with most ranging from five millimeters to five centimeters long. Individual labia may also be different lengths.

Paradoxically, penises have a rhyme about boat size and ocean motion to compensate for *their* differences while corroborating a myth that *our* bits ought to be uniform and Barbie-like. Medically unnecessary "vaginal rejuvenations" and "mommy makeovers" that tighten vaginal muscles and minimize visible labia have become more popular since the late 2000s. One *British Medical*

Journal study on cosmetic labiaplasty found that 40 percent of women went through with them even after doctors told them their labia were aesthetically normal. Moreover, vagina research is roughly a century behind P(enis)hDs, in part because dicks 'n' balls were the scientific standard of what anatomical excellence looked like. For instance, the role of the clitoris in an orgasm was initially misunderstood because its function contradicted the androcentric principle that only an erect penis could provide sexual satisfaction for a healthy adult woman.

It's no wonder Women's Libbers came out swinging at all the body lies they'd been taught and sold. We can also credit second-wavers with rescuing the clit from sexual obscurity. "Until the mid-1960s, most women didn't know how crucial the clitoris was," *Our Bodies, Ourselves* reflected.[12] Published in 1971 by the Boston Women's Health Collective, this breakthrough guide was one of the—if not *the*—first sexual health books by and for cisgender women; later editions take a more queer-friendly, trans-inclusive approach.

Today, feminist educators and artists like Sophia Wallace, with her glorious and validating Cliteracy exhibit, push back on the old, unfortunately not-so-outdated notion that our clits don't mean sh*t. In absorbing messages about penis primacy and enduring shame over our bodies, we wind up holding out on ourselves. Believing we're dirty or that "good girls don't," we don't learn about ourselves or our bodies, we don't learn to ask questions, and we don't learn to advocate for our health, our pleasure, or our safety.

So get unladylike by boldly getting to know your body.

this is what vulvas look like

No two vulvas are alike, but they all share some common—and uncommonly discussed—traits.
Grab a mirror and follow along!

CLITORIS: This beautiful bit of erectile tissue is much bigger than what you see on the outside (that fun bit is called the **glans**, and it can be totally hidden by the **clitoral hood** or poke out). It essentially hugs your vaginal canal, meaning a vaginal orgasm and clitoral orgasm are one and the same. Surprise!

PUBIC HAIR: The coarse, curly texture of pubic hair makes it more prone to becoming ingrown since it doesn't grow straight out of the follicle.

SMEGMA: This is produced when skin cells, oils, and sweat hang out in labial grooves and crevices. If you see some smegma in your vulva, it's totally normal. The vagina is like a self-cleaning oven. Any discharge or mild odor can be freshened up with plain soap and water. If things suddenly look and smell distinctively different, that's when to dial up an expert.

URETHRAL OPENING: The third hole! And it can cause some pain. Around the world every year, bacteria cause 150 million people of all genders to get urinary tract infections.[13]

CERVICAL MUCUS: Estrogen is responsible for production of this fluid, which changes from thick to slick as ovulation approaches. At peak fertility, its egg-white-like viscosity is designed to protect sperm on their way to meet the egg.

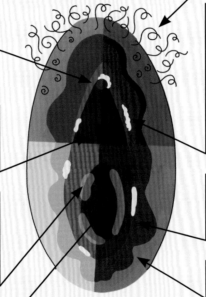

LABIA MINORA: Inner labia come in many shapes and sizes, and may even extend longer than outer labia, requiring tucking into swimsuits and undies to stay put. Totally normal.

LABIA MAJORA: Outer labia are home to your pubic hair, as well as sweat and sebaceous glands.

BUMPS: We're not talking about STI-related bumps like herpes, although they *are* statistically normal—if unwanted—visitors. In addition to the skin around our vulvas being bumpier than elsewhere on our bods, ridges called **vaginal rugae** create a groovy texture inside our vaginal canals.

WRINKLES: The appearance and texture of labia are different for every vulva, from smoother to extra-wrinkled lips.

VAGINAL OPENING: Penetration does *not* stretch out the vagina like an old scrunchie, and if there's sufficient arousal and wetness down there, it shouldn't hurt. (But if we're talking about painful tightness that's even sensitive to tampon insertion, it might be a surprisingly common genital nerve condition, **vaginismus**.) Vaginal muscles are designed to expand and contract without loosening. In fact, when we're super aroused, our vaginas relax and open up like they're lounging on Oprah's couch to make way for penetration. In reality, the fetishized "tight" vagina is more anxious than aroused and could probably use some foreplay to let loose.

DIFFERENTLY COLORED SKIN: Labia come in a rainbow of genetically predetermined pigments including red, pink, peach, purple, blue, brown, and black, sometimes all over or just around the edges. They might even change color with age.

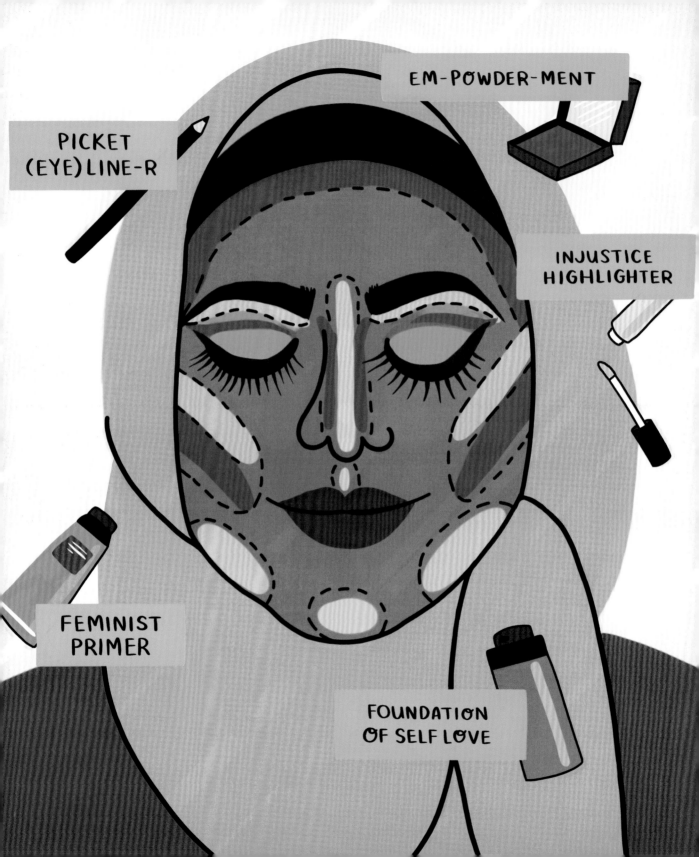

beauty bargains

CONCEALERS, CONTOURS, AND STATEMENT LIPS

Studies have found that people who aren't on board with feminism actually buy into the nonsense notion that feminists are ugly, man-hating, razor-phobes . . . and they don't even have to think hard to make that logical leap. These threatening images are so culturally ingrained that we unwittingly soak up their implicit biases and associations like a contact high. Ironically, research finds that feminists actually exhibit *less* hostility toward men than nonfeminists do.

But research is no match for centuries of dudes slandering self-determined women just by calling them mannish. In the early 1900s, anti-suffragists were all about it, too, depicting pro-voting women as frumpy, bucktoothed spinsters as a warning of what happened to gals who poked at the patriarchy: They'd instantly become sexually unattractive to straight men. Talk about a superpower.

Western beauty ideals are all kinds of high maintenance. Slender ankles. Nipped-in waist. Bootylicious backside. Gravity-defying breasts. Full lips. High cheekbones. Flawless complexion. Long eyelashes. Cascading hair. How does patriarchy cosmetically define us, and how do we reconcile feminism with pressures to conform to beauty standards?

"The single standard of beauty for women dictates that they must go on having clear skin. Every wrinkle, every line, every gray hair, is a defeat."

SUSAN SONTAG
writer, filmmaker, and activist

According to evolutionary biology and psychology, some of these anatomical ideals root back to early humans' most basic imperatives to survive and multiply. Yet there's also a boatload of feminine beauty beliefs that can't be argued away as organic, and attractiveness standards end up coming with all sorts of ugly and exclusionary messages: that our bodies are our most valuable assets. That even basic likability is meted out according to our appearance. That we should mirror the most culturally lauded looks regardless of what it requires in terms of time, money, restricted movement, difficulty breathing, or surgical reconstruction. And that's the real eyeliner rub: When we start bargaining with beauty, the lines between cosmetic uplift and made-up self-worth can quickly get blurred.

Fact: The sum of people's subjective judgments about our bone structure, pore visibility, and other nitpickings do not add up to our individual worth. Also fact: Even if we know that's the truth in our heads, pressurized prettiness still gets up in our faces. The crazy salad of concerns, confidence, and concerns about confidence that it whips up is totally normal and sometimes totally out of our control. We hold the power, however, in how we choose to respond to life's beauty contests.

Engaging with our appearance and taking part in beauty rituals don't automatically make us pawns of patriarchy. Feminists can wear lipstick or not; case closed. On the flip side, scoffing at feminine beauty as stupidly frivolous smacks more of femmephobia (see page 209) than intellectual sophistication. Our task ahead, therefore, isn't to flush cosmetic culture down the toilet but to nonjudgmentally wise up to and detox our personal relationships with Big Beauty to healthfully coexist with it as we age, wrinkle up, and start sagging.

Now that we've applied our philosophical primer, let's blend in some finer contours.

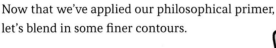

tracey

TRACEY NORMAN's face on a popular box of Clairol hair dye inadvertently produced a pitch-perfect ad for transgender acceptance in the early 1980s. Her elegant headshot modeled No. 512 Dark Auburn, a shade Clairol had mixed up to match Tracey's reddish-tinted locks. The campaign tagline? "Born Beautiful." If anyone besides Tracey caught the delightful subtext at the time, the first black trans cover model and her pristine cheekbones surely would've disappeared from drugstore shelves overnight.

"As a model, I was hiding my truth, and when I got the [Clairol] job it was very exciting for me," Tracey told *New York* magazine in 2016. Her star rose all the way to a 1980 cover of *Vogue Italia*, landing contracts with Avon, *Essence*, and Ultra Sheen cosmetics in the meantime.

After all, attaining the success she'd achieved was already tough enough for a woman of color. For a transgender woman of color? Not even the allure of a thousand Beyoncés could outweigh the transphobia of that era. Tracey was constantly terrified of being outed, which she suspects happened on her last big photoshoot before her work suddenly dried up. Though the fashion industry had been a safe haven for LGBs, the Ts were still often side-eyed for not fitting the narrow image of femininity they were selling.

Still, "I've always said that the person that walks through the door first leaves the door cracked," Tracey said in 2016. "There was a perception that a transgender woman couldn't be passable and work in fashion magazines and land contracts. I proved that wrong. I left the door cracked for other [transgender people] to walk through."

She's right. Today's fashion media feature openly nonbinary and trans faces, such as Carmen Carrera, Hari Nef, and Andreja Pejic. In 2017, CoverGirl introduced its first CoverBoy, and *Vogue Italia* featured its first openly trans cover model. Queer beauty is coming out of the commercial closet, but Tracey reminds us that folks risked everything to model it first.

WHAT TRACY IS DOING TODAY: Standing proud behind her story. "I was reminded that I made history and I deserve to have it printed," she told *New York* magazine in 2015. "And I'm still here."[1]

beauty lessons

From the moment gender assignments are made, those mushy-faced dumplings we call babies become the target of hers 'n' his compliment patterns that reinforce whatever qualities and traits society values most for each gender. Boys swaddled in blue are handsome, tough, and—cringe-inducingly—"little flirts." Meanwhile, for girls, childhood compliments are all about sugar, spice, and everything nice.

"Your infantile projection of personal agency holds promise!" is something no doting stranger has ever told a little girl. Some variation of "My, aren't you pretty?" is more like it. To our girly ears, such concerted attention to appearance subliminally teaches us that our best assets reside on our outsides. We'd even wager that many of us are primed toward prettiness panic before we can tie our own shoes, much less master winged eyeliner.

These earliest impressions of what prettiness is affect how we see our grown-ass selves in the mirror. Psychologist and beauty author Vivian Diller cites those knee-high beauty reviews as one of the top three influencers of self-perception, along with genetics and grooming.[2]

To see what today's little girls consider pretty, head to the nearest princess aisle. The royal squad sets a (usually) white, able-bodied, and romance-needing example of how to get everyone (especially princes) to love you. And from the looks of it, the two leading fairytale ingredients are being beautiful and seeing the whole new world through saucer-wide eyes.

Criminally Unattractive

Amid the disability rights movement of the 1970s, activists first took aim at so-called "ugly laws" across the United States. First passed in San Francisco in 1867 and replicated in Portland, Denver, New Orleans, and elsewhere, these local ordinances forbade visibly disabled poor people from panhandling and occupying public spaces.

Ostensibly passed to curb begging, these laws imposed fines for being seen and deemed "unsightly" or "disgusting" for the sheer benefit of preventing

beauty traps

By the time *Ladies' Home Journal* was launched in 1883, the earliest ad agencies had been established, setting the stage for women's magazines to double as billboards for head-to-toe beauty insecurities. Even the loveliest ladies had plenty to fret about. "Experts" advised women on attractiveness deal breakers including armpit odor, bad breath, stinky scalp, dull complexion, coarse lips, big boobs, small boobs, skinniness, fatness, and the wrong-shaped facial features.

NO GLASSES: The combo of disability phobias and beauty premiums discouraged men from making passes at girls who wore glasses because their blurry vision might mean their wombs are faulty, too.

LONG DARK LASHES: How do you tell boy cartoon animals from girl cartoon animals? Just look for the curlicue lashes. Because our eyelashes become more brittle as we age, we implicitly associate full lashes with youth. A few swipes of darkening mascara also brightens up our sclera, aka the whites of our eyes, adding an extra pop of vitality.

RED STATEMENT LIPS: Freud started a rumor that red lipstick was popular because women subconsciously wanted to make their mouths look like vaginas. (He would've been the world's most awkward dentist.) In fact, we were painting our lips red way back in 10,000 BCE—not to mimic labia, but because of the neuro-erotic appeal of the color red.

ROSY CHEEKS: A swipe of blusher says, "My uterus is young and I'm flush with sexual potential." Or it may suggest a blood-boiling feminist rage brought on by being ogled like a sex object. It's anybody's guess, really!

JEWELRY: Because the only thing more attractive than an attractive woman is a rich, attractive woman. A not-rich attractive woman with excellent taste in the Target jewelry section can also suffice.

WINNING SMILE: Straight, bright teeth connote health and wealth.

HOURGLASS FIGURE: A high hip-to-waist ratio à la Sofia Vergara signals fertility, which heteronormative male brains respond to with a happy hit of dopamine.

MANICURED NAILS: Well-kept nails advertise health and a chill enough demeanor that you don't nervously pick at your cuticles all day.

SLENDER ANKLES: The raised hemlines, thin figures, and dance crazes of the flapper era kicked up the first widespread ankle-fat anxieties.

SHORTER THAN ANY MAN WITHIN A TEN-FOOT RADIUS: In most opposite-sex couples, the man is at least a few inches taller than the woman. Because many same-sex couples share height gaps as well, it's unclear whether it's patriarchy playing matchmaker with petite femininity and protective masculinity, or humans preferring to look up and down for love.

non-disabled passersby from having to look at them. University of California Berkeley professor and disabilities studies expert Susan M. Schweik notes that the combination of an economic recession, permanently injured Civil War veterans, and an influx of immigrants made it impossible to overlook the destitute and disabled populations residing in growing cities. In her book *The Ugly Laws: Disability in Public*, Schweik highlights how these laws amounted to moralizing "bodily difference" and reflected a profound discomfort with coming into any sort of contact with it, as if poverty and disability were contagious diseases.

"The ugly laws were motivated not simply by appearance politics but by the need to control the economics of the underclass and group behavior within it," Schweik writes. The popularity of freak shows as live entertainment reinforced the dehumanizing culture of ableism.

Though the enforcement of ugly laws waned after World War I, it wasn't until 1974 that Chicago became the last city to repeal its local ordinance. But it would still take an additional sixteen years for the Americans with Disabilities Act, passed in 1991, to codify civil protections from the physical and economic discrimination ugly laws represented.

tress taming

The hair on our heads is the original come-hither. Evolutionarily, long tresses represent youth and fertility, which equals sexy. But it's not us, babes; it's our uteruses. That intimate association between hair and reproduction is part of what has coded those protein cords as essential to feminine attractiveness. That visual messaging has been so enduring, in fact, that many religious customs require married women to wear head coverings to signify faithfulness to God and their husbands. Hence, chopping it all off has long been one of the most dramatic statements a woman can make.

Badass Bobs

Short hair has been thoroughly gendered as masculine, but bobbed babes have been chipping away at that standard for decades. In twentieth-century America, women's haircuts heralded independence. Ladies' necks bared all after the 1920 ratification of the Nineteenth Amendment finally granted female suffrage. The New Woman had arrived, and she frankly didn't have time to dry her hair for an hour every day.

Thirty years later on the other side of the world, blunt bobs became the look for women in 1950s and '60s China, though not for personal liberation. The Cultural Revolution enforced a sort of visual gender "equality" by compelling women to shampoo away feminine flourishes like braids and perms. For men and women alike, shapeless pants and tunics known as Mao suits and short hair were a must. Literally.

Buzz Cuts

A woman's shaved head has acquired a fascinating array of meanings because of its comparative extremity. Just ask a 2007 Britney Spears. In certain ultra-Orthodox Jewish sects, brides are shorn once they say their version of "I do." In many cultures across West Africa, Southeast Asia, and the Indian diaspora, grieving women (and fellas) express their sorrow by shaving their heads. Today, Indian Hindu temples are one of the largest suppliers of human hair for the high-end wig market. The Sri Venkateswara Swamy Temple in the Indian city of Tirupati alone collects more than a ton of hair each day from devout women and some men who practice **tonsure**, or sacrificing their locks as a divine offering.

However, involuntary shaving of a woman's head historically connotes disgrace or sexual impropriety. In early America, for instance, shaving enslaved women's heads was a common punishment typically carried out by the white wife of the plantation owner. After World War II, twenty thousand French women suspected of sleeping with German soldiers ("*collaboration horizontale*") were forcibly dragged into town squares and publicly shorn.

But the shaved head has also been appropriated for protection, as in Joan of Arc's case, since her buzz cut was a tactic to desexualize herself. Jumping forward, many women today shave their heads as an exercise in agency and body reclamation. We hear it fills you with the spirit of Imperator Furiosa and her robot arm.

six degrees of "black is beautiful"

Although we most associate it with the 1970s, the Black Panthers, and *Soul Train*, the Black Is Beautiful movement had already been simmering for more than a century when Afros began defiantly blooming on college campuses and city sidewalks. For black women, pursuing beauty historically required camouflaging, not accenting, their features. Black media of the 1920s and '30s published evidence of this determination to outwit Jane Crow, with the most common strategies emphasizing glamour and hair straightening. There were plenty of reasons to invest in these techniques: Beauty meant feminine virtue and worth, respectability, and promise. It meant being seen, not sexualized and scorned. It meant cutting a deal with white beauty standards in exchange for the dignity denied to black womanhood.

To cosmetologist and trailblazing beautician Rose Morgan, all hair was "good" hair. Co-owner of Harlem's Rose Meta House of Beauty, which *Ebony* magazine hailed in **1946** as the "biggest Negro beauty parlor in the world," Rose's personal mission was to dispel the myth of textured hair as inferior and a signifier of racial subordination.

After getting fed up with segregation as America's first professional black model, Ophelia Devore started the Grace Del Marco Agency in **1946**. It was not only the first black modeling agency, but one of the first modeling agencies of any kind.

In its inaugural **1970** issue, *Essence* magazine promised readers that it would "delight and celebrate the beauty, pride, strength, and uniqueness of all Black Women."[3]

In the **1960s**, Motown girl groups like Martha and the Vandellas, the Shirelles, and Diana Ross and the Supremes brought black women to the front and center of pop culture like never before. Their glamorous images permeated even the white mainstream.

From **1961** to **1968**, the Miss Bronze contest crowned women of various skin tones, unlike most black beauty contests, which rewarded only light-skinned contestants. "We used the pageant to make political statements about segregation, being left out, and about complexions and all of that," said Miss Bronze producer Belva Davis.[4]

The only **1968** Miss America protest on Coney Island we hear about is the one that started the feminist bra-burning myth. But down the road at the Ritz, the NAACP held its first Miss Black America pageant to protest Miss America's whites-only policy, codified in a pageant rule that stipulated, "Contestants must be of good health and of the white race."

colorism 101

In the 1920s, sexier flappers upstaged the Gibson Girl, and her porcelain skin became next in line to quite literally fall out of *Vogue*. White American classism was going bronze. "In effect, an all-body tan is a social class marker for the individual—a possession—that represents and symbolizes one's social class standing as well as, incidentally or ironically, a symbol of supposed health," psychologist William Liu points out about the bronzed glow of American classism.[5] That all-body coverage is key to its status symbolism to differentiate sun-kissed luxury from working-class "rednecks" and farmers' tans.

"From a chic note, sunburn became a trend, then an established fashion, and now the entire feminine world is sunburn conscious!" *Vogue* magazine proclaimed in a 1929 four-page spread on what outfits, makeup, and accessories best emphasized white fashion girls' trendy tanning habit. That was the same year Coco Chanel soaked up too much sun on the French Riviera and churned that burn into an epidermal accessory. By then, heliotherapy, or glorified sunbathing, already had doctors' seal of approval as a trendy treatment for depression, disease, and, ironically, cancer.

Also thanks to health and wealth, fair skin made a twenty-first-century comeback. Once the cast of *Jersey Shore* introduced us to "tanorexia," or an unhealthy fear of losing one's tan, the fake bake was officially lowbrow. And oh yeah, there's the whole melanoma and skin cancer thing, too. But an ancient, cross-cultural pursuit of lightness endures. Just don't get it twisted: This ain't all about whiteness.

Welcome to the shady world of **colorism**. Whereas racism systematically discriminates against people based on their race or ethnicity, colorism is an unconscious and institutional prejudice based on skin color. "Physical features such as color and texture of hair, contours of the face and nose, body shape— all of these things relate to colorism," wrote scholar Vetta Sanders Thompson in the anthology *Shades of Difference*. "Skin color is almost never considered without some attention to these other physical features."[6]

Our caste system of skin tones, also known as **complexion privilege**, is most succinctly summed up in the common *un*-compliment "pretty for a dark-skinned girl." That ugly handful of words speaks volumes about the subjective

devaluing of the brownest and blackest skin within ethnic groups of East Asian, African, and Latin American descent. Although especially common in sites of European colonization, favoritism for fair skin had been a cornerstone of Chinese and Japanese beauty standards since well before Marco Polo arrived on the Silk Road. Likewise treasured for its status-signaling in sunny climates, the light-skinned aesthetic motto "One white covers up three uglinesses" was passed across generations of shade-seeking women and girls in East Asia.

Across the Pacific, colorism rippled throughout America, where lighter-skinned slaves were selected to work inside plantation owners' homes and among white family members, while darker-skinned slaves were relegated to the field. Biracial children born from the rape of enslaved women by their owners also sometimes received favorable treatment, such as learning to read and write and eventually being freed. That strategic sorting by skin tone was also a wicked tactic used to divide slaves and thwart revolts.

During the Reconstruction era of the late nineteenth century, lighter-skinned African Americans benefited from their skin tone, sometimes exclusively composing some of the first black communities, associations, schools, and churches. Measures like the paper bag test, ruler test, and comb test might determine whether you were light enough to enter a "blue vein society," like a college fraternity or upper-crust church. Women who were fair enough to "pass" as white might adopt a more privileged identity to gain entrance into segregated spaces.

This double-edged sword still cuts deep when it comes to acceptance within communities of color. While research overwhelmingly demonstrates that lighter skin affords social and economic privilege, it simultaneously marginalizes one's ethnic "authenticity." During the Black Power movement, for instance, lighter skin was perceived as less legitimately African. In those environments, you might not be white enough to dodge racism but also not ethnically identified enough to integrate among your allies.

Despite its global prevalence and harmful pathology, colorism awareness has only recently begun spreading, and it can be a hush-hush topic in Western countries where people of color already combat racism stemming from white supremacy. Communities of color may prefer not to discuss intragroup discrimination for fear it might distract from the fight against institutionalized racism.

why do we wear makeup?

What makes a face objectively hot or not? Cross-culturally, we go gaga for even skin tone; smooth, wrinkle-free skin; clear eyes; and hair lustrous enough to star in its own shampoo commercial. We've always had to care about our faces, but cosmetic appeal is barely a hundred years old, as the 1920s marked a newfound focus on cosmetic appeal and battling acne.

No matter what our skin tone, most of us at some point confront the question of makeup. Should we wear it? Why, or why not? And what resources—time, money, thought, maybe even exposure to harmful chemicals—are we able or willing to pour into the pursuit of pretty? It's worth taking a step back and looking at what, exactly, happens when we face the world with a made-up mug.

While patriarchy deems motherhood as women's most important job, our ultimate patriarchal power supply is beauty. Possess the right kind, and folks will read your high cheekbones and dewy complexion as more trustworthy, credible, and smarter than the average hag's.[7] Psychologists call this the **halo effect**, or our habit of ascribing a glowing list of traits to people based on how nice they are to look at. It's all our lizard brains whispering in our ears, slithering to fitness-based conclusions that prettier people are more likeable, competent, and wealthier than plain Janes.

But with the witchcraft of makeup, Jane can DIY her own halo effect of sorts. How do our brains determine whether a face is feminine or masculine? As any selfie queen knows, it's about lighting. A youthful glow is a cross-cultural hallmark of female beauty. The older you get, the more that glow dims. Scientifically speaking, statement lips and smoky eyes are all about exaggerating those contrasts. As any Kardashian can tell you, applying makeup well is all about contours, contours, contours. "Femininity and attractiveness are highly correlated, so making a face more feminine also makes it more attractive," says psychologist Richard Russell, who's studied gender perception extensively.[8]

The effect? Studies have found that women who consistently wear makeup are considered more competent and make 20 percent more money than bare-faced babes.[9] Just be careful not to make yourself look *too* good because—for women exclusively—crossing the line from attractive to gorgeous arouses *negative* stereotypes about intelligence, trustworthiness, and leadership skills.

Things get way more interesting—and less heteronormative—when we invite queer beauty out of the closet, challenging the very definition of what loveliness looks like. "This processing of potential, pushing past the point of expectation of who you have to be for other people to reach who you want to be for yourself—that's beauty, gone queer," wrote Arabelle Sicardi in *BuzzFeed*, discussing her relationship with makeup as a queer person.[10] Whereas cosmetics are often criticized as masks for a male gaze, they provide just the opposite from a queer perspective. As Sicardi highlights, makeup is also a revelation, a way to be seen in a heteronormative culture. Taken in that light, the possibilities of prettiness are endless.

 **CLAP BACK WITH FACTS**

serious about skin care

"Perfect" complexions are a maddening feminine gender construct, stretching across modern skin care culture.

- According to nineteenth-century beauty rules, concealer could get you slut-shamed because a woman's inherent goodness and piety were supposed to shine through instead.

- Does patriarchy seep into our pores, too? If so, that explains why disproportionately more women than men develop adult acne. As dermatologists established practices way back in the 1890s, girls were already their primary adolescent patients because parents figured boys don't want to marry pizza faces.[11]

- Welcome to the sisterhood of the stationary zits. According to a 2012 study in the *Journal of Women's Health*, around a third of women between ten and seventy years old experience clinical or mild acne. Although teen whiteheads tend to congregate on the forehead, cheeks, and nose, grown-ass-wimmin acne lives her best life on our jawline, chin, and neck.

- Acne is a common side effect of testosterone therapy, but it typically clears up over time. The hormonal fluctuations of pregnancy can also cause uncharacteristic breakouts. Approaching menopause similarly toys with our complexion, so definitely don't treat your pimples like pregnancy tests.

Statement Lips

Betting on beauty products costs women half a trillion bucks globally every year, but can our gender-wage-gapped wallets handle it? According to the **lipstick index**, we appear to think so. This buzzy catchphrase came straight from Estée Lauder chairman Leonard Lauder, who noticed an uptick in the company's lipstick sales in the wake of the September 11, 2001 terrorist attacks and subsequent economic recession. He attributed the boost to women using cosmetic consumption as a comforting indulgence during dour times. Economists and other beauty brands buy the idea, as do our personal stashes of stress nail polishes and face scrubs. "When women use lipstick in times of stress, they're doing it to put forward an image that they are more alive and more vibrant, and not as down in the mouth," psychologist April Lane Benson told the *New York Times* in 2008. "It's part of the uniform of desirability and attractiveness."

But treat yo'self with some fiscal discretion. Impulse shopping—for makeup or otherwise—can overinflate how much we've simply gotta have that $80 vial of revitalizing serum, which is probably half petroleum jelly anyway. "You can keep up with the Kardashians, and that kind of feeling is worth more than what goes into the lipstick," Wharton School marketing professor Z. John Zhang told *Forbes* in 2016.

marking your territory

Before the 1980s, tattoo artists would strongly advise women against getting large, highly visible pieces because of the negative stigma they'd face. And while tattoos are now mainstream and women are actually likelier to have them than dudes, visibly tattooed women still catch all sorts of unwanted comments, questions, come-ons, and touching as a result of their ink. Unfortunately, people seem to think that personal expression/art on a woman's body renders her open and welcoming to public consumption.

That's the patriarchal price of claiming your bodily space. By no means let that deter you from doing you. Tattoo scholar Margot Mifflin totally backs the notion that women and gender-nonconforming people relate to tattoos as a way to flex their autonomy. "I saw that tattooing was an amazing barometer of women's dreams and fears and passions at that time [the mid-90s]—a period when body issues were at a peak of controversy at the end of the culture wars," Mifflin writes in *Bodies of Subversion*.

OLIVE OATMAN

Historically—and even still for some folks—tattoos have been the epitome of unladylike, and anti-ink prejudice in the United States stretches back to European settlers' revulsion at Native American culture. In many tribes across the land, including the Algonquin, Osage, and Choctaw, indigenous women were both the community tattooists and the recipients of sacred markings that might signify their spiritual status or transition from adolescence to adulthood. To European Christians, these tattoos were startling signs of savagery and heathenism. But in the 1850s, Olive Oatman changed everything. Sort of.

Orphaned on the frontier, Olive and her sister were adopted by a Mojave tribe in modern-day California. As a sign of their desire to treat them as members of their community, the Mojave gave the girls ceremonial tattoos of thin black lines from their lower lips to chins, which also symbolized the guarantee of a happy afterlife with their ancestors. But after the US government negotiated with the Mojave for the girls' return, white society interpreted Olive's new facial decor as heartless abuse, not hospitality.

MAUD WAGNER

Because of her high-profile story and shocking tattoo, Olive quickly became a celebrity spectacle. Cashing in on people's prejudice, she traveled around on a speaking circuit that attracted sold-out audiences who wanted to ogle her. Meanwhile, enterprising circus women like Maud Wagner, a performer and the first known female tattoo artist in the US, recognized the profitable opportunities permanent ink could provide. Hence, by the turn of the century, tattooed ladies became a staple sideshow freak. Hail, unladylike queens.

sally ride's space makeup

Sally Ride was one of the six first-ever women selected for NASA's 1978 astronaut class—which also welcomed its first two men of color—and in 1983 became the first American woman sent into space. When NASA engineers were designing Ride's first-of-its-kind female astronaut kit, they knew to include tampons should she get her period in space. But how many would be enough? They initially suggested one hundred. She would be gone five days.

Light-years more sexist was the brogrammers' suggestion of a space makeup kit, presuming gal astronauts would *have* to want to put their faces on each morning. In women's studies speak, the idea that Ride would go to extra lengths to "prove" her femininity in a male-dominated space like . . . space . . . is called a **feminine apologetic**—in other

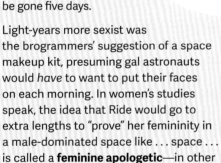

words, women should "apologize" for any masculine behavior by acting overtly feminine. Ride just called it ridiculous.

"You can just imagine the discussions amongst the predominantly male engineers about what should go in a makeup kit," she recalled. "So they came to me, figuring that I could give them advice." When Ride made it clear she couldn't care less, the project was passed off onto two of her female classmates, who probably groaned just as loudly behind the brogrammers' backs.[12]

The safe-for-space prototype they designed never actually made it into orbit, but now sits in the Smithsonian. The mango sherbet makeup bag contains eyeliner, mascara, eye shadow, blush, and lip gloss. Just like Princess Leia's.

nips, tucks, and binding

Brow lifts. Estrogen shots. Tummy tucks. Cellulite lasers. Lip fillers. Eyelash growth serum. Makeup is only the tip of the iceberg. How about more permanent alterations, from nose jobs to Botox, tummy tucks to breast enlargements?

History offers many examples of women permanently altering themselves to conform to contemporary beauty standards. Arguably the most extreme and physically damaging beauty procedure was foot-binding. For nearly a thousand years—from 970 BCE when the practice first took hold among courtesans to 1912 when it was outlawed—three billion Chinese women crushed their arches, mangled their toes, and minimized their mobility in the name of achieving teeny-tiny feet that could fit into teacup-sized, fetishized lotus flower shoes. Generations of all but the poorest feet were subjected to excruciatingly painful binding suffered in the name of feminine allure, lest their owner be criticized as lewd or disgusting for walking around on unbound feet.

Foot-binding was about far more than satisfying the male gaze, though. It reinforced patriarchal power by tethering women to their husbands and homes. How could a lady run away if she could barely totter out the front door? At the time, Chinese women's legal status was virtually nonexistent, educational opportunities slim to none, and immigration status a moot point since travel was so physically demanding.

Chinese foot-binding offers a stark example of what to watch out for amid the bombardment of beauty dos and don'ts. It's easy to get caught up in the *what* of beauty debates, à la questioning whether lipstick and cleavage are limiting or liberating. But as the history of foot-binding makes clear, it's the *why* and *to what effect* that deserve our attention. Lipstick and cleavage aren't the enemy, in other words. It's the forces that popularize and reward trend loyalty that need to be plucked out and examined like random nipple hairs, because that stuff can get stuck in our heads.

Research has consistently found that a **growth mindset**, or believing that we can improve in some way, yields rich benefits. And it's true that approaching intelligence, peacekeeping, and even romance from a perspective that our

natures and environments are malleable leads to smarter, more unified, and more committed outcomes. When it comes to beauty and women, however, the opposite is true.

An October 2014 study found that ladies who believed they could attain higher standards of beauty if they just tried hard enough and struggled through enough YouTube smoky-eye tutorials fared much worse than those who were more like, "I'm gonna do me."[13] Imagining that we can and must look as good as Natalie Portman or Kerry Washington is strongly linked with appearance-related anxiety and low self-worth, which can bankrupt our confidence.

One big clue that this is a gender-specific beauty trap? The researchers found no such pattern among men. Dudes certainly aren't immune to media messages about how they "should" look, but they also don't have centuries of cultural objectification baggage to intensify their aspirations.

To flip the prettiness script we've been memorizing since forever, we need to redefine beauty as a fluid expression rather than a static state. Or, to put it in growth mindset terms, let's "make over" beauty as a subjective and infinitely malleable by-product of our identity, instead of the other way around. Facets of who we are, including gender, physicality, ethnicity, and sexual orientation, can all contribute to what we accept as aesthetically pleasing.

Getting called pretty or even feeling pretty doesn't need to be the end goal. The point of doing our hair (or not), putting on a wild outfit (or not), and contouring the living hell out of our cheeks (or not) becomes more about meeting ourselves in the moment. By honoring it and taking comfort that since no *single* look can possibly capture all of who we are—now or ever—a predetermined "pretty" is powerless.

beauty on the clock

The American Time Use survey confirms what you probably already suspected if you've ever flipped halfway through a women's magazine. Femininity demands more time in front of the mirror. On average, we clock nearly an hour each day getting our groom on, around 50 percent more than dudes.[14] Women also average a few extra minutes of sleep per night, so maybe "beauty rest" is real after all.

 **CLAP BACK WITH FACTS**

when guys say you're prettier without makeup

For approximately 99.9 percent of our heteronormative history, men have decided what's hot or not. Let's reclaim our face space.

- Developing research finds that average made-up faces are usually rated more attractive than bare faces, albeit slightly. However, the more conventionally attractive your face, the less makeup amplifies your supermodel assets because you already have the features makeup is designed to suggest. In other words, pretty faces are pretty with or without makeup.[15]

- Regardless of how many bros tell us we shouldn't care about makeup, we're doubling down on our cosmetic skills nonetheless. In 2017 alone, views of YouTube beauty tutorials, hauls, and primping videos soared 60 percent. On Instagram, the number of male-identified accounts that mentioned "makeup" increased 20 percent in 2017.[16]

- Women are wearing makeup as fast as Fenty et al. can pump out new products; between 2015 and 2017, cosmetics consumption ballooned 25 percent. Athleisure and the 24/7 leggings lifestyle has even spawned "active cosmetics" designed to withstand workouts—and the requisite #gymselfie.[17]

- According to beauty-industry analytics, more than a third of women eighteen to fifty-four wear at least five daily makeup products. But collectively, we're doing it more for satisfying selfies than the analog male gaze.

- Even if women were objectively prettier without makeup, the look wouldn't last for long. That's what happens in Hollywood, at least. When *Vulture* compared Harrison Ford, Denzel Washington, and other male A-listers' ages with the ages of their female romantic costars, and even as the guys hit their fifties and sixties, the women consistently hovered around thirty years old.[18]

creep factors

VIRGINS, CHIVALRY, AND SEX OBJECTS

Are you ready for a male gaze makeover? Ready or not, here it comes, unladies.

Glass half-full: It's *so* easy to get started. You already have everything you need since you possess a female-identified bod. Whoop whoop! Just remember, it *is* a wonderland, a temple, and a vessel for human life. Truly incredible. Oh, and don't forget it's also a sex object. Got that?

Along the way, you'll get catcalled, boob-ogled, and possibly trapped on a Tinder date with a men's rights activist. If you're looking for an "edgier" adventure, wear something skimpy and a statement lip. That'll give you an all-access pass to asking for it.

Women have always been both too much and not enough eye candy for patriarchy. True, philosophers, clergy, doctors, and scientists have wasted countless hours over the ages mansplaining all the ways we were little more than defective, menstrual-disease-ridden skin sacks. Yet we were also the sexiest, most irresistible, and satisfying skin sacks cis-hetero male entitlement had ever seen. So, what were men supposed to do about these sex objects?

"It is necessary to realize that the most sacrosanct article of sexual politics in the period, the Victorian doctrine of chivalrous protection and its familiar protestations of respect, rests upon the tacit assumption, a cleverly expeditious bit of humbug, that all women were 'ladies' . . . "

KATE MILLETT
feminist writer and activist

In 2015, Nobel Prize winner Tim Hunt exposed the thin line between genius and sexist jackassery when he publicly whined about the "trouble with girls" in laboratory settings. "You fall in love with them, they fall in love with you, and when you criticize them they cry," the biochemist told a conference crowd. On Twitter, women scientists flipped off that misogynistic nonsense with viral #distractinglysexy workplace selfies. "Here I am shoulder-deep in cow rectum, so seductive!" a veterinarian tweeted. "I did an entire liver transplant without crying or falling in love," a doctor chimed in.

 The **male gaze** of female sexuality is so deeply embedded in culture, we no longer even recognize it as biased; it's just the way things are. If you start looking at yourself through a cis-hetero male gaze, suddenly, you're a sex object. Unfortunately, it's a lot easier to do this than we might like, and it can inform all kinds of decisions we make regarding how we dress, wear makeup, and act.

 In 1997, psychologist Barbara L. Frederickson developed **objectification theory** to shine a light on how we process, internalize, and externalize sexism, misogyny, and a sexually subordinate status. She notes how we do this to ourselves in monitoring and rituals that probably sound familiar. When we sexually objectify ourselves *through a patriarchal lens*, it increases anxiety over how we look, lowers our body awareness, and sharpens our self-shaming.[1] When seen through the #distractinglysexy gaze patriarchy foists on us, intersectional sexpectations reveal themselves.

unsafe faces and spaces

Dudes are the creepier sex. That isn't just our misandry talking. Creepiness speaks for itself.

"Creepiness is often judged to be a male problem, like baldness or the wearing of loafers without socks," Nathan Heller wrote in a 2015 *New Yorker* book review of Adam Kotsko's *Creepiness*. "That's probably because creepiness carries a vague, erotically tinged threat, and men are classically predatory."

Et voilà, women tend to perceive ick vibes as sexual threats. At its core, that suspicion—sometimes baseless, granted—is seeded by the low-key, patriarchal power dynamics that constantly whirl around us. We're typically raised with an implicit understanding that bad men might do bad things to us; parents openly fret over their daughters' safety way more than they worry about their sons. We're taught to be vigilant to the point of being blamed if we don't superhero-style dropkick every predator who comes our way. The patriarchal power imbalance collides with the socialized expectations of our feminine politeness to throw us for some serious loops.

Think about how routinely women who report sexual harassment are immediately asked why they didn't aggressively defend themselves against their creep, and how routinely the truth is because they felt frozen in place and had no clue what to do. Often, you can barely think clearly until after you get away and can process. Psychologist and creepiness researcher Frank McAndrew conducted the first empirical research on how and why we get creeped out, and his initial findings document that chilling cycle.

"[Getting the creeps is] about the uncertainty of threat," McAndrew told *Smithsonian* magazine. "You're feeling uneasy because you think there might be something to worry about here, but the signals aren't clear enough to warrant your doing some sort of desperate, lifesaving kind of thing."

It's as if creepiness creates a brain fog of social etiquette versus personal comfort. In the moment, it's entirely plausible that we simply won't know the right way to respond—or whether you should respond at all! Maybe you're just being crazy, right? Maybe he's just trying to be nice, right? Here's the snag: Creepiness revolves around the *possibility* of something bad happening, so acting on it is a bit of a dice roll, especially if the creep is someone you should be able to trust like a family friend, teacher, or boss. Plus, girls and women might worry they'll be written off as thirsty if they tell anyone—especially if their outfits were "asking for it" at the time. Patriarchy pressures women and girls to second-guess whether we could've dodged horny dudes, and sets off society's skeptical follow-up questionnaire:

- What were we wearing?

- Had we been drinking or getting high?

- Did we go home with that person?

- Did we fight back?

- Did we tell anyone immediately? If no, why not?

In short, we're socialized to wonder whether we'd been exercising enough modesty.

is modest hottest?

By linking chastity (i.e., female worth) to the concept of modesty and clothing coverage, patriarchy puts the onus on gals to keep their lust magnets hidden from the male gaze. And to keep women complicit in their own sexual objectification, any transgressions were traditionally punished via public shaming. In her book *Pantaloons and Power: A Nineteenth-Century Dress Reform in the United States*, Gayle V. Fischer notes that if a nineteenth-century woman lifted her skirt to climb into a carriage and flashed her ankles in the process, she could expect any surrounding men to loudly and lewdly let her know.

Even supposedly progressive suffragists tsk-tsked other women for associating with "evil companions" (as turn-of-the-twentieth-century social worker Jane Addams put it) who might drag otherwise upstanding female citizens into the muck and mire of prostitution. Those weak-willed women might corrupt your equally weak mind! Popular turn-of-the-century novels were full of this sort of propaganda. Products of the sexist, racist, and classist anxieties of their time, many—like 1910's *The House of Bondage*—were full of the weak-woman-as-vile-corruptor trope. Women seduced "friends" to their doom with liquor or opium, preyed on their vanity and materialism with fancy dresses, and used their feminine wiles to compete over men, dragging the whole group into a downward spiral of competitive depravity.

In the Roman, Byzantine, Assyrian, and Persian empires, upper-class ladies covered their hair in public to deter dudes from ogling them. And we're not talking about whistles and catcalls; simply being looked at and lusted over by a random guy on the sidewalk could sully a woman's respectability and, by extension, her family's. Interestingly, one group of women at this time didn't—and sometimes legally couldn't—toss on veils: prostitutes and enslaved women. So thoroughly marginalized were these women, they were symbolically stripped of agency and their bodies commodified.

What about religious modesty? Through secular eyes, head coverings in particular are often interpreted as artifacts of female subjugation. But the

FIELD NOTES

modesty vs. science

Not convinced modesty is a flawed concept? Let's take red—the most immodest, unladylike color—as an example. A stack of studies agree there's something about burgundy, crimson, and ruby on a woman that signals s-e-x to normatively straight, male brains. Behavioral psychologists call it the red dress effect.

If you've watched *The Bachelor,* you've witnessed this theory in action. For more than twenty seasons, rose huntresses are most likely to roll up to the reality show mansion in red. That siren shade also applies to lipstick; a French social psychologist found that when pink, brown, and red statement lips walked into a bar, the latter got the most male attention. (The study failed to note, however, whether the woman wearing the lipstick wanted said attention.)

The magic of red highlights the fundamental failure of the modesty doctrine: assigning all of our meaning and value onto *clothing* and how we wear it (or don't), instead of on the bodies they're meant to hide. See, it's not the color itself that attracts the male gaze. Rather, it's a learned connection between red and sexual receptiveness. Awash in cultural images and innuendo that feminine plus red equals bed, straight men subconsciously perceive that women wearing it are more down for sex. Just as guys still tend to misread polite smiles as flirtation, the red dress effect tells them *come hither* when it might actually mean it's laundry day.

As even more proof that context is everything, red has the opposite effect on women. For us gals, masculinity plus red does not equal sexy, but menacing—evoking male rage and violence—and is likely to send us in the opposite direction.

LEGAL EAGLE

BENEVOLENT SEXISM

The verdict: It's better for everyone when women stick to their "paramount destiny" and manage the household. The National Women's History Project takes it away:

- **1873:** The US Supreme Court (SCOTUS) gives a majority thumbs-up to Illinois's refusal to admit women to the state bar, arguing that "the paramount destiny and mission of woman are to fulfill the noble and benign offices of wife and mother."

- **1908:** SCOTUS is cool with an Oregon law restricting women's machine labor in the name of protecting the "proper discharge of [their] maternal functions."

- **1961:** In *Hoyt v. Florida,* SCOTUS upholds state laws making it far less likely for women than men to be called for jury service on the grounds that a "woman is still regarded as the center of home and family life."

millions of Muslim, Jewish, Catholic, and other Christian women around the world who publicly cover their hair would probably disagree. As Arab and Islamic studies professor Sahar Amer underscores in her primer, *What Is Veiling?*, Islamic women veil for a variety of reasons, including piety, familial respect, and expressing one's hijabi fashion sense. In Iran, Saudi Arabia, and parts of Iraq, wearing a hijab is legally mandatory, but far more women opt for a hijab or niqab because of personal piety, thrift, cultural preservation, confidence, and solidarity.

Still, it's worth asking who defines these dress codes. Where does expression end and compulsion begin? To be clear, there's nothing wrong with covering up—whether with a hijab or anything else—if that's what makes you the most comfortable. There is no approved feminist uniform of liberation. If you're unsure whether your closet is repressive, check the motivation. Prim fashions aren't the enemy; it's subjective modesty doctrine that needs to be taken out of rotation because it assumes that we can bend social status to our will if we present ourselves in just the right way. It may be true to a point, but it's by no means a cure-all.

knight in rusted armor

Ladylike modesty doctrine is in a codependent relationship with chivalry. While naysayers contend that feminists have killed off the perfectly good chivalrous perks of opened doors, free dinners, and heavy things lifted, the fact is that today's society remains firmly attached to the idea that protectiveness is not only an innate male trait but also a masculine responsibility. By the same token, chivalry ultimately expects ladylike deference and sexual availability in exchange.

And that, dear friends, is what we call **entitlement**, and it is far from a relic of the past. For an idea of how it works today, let's meet a couple of super uncool characters: Nice Guys™ and pickup artists.

The trademarked Nice Guy reeks of chivalry: There's an expectation of sexual availability in exchange for treating women like ladies, unlike the dark knights they're convinced conventionally beautiful girls usually fall for. Who else in her life could provide a masculine refuge *and* know her better than she knows herself? These nefarious characters are known to meet sexual or romantic rejection with deep misogynistic anger, upset that being "nice guys" doesn't equal sexual access to the women they desire.

Pickup artists, meanwhile, practice what they call "the art of seduction" to strategically prime women to have sex with them. One of their go-to tactics is negging, in which they low-key insult a woman who's attractive enough that she probably won't expect it. The insecurity she then feels will supposedly lower her defenses and make the guy more attractive because he's masculine enough to put her in her place, or whatever. It's super gross, but PUAs insist it's a confidence-salvaging tool in a world where only conventionally handsome, muscular Toms, Dicks, and Harrys get the girls. So why not employ some subliminal subterfuge to win a sex object to put your penis inside? OH YEAH, TOTALLY OKAY.

six hallmarks of highly toxic masculinity

Power breeds entitlement, regardless of gender. The wider the gap between those who have it and those who don't, the more entitled those in power tend to feel. In capitalist patriarchies like ours, it's a rich man's world. Upper-income Americans were seventy-five times wealthier than low-income families in 2016, according to number crunching from the Pew Research Center. That combo of macho and money mixes up into a problematic stew—our least favorite *men*-u item.

1. **Superstars:** The Equal Employment Opportunity Commission calls them "superstars" because of the lengths organizations will go to look the other way or protect these high performers from being punished for their pathological dick swinging. Even if they're workhorses, the cost of keeping their toxicity around outweighs the bottom line benefits by more than two to one. Uber founder Travis Kalanick, who steered the bajillion-dollar startup into an emblem of Silicon Valley misogyny, is a leading member of this patriarchal class.[2]

2. **Locker room talk:** Donald Trump won the presidency despite—or thanks to—"locker room talk." That, of course, was his nauseatingly effective excuse for being caught on an *Access Hollywood* tape bragging to Billy Bush about pussy grabbing. Sports sociologists who've studied the jock-strapped realities of men's locker rooms have identified an unsurprising script. These are "verbal exchanges whereby male athletes celebrate heterosexual aggression against women as a common method of oppositional self-definition."[3] Chest bump.

3. **Bro apologetics:** A term coined by Stanford University law professor Michele Dauber that also describes the underlying message of Trump's "locker room talk" excuse is that, hey, that's just how men talk about women behind their backs. Boys will be boys. Deal with it. When we accept those apologetics, it effectively allows the bad actors to shape our realities.

4. **Bro code:** Ironically, all that locker room banter cultivates a culture of silence that sounds an awful lot like bro code. Speaking like a sociologist, "a longstanding rule of male culture in general is that guys are supposed to abide by the unspoken but understood oath not to disclose, denounce, or disrupt the bad behaviors of other men."[4] You could also call it enabling.

5. **Girl-watching:** Business bros plying other bros with steak dinners at strip clubs are attempting to impress one another by girl-watching, or openly checking out women, usually in the company of another bro.[5] Think of it as organized sexual objectification. Get a better hobby, fellas.

6. **Aggrieved entitlement:** This is the favorite crutch of men's rights activists who perceive feminism as poison, men as culturally cucked, and women as duplicitous sluts. Like a gendered take on whataboutism (i.e., deflecting critique with "well what about"–style false comparisons), these boo-hoo boys deny feminist platforms by essentially whining that men have it just as bad if not *worse* than anybody else.[6]

These cultural carcinogens seep into our collective perceptions of female sexuality and sexual victimhood. Because of that toxicity, when the worst-case scenarios happen, as they constantly do, way too many factors determine who gets sympathy, help, and justice, as well as who gets slut-shamed and victim-blamed to the side.

missed opportunities

Around the world, 235 million women in sixty-eight countries are particularly vulnerable to sexual harassment because their governments lack laws barring it in the workplace.[7] In a world where women already make up less than half of the workforce, and their presence across male-dominated industries and in leadership positions still isn't normalized, harassment is a weapon to keep more of them out and send even more back home. Sound paranoid? How about if a man says it?

Tweeting in November 2017, University of Virginia media studies professor Siva Vaidhyanathan asserted, "All men have benefited from the reduced competition of women who have been dissuaded from certain careers or certain companies."[8]

Whether it's the student who can't access safe and productive time with a sleazy professor, or an employee with a creep of a supervisor who passes up ladder-climbing opportunities, women will often opt for a different path over dealing with demoralizing harassment. "If a woman has a bad experience in graduate school and decides not to become a professor, that is one less woman who applied to the same jobs I did, and that meant more room for me," Vaidhyanathan wrote of opportunities in the United States, where sexual harassment actually *is* classified as discrimination—but still *does* force women off their career paths and into a poison ivy patch of sexist bullsh*t and trauma.

risk factors

Sexual harassment is a side effect of power dynamics and skewed views of gender norms, and it's certainly not limited to situations in which a man has higher authority. In fact, Australian researchers in 2016 found that in some workplaces, female supervisors in their thirties and forties are more likely than their lower-ranking female peers to face sexual harassment.[9] They call it **contrapower harassment**, a tactic for tearing down women who dare to step outside their assigned lower rung in the gender hierarchy, particularly in male-dominated fields.

Regardless of who's at the top of the org chart, sexual harassment is most prevalent in tip-based service positions like waiting tables; isolated roles like housekeepers and farmworkers; and in decentralized workplaces like retail outlets or distribution centers where employees might not understand the chain of command.

And a glaring risk factor for any workplace in any industry is having a Harvey Weinstein or a Bill O'Reilly: a powerful superstar performer who's managed to rise to the top based on stellar performance, achieve equally extraordinary benefits and paychecks, and develop an overblown sense of being above the law. Employers' fears of losing the superstar's contributions and connections—or of losing their financial investment in him—can present a hurdle to punishing the

this is what male entitlement sounds like

Dating apps have lowered the threshold to getting laid, but algorithms haven't cracked the patriarchal code of sexual conquest. Even if women make the first move a la Bumble, dudes often mistake swiping right as implied consent to whatever happens next, leaving many women—42 percent, according to a 2016 Pew Research study—feeling harassed or uncomfortable on dating sites and replicating all-too-familiar offline sexpectations.[10]

- **BLUE BALLS:** When bods get sexually aroused without orgasming, the pressure of engorged genitals can get uncomfortable whether you're working with testicles *or* labia. Luckily, there's a cure called masturbation.

- **CON-DAMNATIONS:** Badgering partners into unprotected sex is called **coercive condom resistance**, and studies suggest most straight guys have done it.[11] But dudes doth protest too much considering condom-related boner loss affects less than a quarter of men and can often be remedied with better-fitting coverage.[12]

- **SLIP-UPS:** In 2014, a *British Medical Journal* study of teens' anal sex habits found that when girls were hesitant to try it, guys were likelier to initiate penetration and claim that "it slipped." (No, it didn't.)

- **UNSOLICITED DICK PICS:** Almost half of all women in a 2016 Match.com survey said they'd received one of these, which are often sent to shock, seduce, or solicit nudes in return. Emerging research describes these surprise selfies as cocktails of online disinhibition, aggressive hookup strategies, and exhibitionism.[13]

harasser or blowing the whistle, despite the fact that his toxic behavior puts a dent in other workers' productivity, mental health, and safety, not to mention the company's bottom line.

Employers who want to reap the benefits of keeping a powerful abuser around have plenty of ethically questionable legal tools at their disposal, such as nondisclosure agreements (you won't tell anyone except in court or we'll sue you) and forced arbitration clauses (you won't speak out or take the issue to court at all). These tactics serve to silence, intimidate, and confuse people who have endured workplace harassment.

LEGAL EAGLE

HARASSMENT AT WORK

In 1974, Mechelle Vinson was hired to work as a teller at a Philadelphia bank. She worked her way up the ranks, but in 1978, she was fired for taking "excessive" sick leave. Vinson sued, saying she'd had to deal with incessant sexual harassment from her boss, who had not only fondled her in front of coworkers, followed her into the bathroom, and whipped out his junk in front of her, but who had also repeatedly pressured her into sex and demanded sexual favors.

The case *finally* made it to the Supreme Court, and in 1986, the court recognized sexual harassment, which created a "hostile work environment," as a form of sex-based discrimination under Title VII of the Civil Rights Act of 1964.[14]

fending them off

In April 1975, Cornell University instructor Lin Farley lit a match. Testifying at a New York City Human Rights Commission hearing on women in the workplace, she used a term unfamiliar to most people outside feminist academia to describe what women were dealing with but were often too embarrassed to speak up about. "Sexual harassment of women in their place of employment is extremely widespread," she said in a statement that still sounds fresh. "It is literally epidemic."[15]

In describing the hearing in an August 1975 article, the *New York Times* also interviewed several women fed up with harassment's effects on their wallets. A sociology student earning money as a waitress asked, "Why do women have to put up with this sort of thing anyway? You aren't in any position to say, 'Get your crummy hands off me' because you need the tips . . . Women are the ones who are punished. They have to leave a job because of a man's behavior and the man is left there, sitting pretty."[16]

In her 1964 book *Sex and the Office*—which, it's worth mentioning, was reprinted as recently as 2012—*Cosmopolitan* editor-in-chief Helen Gurley Brown wondered why you'd leave your job when you could just play the game, ladies! Brown advised women dealing with sexual harassment—those being grabbed, pinched, chased

anita

In October 1991, law professor **ANITA HILL** captivated the country. She testified before an all-white, all-male Senate Judiciary Committee that Supreme Court nominee Clarence Thomas had subjected her to endless workplace come-ons and sexual humiliations when she had worked under him at the federal Department of Education and, ironically, the Equal Employment Opportunity Commission.

American mistrust and disregard for unmarried black women—and arguably black womanhood at large—was exhibited on public-spectacle scale. Anita's agonizing testimony of sexual harassment triggered cultural shock waves that still resonate. Yet, after Anita and Thomas both delivered their testimonies, only 27 percent of Americans viewed Anita more favorably.

Saddled with the triple threat of being unmarried, child-free, and African American, Anita found her credibility as an upstanding law professor was no match for the lie that women "like her" just aren't to be trusted. In spite of—and partly because of—the media blitz and predictions of women's widespread outrage and support of Anita, the abuse she endured while working for Thomas seemed to bounce off most people. Both before Anita became a household name and after Thomas accepted his Supreme Court appointment, a solid 70 percent of public opinion favored him.[17]

But according to the unscientific Feminist Law of Energy, outrage cannot be created or destroyed; it merely changes form. Most recognizably, it shape-shifted into new language to identify old abuses in the workplace. During the 1992 elections, it also won a record number of female candidates a record total of just over 10 percent of House and Senate seats.

Her testimony might not have brought down her abuser, but in coming forward in 1991, Anita became an inextricable part of a larger movement and a hero to countless women.

"I don't think of 1991 and 2017 as isolated moments in history," she said during a December 2017 panel organized by the National Women's Law Center. "I see them as part of an arc, and an arc that has been bending towards justice."[18]

WHAT ANITA IS DOING TODAY: In December 2017, amid the #metoo movement, Anita was picked to lead the Commission on Sexual Harassment and Advancing Equality in the Work-place, a nongovernmental effort to squash the festering bullsh*t that springs from unequal power dynamics in the entertainment industry.

around desks, pressured into sex, and called names—to use flattery to somehow charm the harasser into stopping his disgusting gender-based power play. And if that doesn't work, just tell him the man in your life, the one who's "buying you a mink coat for Christmas," wouldn't like it![19]

Cue dead-eyed feminist stare.

Playfully telling your boss, coworkers, or customers about angry men and mink coats hasn't really panned out as a solution. In 2015, a third of the US Equal Employment Opportunity Commission's claims involved workplace harassment. At least people are reporting it, right? Sure, but in the case of businesses and private employers—as opposed to government employees, for instance—the EEOC doesn't step in unless those companies have at least fifteen employees. That means many women who work for smaller companies or in roles such as housekeepers and home-based caregivers have little legal recourse.

Not to mention, those reports are from only a fraction of the women in the United States who are being harassed. Most women don't report workplace harassment, and three-quarters of those who do have to deal with the added— and also illegal—layer of retaliation.[20]

Many women, feeling they have nowhere to turn, afraid they'll be dismissed, disbelieved, victim-blamed, or retaliated against, turn to more under-the-radar tactics to at least try to warn other women to stay far away from potential abusers. **Whisper networks** made headlines as big-name harassers fell like dominoes in 2017, with the unsurprising news surfacing that women do, indeed, talk to one another, and in cases of dealing with assholes, they take notes. Whether transmitted over brunch, email, or anonymous spreadsheets, whispered warnings about harassers are a way to informally exercise power and fill in the gaps left when HR reporting protocols fall short or don't exist in the first place. They validate concerns, help out people in our networks— and are evidence that our current system doesn't work.

WTF Do I Do?

The path to change, of course, starts with believing women and ending patriarchal systems of oppression that allow harassment to fester. On our way there, assuming we're not all high-powered legislators, attorneys, and CEOs already, we can keep some other routes and strategies in mind to make sure women feel safe and supported within our shaky systems.

1. KNOW YOU'RE NOT CRAZY

Recognize right now that sex- and gender-based harassment is never okay, and if it's happening to you, it's not your fault. If your gut tells you something feels unsafe or uncomfortable, trust your instincts rather than dismissing your feelings as an overreaction. That can be easier said than done after a lifetime of watching people slam accusers as crazy, slutty, or money-grubbing, so start working right now to reframe your thoughts: Women do not deserve to be harassed. The only thing we're *asking for* is to be able to go to work and earn a living with dignity.

2. SEE IT TO BEAT IT

Seek out and highlight stories of women who are kicking ass in their respective fields, or share your own experiences with girls and women looking for some inspiration. The oft-repeated "see it to be it" has significance beyond heartwarming optics; when girls and women recognize an avenue exists and is open to them, they can follow their role models.

Getting more women into workspaces means their presence is normalized and provides less fertile ground for harassment than in more homogenous organizations. With less harassment forcing women off track, more of them potentially can rise to higher paying leadership roles. After all, values come from the top down. It's not enough to show anti-harassment videos. Leaders who demonstrate inclusive, respectful behavior and who institute across-the-board systems to make sure people facing harassment are heard and taken seriously—and that hold abusers accountable—will be more successful in combating it.

3. SPEAK UP

If you're a bystander, take note of your coworkers' reactions to jokes, hugs, and other gray-area behavior. Is she laughing nervously? Does she seem uncomfortable? Was the offender's comment or action obviously gross? Call it out! You don't have to make a dramatic citizen's arrest; simply follow your gut and say what's on your mind: "Hey, dude, that's really weird. Cut it out." Or, "I'm uncomfortable; let's end the meeting." Then try gently talking with your coworker in private to find out if she's okay. If she's not, you might offer to walk through the appropriate chain of command with her as a witness, or report it yourself with or without her name attached. Without pressuring her either way, let her know you're on her side. Keep notes and screengrabs about the interaction.

love shouldn't hurt like that

In the summer of 1993, Lorena Bobbitt exacted astounding revenge on her violently abusive husband and triggered a culture-wide penis anxiety attack. After cycling through six years of spousal torment from John Wayne Bobbitt, Lorena survived being raped by him for the last time when a few hours later, she grabbed an eight-inch carving knife from the kitchen and chopped of her sleeping abuser's penis.

Vanity Fair crowned her "a national folk heroine" for daring to commit "the ultimate crime against manhood"; feminists heralded her as a tragic symptom of silence around intimate-partner violence, while right-wing shock jock Rush Limbaugh cast Lorena as an arch feminazi just like then-First Lady Hillary Clinton. In 1994, a Virginia jury acquitted Lorena, and not coincidentally, the US Congress passed the Violence Against Women Act later that year, earmarking more than $1 billion for domestic violence and assault prevention and response programs. Lorena eventually remarried, had children, and remained a committed advocate for fellow survivors of intimate partner violence, which had driven her such desperation for the sexual dignity we all deserve.

Serial abusers like John Wayne Bobbitt don't rely solely on physical violence. They might also use psychologically manipulative tactics to control another person. The most common tactic? Isolation. It often involves blocking or reducing the partner's contact with her friends and family so she becomes increasingly dependent on the abuser for money, attention, and/or resources. Other forms of **symbolic violence** include destroying property, hurting pets, kicking and throwing things, or even just driving recklessly while the other person is in the car.

Abusers might also try **gaslighting**, telling their partner she's nuts or too sensitive for pointing out abuse, manipulation, or negativity. The term comes from the 1944 film *Gaslight*, in which a husband tries to convince his wife she's losing her mind by literally messing with, among other things, the lights in their house.

 **CLAP BACK WITH FACTS**

getting out of danger

It's not always easy to leave or spot an abusive relationship, so it's important to know the facts.

- **TRYING TO LEAVE:** On average, it takes women five to seven times of walking away from an abusive relationship before the decision sticks. With each attempt to leave, the potential for danger grows. Seventy percent of abuse occurs after a woman leaves, and women are 75 percent more likely to be killed once they leave the relationship. It's especially important for friends and loved ones of a victim of abuse to be patient and not turn away from the victim if she goes back to her abuser.

- **LEARNED HELPLESSNESS:** Some abuse victims rely on a coping mechanism in which they give up, passively accept the pain and suffering, and retreat into themselves in an attempt to avoid further violence rather than risk being turned away at a shelter.

- **FATAL CONSEQUENCES:** In the United States, men kill more than 1,600 women every year. Of the women who knew their attackers, 63 percent were killed by a spouse or intimate partner, equating to about 870 women a year.

- **LOOKING FOR HELP:** Of the LGBTQ survivors who seek out a shelter, about 44 percent of them are turned away.

- **GENDER TROUBLE:** Nearly three-quarters of those denied shelter say it was because of their gender identity. Cis and trans men struggle to find shelter services for a range of reasons, but often sex-segregated shelters focus their attention on cisgender women. One survey indicated that just 30 percent of homeless shelters would be willing to help trans women alongside cis women, while 21 percent said they'd refuse entry altogether.

A cycle of abuse unleashes a torrent of chronic stress throughout the victim's body. Stress hormones like cortisol flood the abused partner's system, which is basically put on high alert. That chronic, constant fight-or-flight status takes its toll on her health, particularly her heart and immune function.

There *are* protective factors. Having higher self-esteem, more economic security, a stronger social network, and the ability to maintain a separate identity predict better outcomes for women who might otherwise become isolated or abused. But it's still important to stay vigilant—for yourself and your loved ones. Emotional abuse is often a precursor to physical violence. If you suspect your partner is manipulating you, confide in someone; a friend or therapist might be able to help you put the situation in perspective and see that you are *not* losing it.

how rape culture happens

Time to face grim facts. According to the US Centers for Disease Control and Prevention, one in five cisgender women and one in seventy-one cis men will be raped. In other words, there's a solid statistical chance that you or someone you know will be sexually assaulted or raped at some point. We don't say this to scare you. It's just the opposite: The more we can confront rape as a global public health concern, the more research and data we can marshal to better understand why it happens, who commits it, and how to respond.

Although rape has existed at least since civilization's oldest laws were enforced, its meanings have changed since ancient times. Plus, much of what we do know about why rape happens comes from research that's largely been limited to South Africa and America, where disproportionately white college students and disproportionately black prisoners make up the bulk of study participants. Chronic underreporting adds more challenges to rape prevention.

From our limited public health perspective, **rape culture** isn't a product of football teams, fraternities, and military boot camps. Sure, it's easier for it to thrive in those environments, but on a global scale, rape culture is a broad-brush problem of social injustice and dysfunctional gender roles. The three most fertile breeding grounds of rape culture are as common as table salt:

1. **War:** The history of war is one of widespread sexual violence, including rape, forced prostitution and sexual slavery, and forced pregnancy.

2. **Bro-coded cultures:** Cis, hetero, man-on-top gender hierarchies that encourage female subordination and sexual one-upmanship are a recipe for crossing not-so-blurred lines. To put a finer point on it from a cross-cultural psychiatric study on rape culture published in the *Lancet*: "If a woman resists sexual intercourse, it may be perceived as a direct threat by men to their masculinity, triggering a crisis of male identity and contributing to sexual control and violence as it is seen as a way of resolving this crisis."

3. **Enabling communities:** Whether neighborhoods, friends, family, or law enforcement, bystanders who turn blind eyes to abuse, slut-shaming, silence, and inaction perpetuate rape culture. To find one, head for the nearest college frat house.

 **CLAP BACK WITH FACTS**

street harassment

Hollering at female-identified folks on sidewalks and public spaces is arguably the most obnoxious form of gender policing. It's also existed since approximately forever because patriarchy is an old dog that hates learning new tricks.

- In 2014, the online magazine *Matter* asked women in 10 major global cities to keep a street harassment log for a week. When they swapped notes, a familiar pattern emerged. You're likeliest to be catcalled when you're A) alone, B) passing two or more men, and C) not smiling. Fact check: Demanding a smile isn't a compliment; it's a power trip.[21]

- It trips up our jogs. A 2017 reader poll conducted by *Runner's World* magazine found that 58 percent of women under thirty regularly experienced mid-run street harassment.[22]

- Public awareness of catcalling and street harassment first coincided with the turn-of-the-twentieth-century rise of unmarried, white, young women working as sales girls, typists, and waitresses. By 1920, pavement predation had become a potent enough problem that more than two hundred American cities collectively hired more than three hundred women police officers specifically to thwart catcallers.

asking for it

Ladylike law decrees that women and girls should do everything in their feminine powers to preemptively thwart any inappropriate thoughts, looks, or come-ons from horny gents. If they can't satisfy that impossible burden of proof, too bad—if they hadn't *really* wanted it, they would've fought him off. Sociologists call this insidious prejudice **rape myth acceptance**.

WHAT WERE YOU WEARING?

CLAP BACK: Research on victim-blaming finds our sympathy for a survivor changes with their outfits, and more revealing means less appealing. Those first impressions of trustworthiness, then, are mere fashion statements. Another ugly twist? Prettier rape victims are also likelier to be blamed for the crime.

HAD YOU BEEN DRINKING?

CLAP BACK: Along with boredom and sexual entitlement, getting wasted is cited as one of the primary catalysts of cis male–perpetrated rape. Yet when alcohol contributes to assaults, it's considered *women's* fault to the point that victims blame themselves more than the perpetrators.

DID YOU GO HOME TOGETHER?

CLAP BACK: Probably. In the US, an estimated seven out of ten sexual assaults involve perpetrators who know their victims, and over half of those are intimate partners. In fact, 2.6 billion women around the world live under marriage laws that effectively grant husbands on-demand sexual access to wives.

DID YOU PUT UP A FIGHT?

CLAP BACK: In criminal justice and civilian contexts alike, victims' credibility has always been judged in direct proportion to how visibly brutalized they appear, rather than taking their word for it. Even though courts have struck down standards of victims proving "utmost resistance" in order to convict their rapists, they're still steeped in a fundamental wariness of women.

SHOULDN'T YOU HAVE KNOWN BETTER?

CLAP BACK: Chronic victim-blame comes out of what psychologists call a **just world belief**. As in, a commonly held conviction that everything happens for reason. Combine that with patriarchy, and the just-world reason for rape is women asking for it, like Occam's razor for bros.

title IX and white male privilege

During the 1970s, the Women's Liberation movement called national attention to sexual violence like never before and effectively redefined rape from a crime of passion to a violent crime. Feminists had begun discovering shared experiences of rape and the subsequent shaming survivors often experienced afterward in hospitals, police stations, and even at home. Safe spaces didn't really exist, which left survivors to recover on their own and likely in secret. But they knew better than to wait around for lawmakers to listen and heed their demands. Instead, and often without intentional collaboration, groups around the country from the grassroots to the global began building out rape survival resources and politically pestering the justice system to catch up already.

For unsung instance, while the 1972 passage of Title IX is best known for compelling schools to fund girls' athletics, it's also had a profound effect on how we talk about rape. Rape on US university campuses went largely unchecked and unspoken about until 1990, when Congress passed the Clery Act, compelling colleges and universities to submit annual security reports and on-campus crime statistics, including sexual assaults. The legislation was prompted by the 1986 torture, rape, and murder of Jeanne Clery, who was attacked while asleep in her dorm at Lehigh University.

Enraged that Lehigh University security failed to protect their sleeping daughter, the Clerys marshaled the resources and public outrage reserved for attractive, white female victims of crime and established a nationwide initiative to crack down on campus security and reporting. But in 2006, nearly twenty years after the Clery Act's enactment, a statistically implausible 77 percent of American schools reported that no rapes had occurred in the previous year. Zero, zilch, nada.

Those shady stats were thrown into starker relief after the Obama administration in 2011 threatened to withhold federal Title IX funding—meant to protect against sex discrimination in school programs and activities—if campuses didn't step it the hell up with sexual assault prevention programs, response protocols, and annual reporting. The result was a major backlash on behalf of the accused. At no other time in American history have alleged and convicted rapists garnered so much public sympathy. It's also—surprise, surprise—the first time in our white supremacist culture of rape that the presumed perpetrators weren't black and brown bogeymen lurking in the shadows, but young white men from middle- and upper-class families hanging out on the quad, contradicting our racist narratives about what rapists look like.

The feverish outcry that Title IX has become a threat to young men's promising futures exposes the white supremacist patriarchal foundation upon which our rape culture is built. And as we've learned time and again on our unladylike journey, backlash roars loudest when economically advantaged white livelihood is at stake.

six degrees of dignity

Like #MeToo and #TimesUp, America's first anti-rape reckoning started with women talking to one another and realizing they weren't broken, crazy, or alone. Fed-up feminists knew better than to expect police, politicians, and the public to give a sh*t. Instead, unladylike sisters did it for themselves. In the 1970s, Women's Lib consciousness-raising groups evolved into public protest and legal activism that yielded rape survival resources and a whole new language to describe the unspeakable—and patriarchy's indifference to it.

Rape Crisis Centers

When Oleta Kirk Abrams' fifteen-year-old foster daughter was raped, doctors treated her with such insensitivity that Oleta rallied two girlfriends and founded one of the first-ever rape crisis centers, Bay Area Women Against Rape, in 1971. The feminist grapevine caught wind, and within five years, four hundred other rape crisis centers had opened across the country, providing medical care, victim advocacy, therapy, self-defense classes, and models for survivor-centered responses to sexual assault and abuse.

Sexual Assault Nurse Examiners (SANEs)

In the late 1970s and '80s, nurses independently brought much-needed SANE-ity to emergency rooms where predominantly male doctors had little bedside regard for rape victims. Officially recognized in 1991, these feminist Florence Nightingales focus on physical and emotional trauma and recovery, specializing in harm prevention, STD and pregnancy risk evaluation and testing, and counseling.

Rape Crisis Hotlines

Social workers spearheaded the earliest hotlines, connecting advocates and survivors to community resources. Those phone numbers also reached women with the least access to feminist support networks, like Los Angeles's first Spanish-language rape hotline founded by Chicana activists in 1976, and a multilingual hotline for non-English speaking Asian and Pacific Islander women established two years later.

Rape Shield Laws

Legal-eagle second-wave feminists championed the adoption of rape shield laws, which prevent victims' sexual history from being used as character evidence against them in stranger rape cases. However, they typically include loopholes for when that sexual history includes the perpetrator.

Forensic Rape Kits

In the early 1970s, after discovering the absence of protocol for collecting forensic evidence of sexual abuse, Chicago assault survivor Marty Goddard invented the rape kit. Reliable scientific evidence would provide courtroom credibility to victims, but other philanthropies wouldn't come near such a taboo issue. Scrappy Marty called in a favor to her galpal Christie Hefner, and the Playboy Foundation ended up underwriting the first standardized rape kits, which arrived in emergency rooms in 1978.

Shades of Rape

Men didn't criminalize husbands' "marital privilege" until second-wavers led by activist Laura X (no last name to symbolize she's no man's property) called it for what it was and didn't shut up about spousal rape until legislatures listened. In 1979, it was recognized as a crime for the first time. In the meantime, feminists began confronting victim-blaming of sexually active, single women who drink by identifying date rape and acquaintance rape for the first time in the late 1980s.

sexual healing

To cultivate sex positivity, we have to stop playing Bad Sex Baseball. Y'all know that game: Whoever gets from Frenching to penetration first wins. But that goal-oriented approach puts major pressure on all of us to sexually perform instead of staying present. And while we can't magically wring out those adolescent attitudes from every sexual encounter we have, there's plenty of work we can do for ourselves whenever we're down to get down.

Step 1: Expect Unflattering Angles

More than half of straight women have faked an orgasm at least once, usually as a way to end sex without bruising egos. Faking makes no one a bad feminist, but wouldn't we all benefit from retiring the myth of the always-orgasmic vagina? Or as Indiana University sex educator Debby Herbenick advises, "throw away the measuring stick" and prioritize quality over quantity. Same goes for how we think sex *ought* to look; worrying about whether our random nipple hairs, flesh rolls, and birthmarks are turnoffs is called **spectatoring**, and psychologists say that mindfulness, or staying in the moment, is the only cure.

Step 2: Don't "Just Relax"

As many as 15 percent of vulvas chronically hurt, and in a National Survey of Sexual Health and Behavior, sex was painful for 30 percent of women. **Vulvodynia** and **vaginismus** can make it even too painful to wear pants. Also beware gaslighting gynecologists who insist you're just "too tight" and need to relax; healing has nothing to do with lying back and thinking of England.

Step 3: Don't Apologize For Not Being a Sex Machine

Pumping the sexy brakes doesn't make you a bitch, prude, or "bad in bed." It makes you someone who knows what they want and how to ask for it. Consent is an ongoing negotiation from start to whenever either or all y'all are finished, regardless of orgasms. If someone doesn't want to take no for an answer, remind them that if their parents burst in, it would *definitely* be possible to stop right then and there. So there.

taxonomy of slut-shaming
(aka oh, the slutty places you'll go!)

Patriarchy's sexual double standard decrees that boys will be boys, and girls will be sluts—or one of the two hundred twenty other English slang terms for promiscuous women.

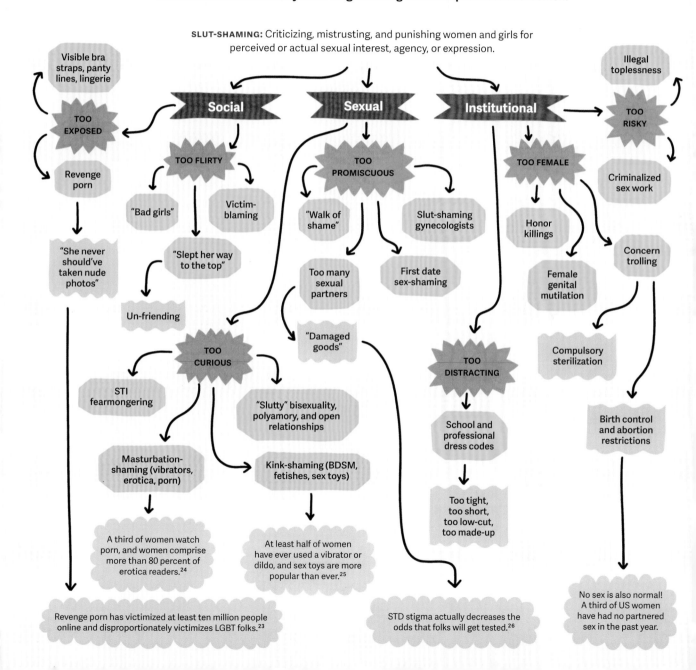

SLUT-SHAMING: Criticizing, mistrusting, and punishing women and girls for perceived or actual sexual interest, agency, or expression.

Visible bra straps, panty lines, lingerie

TOO EXPOSED

Revenge porn

"She never should've taken nude photos"

Social

TOO FLIRTY

"Bad girls"

Victim-blaming

"Slept her way to the top"

Un-friending

Sexual

TOO PROMISCUOUS

"Walk of shame"

Slut-shaming gynecologists

Too many sexual partners

First date sex-shaming

"Damaged goods"

Institutional

TOO FEMALE

Honor killings

Female genital mutilation

TOO RISKY

Illegal toplessness

Criminalized sex work

Concern trolling

TOO CURIOUS

STI fearmongering

"Slutty" bisexuality, polyamory, and open relationships

Masturbation-shaming (vibrators, erotica, porn)

Kink-shaming (BDSM, fetishes, sex toys)

TOO DISTRACTING

School and professional dress codes

Too tight, too short, too low-cut, too made-up

Compulsory sterilization

Birth control and abortion restrictions

A third of women watch porn, and women comprise more than 80 percent of erotica readers.[24]

At least half of women have ever used a vibrator or dildo, and sex toys are more popular than ever.[25]

Revenge porn has victimized at least ten million people online and disproportionately victimizes LGBT folks.[23]

STD stigma actually decreases the odds that folks will get tested.[26]

No sex is also normal! A third of US women have had no partnered sex in the past year.

sexual frustrations

HANG-UPS, HOOKUPS, AND HEARTACHES

A popular gynecological guide from the 1850s reassured readers that "the majority of women (happily for them) are not very much troubled by sexual feelings of any kind." Except, that is, for "loose women and prostitutes," whom the author blamed for being irresistible, adulteress sirens for married men. How original. Particularly as farming communities gave way to urbanization, housewives' monogamous sex roles became more pronounced.

The anti-masturbation panic and lesbophobia that intensified in the nineteenth and early twentieth centuries might seem quaint to us now, but girls' and women's vaginal explorations became a fundamentally radical act of gender role rebellion. Pooh-poohed pastimes included:

- **Masturbation:** Duh, right? In the late 1800s, girls' boarding schools were declared hotbeds of female masturbation, which was a worrisome sign of moral decay. Hands off!

- **"Immature" clitoral orgasms:** As part of ruining pretty much everything, Freud exalted vaginal orgasms as the only variety of orgasms had by well-adjusted, mature women.

"I'd rather be a free spinster and paddle my own canoe."

LOUISA MAY ALCOTT
novelist, poet, and the
original little woman

151

- **Intimate friendships:** When marriage radically pivoted from an economic to a romantic arrangement during the industrial revolution, emotional and physical "romantic friendships" between girls, women, and wives became taboo.

- **Riding bikes:** Many turn-of-the-century doctors fretted that bicycle seat friction would lead to, as Dr. Theresa Bannon put it in 1895, the "evil results" of sexual arousal.[1] Pump your brakes, Dr. T! The pro-bike advocates weren't exactly pro-independent women, though, spinning cycling as good exercise to keep women's uteruses fit for future pregnancy.

- **Reading novels:** In the late 1700s, reading for pleasure was considered a dangerous distraction for women. Pierre-Antoine Baudouin captured it most vividly in his steamy 1790 painting, *The Reader*, featuring an aristocratic woman with her hand up her skirt and novel at her side.

The industrial revolution's innovative spirit further backfired on female sexuality. "We decided that men were sexual," sociologist Lisa Wade writes in *American Hookup*. "Women got the distinct privilege of being the object of men's desire." In a world where men basked in virtually complete control over public and private matters, they stacked the bedroom deck to their advantage, too. Patriarchy's dream girl was expected to want for nothing more than to please and be pleasant; she was the feminine foil to masculine lust. Providing sex on demand to breadwinning husbands was really the *least* she could offer. Even early women's magazines like *Ladies' Home Journal* heaped praise on submissive "domestic angels."

In light of this crappy legacy, your unladylike mission is to masturbate more. Today, vibrators and masturbating are pop-culturally normalized, but research suggests that we're still toting around solo-sexual baggage. A 2017 study published in *PLOS One* found that 21.8 percent of women had never masturbated.[2] Never. Vaginal sex was actually more common among women versus solo masturbation. Among folks who *had* masturbated, only half had treated themselves in the past month.

purity ring of hell

If there were an historical award for the most subjective, repressive sexual status of all, virgins would surely take home the lily-white trophy. Even today, virginity continues to hold a tremendous amount of sway in many parts the world.

Abstinence-only sex education is the norm in American public schools. In parts of Africa, an estimated eight million girls undergo female genital mutilation each year in a gruesome attempt to curb their sexual feelings and preserve their virginity. In Afghanistan and Indonesia, some women who want to become police officers have to undergo "virginity tests" to determine whether their hymens are still intact (and, no, aspiring male officers don't endure the same kind of physical intrusion).

Regardless of whether having sex outside of marriage is a big deal to you, it is for millions of affected women and girls around the world each year.

Yet as Hanne Blank, author of *Virgin: An Untouched History*, points out, virginity is nothing more than a cultural construct. As she explains: "Anthropologists have found examples of too many other cultures that do not value virginity or which value it very differently than we do, including cultures in which both private property and virginity are essentially nonexistent concepts, for us to claim that the way our culture does it is either the way that humans are 'supposed to' do things, or the only way they can be done."

orienting sexual attraction

Whether we're living single or with a partner, with kids or without, in our parents' home or on our own, one thing all humans navigate throughout our lives is the question of sexual attraction. Most of us figure out whom (if anyone) we're attracted to around the time puberty hits. But why do we tend to assume that attraction is set in stone, rather than able to ebb and flow?

At the heart of **sexual fluidity** is acknowledging that sexual orientation is a spectrum and attractions and sexual behaviors can shift, rather than subscribing to some rigid gay/straight binary. And it's particularly pronounced among women. University of Utah psychologist and sexual fluidity researcher Lisa Diamond defines fluidity as "situation-dependent flexibility in women's sexual responsiveness." This does not mean, necessarily, that women's sexual orientation identity has changed, nor does it mean that the women she studied woke up and *decided* to change how they felt romantically and sexually about other women.

Rather, she argues, women have the capacity to roll with the erotic tide, even if those feelings are temporary or limited to one person or one encounter. In other words, you might identify as straight, but circumstances might lead you to feel **heteroflexible** and overwhelmingly hot for another lady. You no more choose to feel that attraction than you would to a man in similar circumstances.

In a study of lesbian, gay, bisexual, and straight adults, women were more likely than men to recall having experienced changes in their sexual attractions, with bisexual women experiencing the most. Researchers attributed gay, lesbian, and straight people's somewhat less fluid responses to the **anchoring effects** of identifying with an either/or label. Many folks on Diamond's bar graphs might identify one way or another but experience levels of erotic or romantic feelings and behaviors that don't always fall in line with their espoused identity. Perhaps our labels—rather than our love or lust—just get in the way of a good time.

For an example of sexual fluidity in action, look no further than early American college girls. As more young women entered all-female colleges in the nineteenth and early twentieth centuries—without the meddling influence of dudes or parents—they developed intense friendships with classmates. These so-called **smashes**, whether playfully platonic or amorously affectionate, involved courtship rituals of traditional romance, but without the possibility of marriage. Freshman girls kept pictures of seniors they admired, who in turn penned love poems, presented the younger women with bouquets, and escorted them to dances, sometimes dressed in men's formalwear. "Men are not missed, so well are their places filled by the assiduous sophomores," the Smith College newspaper reported in 1895 about the annual Freshman Frolic all-girls dance.

Initially, women's college instructors and administrators tolerated romantic friendships as a normal part of young women's development; plus, it was assumed that women didn't have much of a sex drive, anyway. But by the turn of the century, Victorian sexual ambiguity was giving way to newfangled psychology and sexology research, with influential psychologists like Havelock Ellis and Sigmund Freud preaching that same-sex attraction was a form of perversion. Ellis went so far as to call women's colleges "the great breeding ground" of lesbianism, a stereotype that endures. By the 1910s, doctors, faculty, and parents hopped aboard the Freud train, sending girl-on-girl smashes and outright same-sex attraction into the closet. "Intimacy between two girls was watched with keen distrustful eyes," writes Wanda Fraiken Neff in *We Sing Diana*, her 1928 novel about Vassar. "Among one's classmates, one looked for the bisexual type, the masculine girl searching for a feminine counterpart, and one ridiculed their devotions."

Another example of sexual fluidity was offered by the sex radicals, a culturally diverse hodgepodge of writers, artists, and activists in the 1910s. This group philosophically converged around a stunningly revolutionary concept: Women deserve equal-opportunity access to sexual pleasure. Since the Middle Ages, denying women the right to sexual satisfaction had formed

LEGAL EAGLE

PROUD MARY

In 1915, suffragist Mary Ware Dennett couldn't find quality sex education info for her sons, so she wrote some herself and called it *The Sex Side of Life: An Explanation for Young People*. Along with her hand-drawn diagrams of reproductive organs (pube tufts included) were reassurances that genitalia are truly wonderful despite their proximity to our "sewerage system," and that our early sexual urges are nothing to fear.

The Sex Side of Life landed public endorsements and flew into classrooms, social work agencies, and doctors' offices. Anti-vice alarmists freaked because the obscenity laws of the day banned mailing anything "designed, adapted, or intended for preventing conception or producing abortion."

In the early 1920s, the US Post Office charged Dennett with circulating obscenity. Undeterred, Dennett surfed her defense all the way to the Supreme Court, which ruled in her favor. That decision legally exempted birth control and contraceptive information from obscenity laws.

the bedrock of Western, domestic sex lives. But inspired by suffrage, socialism, and bohemian values, these early proponents of free love rejected conventions around marriage, sex, and gender roles, and got political in order to live however and love whomever they wanted.

GLADYS BENTLEY

Although they didn't have the language we use now to describe the spectrum of attraction, identity, and coupling, the sex radicals' fundamental belief in shame-free sexual individuality and respect echoes today's growing recognition and validation of sexual fluidity. Ironically, considering pop culture's chronic denial of bisexuality, openly bi women like Emma Goldman and Virginia Woolf were far more visible than exclusively women-loving women at the time—except, that is, on the blues stage. Tuxedoed African American blues singer and pianist Gladys Bentley, for example, wore her lesbian identity on her sleeve, strutting the New York stage in men's suits and top hats and even marrying her white, female lover in a public ceremony. And she wasn't alone. Fellow Harlem Renaissance Star Gertrude "Ma" Rainey sang about wearing men's clothes; singer Ethel Waters lived and performed with her lover, dancer Ethel Williams; and the bisexual, married-to-a-man Bessie Smith crooned about "those parties where women can go."

The lessons from these self-empowered women? If you feel pulled in a different direction than usual, don't be afraid to explore unexpected attractions. Open your mind and your feels! Labels might help you find like-minded folks and simplify dating apps, but strictly adhering to them might mean you miss out on experiences with someone worth your time and your lucky underwear.

settling for sh*tty 'ships

When we don't think much of ourselves and are insecure about our ability to find better bonds, it's easy to settle for friendships, family connections, and partners who don't bring much to the table. Rather than giving ourselves the time and space to get in touch with our real wants and needs, we might stick it out with bad buds or lame lovers for fear that we can't do better and might wind up alone.

When it comes to love, author Lori Gottlieb, who penned the 2008 *Atlantic* essay heard 'round the world, "Marry Him! The Case for Settling for Mr. Good Enough," would emphatically disagree that settling is a trap. Gottlieb argued that it's better to lower your standards and ignore the usual red flags, including lack of passion, if you have your eyes on the family-and-baby prize. At least you won't grow disillusioned like those *poor women* who marry for romance, or, worse, wait around for romance and end up turning to dust in the process.

There are other options out there that might work better than waiting passively for a soul mate or letting someone like Gottlieb send you into a panic about finding a sperm donor for life. Love might not be entirely about the "divine spark," as she calls it, but it's certainly not all about finding someone just to take the kids off your hands while you eat lunch (a perk she highlights). Can we give ourselves and our potential partners a little more credit? As long as you accept that both you and your partner are imperfect people, together you can craft a relationship based on love and respect, and make a constant, conscious effort to prioritize your relationship and communicate your feelings honestly. Work on the soul mate thing together.

living single

In agrarian communities about six hundred years ago, **spinsters** were self-made women who played an essential role in their homespun local economies, spinning cotton, wool, and silk. While they certainly weren't as lauded as mothers, their contribution garnered a desexualized respect, neither attractive nor distinctly fugly, as culture would eventually stereotype them. Despite their eventual old-maid connotations, seventeenth-century spinsters were, by definition, twenty-five or younger. Upon blowing out the candles on their twenty-sixth birthday cake, unmarried women were downgraded to prickly **thornbacks**.

In the 1930s and '40s, fears about how spinsters and thornbacks spent their downtime were exacerbated by studies that described young women wandering the streets, visiting pubs and dance halls, treating themselves to trips to the cinema, and even reading romance magazines with headlines like "I Married a Barbarian Pursued by Women" and "Should I? No Girl Knows the Answer."

The horror! These women would never grow into proper citizens if their brains were constantly bombarded with movies and mags that reinforced materialism and selfishness, not to mention an obsession with romance. They'd make much better marriage material pursuing an unarousing leisure hobby like needlework instead of gambling with their virtue.

Even today, single women's decisions are doubted and their capabilities called into question, especially if they dare claim the **single by choice** label. When sociologist and relationship researcher Kinneret Lahad studied reactions to women who proudly claim singleness, she found that online commenters were all too eager to spew such standard lines as: "You just don't know what you're talking about"; "You're going to end up lonely without anyone to care for you"; "You're too choosy"; and "You're just afraid and should get thee to a therapist's couch." One of the main tactics outsiders use to delegitimize single women's choices is the insistence that they're lying to themselves about what they really want, and that they've been forced into singledom rather than choosing it for themselves.

 **CLAP BACK WITH FACTS**

the science of attraction

Whether you're single, attached, or somewhere in between, it never hurts to have some sexy science on your side.

- **HEADS UP, STRAIGHT WOMEN WHO GET PERIODS:** When scanning the room for a hookup, ovulating women tend to be drawn to men with traditionally masculine features, including symmetrical bodies and faces.

- **STOP SNIFFING AROUND:** Humans can't actually smell one another's pheromones. You'll probably have better luck with some deodorant.

- **MYSTERIOUS IS SEXY:** Mysterious people are exciting because humans like novelty, a trait that sparks dopamine activity in the brain. And dopamine boosts sexual drive, arousal, and performance.

- **FRUSTRATION INFLAMES THE EQUATION:** Romeo and Juliet were onto something. This isn't exactly a dynamic to aspire to, but once two people pair up, adversity only further inflames their passion.

ditching the duds: your breakup guides

Some badass women have walked the sh*tty breakup path before you.

Fanny Kemble

The English stage-actress superstar fell hard for wealthy American Pierce Butler in 1834, but the charm wore off quickly. After making her ditch her career, Butler brought abolition-leaning Fanny and their two kiddos south to his sprawling Georgia plantation, where she was horrified by the treatment of the enslaved people working the land. Fanny swore she'd testify to the abuse, and after several separations, the couple divorced in 1849. Fanny returned to the stage to support herself, and in 1863, she fulfilled her promise and published *Journal of a Residence on a Georgia Plantation in 1838–39* to shed a light on what she'd witnessed as Butler's wife.

BREAKUP INSPO: Don't settle for someone whose values are the polar opposite of yours, and who wants to change everything about you. You're worth more than that.

Qiu Jin

The Chinese revolutionary came from a privileged, conservative background, complete with foot-binding and an arranged marriage. A few years into that marriage, however, Jin got pissed off and got out. In 1903, she sold her dowry, unbound her feet, and went to study in Japan. She threw herself into education and exercise, convinced that having a strong mind and body was the only way to help stage an anti-imperial revolution in China. From Japan, the sword-toting Jin divorced her husband and launched a newspaper in which she attacked traditional marriage and gender roles, encouraging women to get an education and earn a living. She returned to China to launch a revolution, but her plot was foiled and she was executed in 1907.

BREAKUP INSPO: Love doesn't always conquer all if one partner's priorities drastically shift. If your partner is actively, deliberately standing in the way of your dreams—particularly if you're trying to spark a feminist revolution—it might be time to leave.

Emma "Grandma" Gatewood

After enduring decades of abuse at the hands of her husband, Emma divorced the maniac—but she wasn't ready to settle down quietly. Inspired by a *National Geographic* article about the Appalachian Trail, and challenged by the fact that no woman had walked it before, sixty-seven-year-old Emma set off on "a walk" in 1954. After all, she said, "If those men can do it, I can do it." This little stroll made her the first woman to hike the entire 2,050-mile trail. In 1957, she did it again, becoming the first person, regardless of gender, to hike the trail twice, inspiring other women to take up hiking—and take a hike from unhealthy relationships.

BREAKUP INSPO: Abuse crushes self-esteem and leaves survivors feeling helpless. Trust that you are worth saving, and start saving yourself by reaching out to allies, whether that's a friend or a thera-pist. Finding something you are passionate about can also help motivate you to make a needed change to your relationship status.

Whether the people spewing their assumptions all over single women are anonymous commenters or nosy neighbors, their emphatic accusations that single people are *less than* almost force single women to take an assertive, political stance, insisting that—*yes*—I'm a happily single human, damn it! Maybe you are, and maybe you really do wish you could find a partner, but either way, when others point fingers they are forcing an identity on you. Putting you in a "sad, single woman" box alleviates their discomfort and confusion over a woman of marriageable age on her own and relegates you to a tidy, pitiable position they can ignore.

On the flip side, forcing the choice narrative also silences the women who legitimately don't have the option to stay single, whether because of culture, religion, or finances. So now it's not just single versus coupled, but singles with agency versus those without.

The moral of the story: Own your story and your path. You don't owe anyone an explanation.

going with the group

Another group that's often harshly judged is actually a group of groups: poly people.

Folks in **polyamorous** relationships focus on building and stoking loving connections in the same way anyone would with a long-term partner—but with more than one person. There's an understanding that falling in love with new people takes nothing away from their relationship with their primary partner or other partners in the relationship.

Falling under the umbrella of **consensual nonmonogamy**, polyamory is hardly new, but the term itself didn't show up until 1990, when pagan priestess Morning Glory Ravenheart Zell popularized it as a replacement for the more clinical-sounding synonyms of **ethical** or **responsible nonmonogamy**.

Consent? Ethics? It sounds like poly peeps are onto something that could benefit humans regardless of relationship status. It's easy—and incredibly common—to dismiss members of the poly community as greedy, slutty, or noncommital. But those harsh judgments overlook the very real and extensive work, trust, and communication that goes into fostering such relationships. After all, maintaining a poly lifestyle involves balancing and caring for multiple partners' expectations and emotions. And a crucial element of the poly community that members strive for is **compersion**, which is the warm, fuzzy, supportive feelings you get when one of your partners meets another Ms. or Mr. Right.

Missing from the description? Coercion. Polyamory might work beautifully for some, and we can all appreciate the importance of clear and honest communication with our partners, but it's okay if you're not into it. Polyamory isn't better or worse than traditional pairings, and if someone tries to pressure you into opening up a relationship when you're neither willing nor ready, your red flag should fly.

Even famed anthropologist Margaret Mead struggled with unconventional relationship structures, writing, "The logic of human relationships is not as simple as you think." Mead helped open minds and usher in the sexual revolution with her research in the 1920s, but her personal life was a revolution all its own. Married and divorced three times to men, Mead maintained a loving relationship all the while with fellow married anthropologist Ruth Benedict. Subscribing to a philosophy of free love, Mead believed we're capable of loving more than one person, male or female, at a time.

For polyamory—or any relationship, TBH—to work, partners must commit to open, honest, and constant communication. It's like a nonstop verbal trust fall.

asexuality 101

It's estimated that about 1 percent of people identify as asexual. Asexual folks are usually not sexually attracted to other people, experience a low sex drive, and don't find the thought of having sex with others appealing. However, roughly a third of asexual people do masturbate and pursue long-term relationships. Yes, you can be *romantically* oriented toward one group and still not want to have sex with them—maybe you don't want to have sex at all. If you're on the "do not pass go" end of the sexuality spectrum, know that however you want to live your truth is totally okay. If you don't date or have sex, that's cool. But if you are interested in dating, do be straightforward about your preferences if you find yourself getting close to someone—just like anybody else!

figure out what you want

Across cultures, we get the memo early on that romantic relationships are the goal and that there's a soul mate out there waiting for us. All too often, we feel ashamed or embarrassed of our single status without questioning those feelings. Ditch the "shoulds" and tune into what *you* want, whether that's singleness, random sex, or relationship bliss. It's okay not to be sure, but don't go with the flow if it's taking you somewhere you don't want to be.

It can be easier at times to put up walls and tune out your own emotional or sexual needs if it means you can coast along without too many emotional demands. After all, solitude doesn't necessarily mean loneliness. But if you realize you've been stuck at home or at work too long without a friendly face and think your subconscious is building emotional barriers, it might be time to reach out. Society tends to prize intimacy as an element of romantic relationships, but it's an integral part of friendships and family ties, too. Find people you can count on for fun nights out or chill nights in who don't need to make every hangout about couple time.

Talk the issue out with a trusted friend or therapist and, in the meantime, do a fear-of-intimacy check:

- Do you make time for everything—work, friends, hobbies—except a partner?

- If you do make time for friends, do things stay pretty surface level?

- Does a fear of getting hurt, tied down, or bored lead you to keep one foot out the door when you date?

- When you're with someone, do you act like a control freak who uses manufactured disappointment as an excuse to leave?

If any of this sounds familiar, you might be throwing up intimacy-blocking booby traps to keep yourself "safe" from the potential pain of vulnerability and failure. Maybe you don't fully believe you're worth investing in. Maybe you're a workaholic who doesn't want to make room for others' needs and feelings. Maybe you're holding on to some fantasy of a perfect, imaginary partner. But, communicating your fears—that you're afraid of losing control or getting hurt—can help deflate them.

don't lose yourself

Getting stuck in infatuation mode in a relationship can make it especially hard to communicate about boundaries. You might wind up suffering from **disappearing woman syndrome**, a term coined by psychotherapist Beverly Engel.[3] Conse- quences range from feeling unable to maintain a separate existence, which already sounds exhausting, to completely losing yourself in *any* relationship, adopting a friend's, coworker's, or lover's likes and dislikes to make up for weak or nonexistent self-worth. In letting others define you, or trying to live vicariously through them, you might be settling for a relationship that's not right for you in an effort to feel loved and validated.

It's possible and necessary to balance the drives for individuality and together-ness, which can be uncomfortable if you've internalized messages that wanting, needing, or enjoying time apart means something's wrong in your relationship. But it's especially important in romantic relationships to carve out space to grow individually and then return to each other to thrive as a pair—if you don't, your relationship balance will get all wobbly.

Take a cue from aviatrix Amelia Earhart, who made it a point to be crystal clear with her soon-to-be husband, George Putnam. "There are some things which should be writ before we are married," she wrote in a letter to Putnam on the eve of their 1931 wedding. Earhart expressed deep ambivalence about getting married, fearing it would interfere with her beloved flying. She promised not to hold either one of them to any "midaeval [sic] code of faithfulness." She said she'd do her best to give him what he wanted, and had a single request: "And that is you will let me go in a year if we find no happiness together."[4]

Here are a few ways to nurture positive communication and maintain healthy time apart and together—or recognize when it's time to split for good:

- **Do your own thing.** Talk about your interests and figure out what works well to try together—and apart. You don't have to do everything together, nor do you have to enjoy all of the same things. Pursuing your own hobbies is refreshing and invigorating, and it just means you'll have that much more to talk about when you hang out together later.

- **Cultivate emotional transparency.** It's crucial to be open about what you want, enjoy, and are comfortable with, in addition to what might be causing you pain or stress. Communication is necessary to manage any pangs of jealousy, check in with everyone's emotions, and help ensure you're healthy and happy.

- **Set expectations.** Be clear about your passions, goals, and what you want from your relationships and your life. A solid person will help you achieve your goals. Being open allows you both to get on the same page about everything from career dreams and future plans to chores and quality time.

- **Try to compromise.** Try to see things from the other's perspective to determine whether you can meet each other's needs in a healthy way. Just because your goals might not match up perfectly at first doesn't mean you can't work to align complementary actions to help support each other's dreams.

- **Identify incompatible priorities.** It's far more difficult to resolve conflict and support a partner when their goals stand in the way of your own, or make you feel ambivalent about going after them at all. If one partner wants to travel the world unencumbered while the other wants to stay put and have kids, it will take a lot of soul-searching and negotiation to find out whether those visions can be reconciled or whether it's better to go separate ways. The chronic, unresolved conflict and resentment that stems from settling or giving up is harder to bounce back from, particularly if it interferes with your identity and sense of well-being, leaving you feeling powerless, unheard, and unfulfilled.

- **Be realistic.** If someone is being abusive, neglectful, or manipulative, they are unlikely to change without a powerful combination of self-awareness, repentance, and therapy. Change is far from impossible, but you can't force anyone to fit the mold you want. Understand that you are not responsible for other people's behavior, but you *can* take responsibility for yourself.

keep your name (if you want to)

One of the biggest loaded questions you'll inevitably encounter if you decide to get hitched is what to do about your name. Keep it? Change it? Hyphenate it? It's a complicated question for many folks, and it can rack even the most self-assured unladylike feminist with doubt.

For seventeenth-century historian William Camden, a woman keeping her own name wasn't even a question—he fretted that women would appear "over-pert and too forward" if they opted not to take their husbands' names.[5] By the time Camden was writing, the practice of taking a husband's surname had evolved from a sign of outright lady-ownership to a religious signal that the couple was a spiritual and legal unit. Baby steps!

When the Enlightenment sparked ideas about equality and marrying for love, and women started getting educations, those who were powerful enough to have a platform started to question lots of man-mandated traditions. In 1797, feminist author Mary Wollstonecraft, the new bride of philosopher William Godwin, signed a letter "Mary Wollstonecraft *femme* Godwin."[6] Literal translation: Wife of Godwin. Louder translation: I'm married, but I'm still my own woman with my own name.

These days, roughly 70 percent of married-to-men women in the United States take their husband's names.[7] Those who don't tend to be older and more financially and professionally established—we can't just go around changing *all* of our social media handles, email addresses, and URLs!—or lack patience for all the paperwork involved. But a 2017 survey revealed that not only do 70 percent of American adults think women should change their names when they get married, but also, horrifyingly, a full 50 percent think the change should be required by law. The top reason cited? You selfish, independent women should prioritize your marriage and family ahead of yourself—as if you can only love people with whom you share a name.[8]

This view isn't held evenly across all demographic groups: For the most part, highly educated men and women don't give a hoot whether women change their names, while men with lower levels of educational attainment have pretty negative views of women who don't take their husbands' names, seeing it as a lack of commitment. This jibes with earlier research linking men's low education with a desire to cling to the traditional gender hierarchy. Idealized beliefs about "true" masculinity and gender norms relate to these men's desire to claim power when other avenues—education and income—aren't open to them. Basically, they're compensating.

To women around the world, the which-name-is-less-regressive argument might look ridiculous or not even register on their radar. Whereas it's customary for women in Malaysia and Korea to keep their own names, women in Quebec are *legally required* to do so, thanks to the 1976 provincial Charter of Rights statement on gender equality. Greece passed a similar law in 1983, though a 2008 tweak lets spouses decide whether they want to add their partner's name to their own and which name, if not both, to give to their children.

And why worry about changing your name when your partner could change theirs, or you both could come up with a new name together? Whatever you decide to do, the name-change thing is pretty personal. It should be up to you whether and how you want to switch things up on all that paperwork, but whatever you decide, be ready to clearly communicate it to your boo—and deal with the inevitable nosy questions and comments from others.

lucy

The first woman in Massachusetts to earn a college degree, **LUCY STONE** (1818–1893) was an antislavery women's-rights crusader who broke with powerhouses Elizabeth Cady Stanton and Susan B. Anthony after they opposed the Fifteenth Amendment to the Constitution, which granted black men the right to vote. She had no time for racist or sexist nonsense. That included marriage, which she considered a way to shackle women into subordinate positions to their husbands—a dynamic she'd experienced in her own family growing up.

Fellow progressive Henry Blackwell changed her mind, but not without agreeing to cowrite a document protesting traditional marriage and reading it to guests on the morning of their wedding. Together, the couple asserted that they were against the legal framework that gave the husband ultimate authority over not only his wife and children, but also his wife's money, property, name, and individuality. After all, Lucy had already made quite a name for herself as a professional lecturer for the Massachusetts Anti-Slavery Society. On her wedding day, Lucy placated her mother by agreeing to include "love and honor" in her vows, but she would not say "obey."

The badassery continued after the marriage, of course. After using the Blackwell name for a year, Lucy met with several lawyers who assured her there was nothing illegal about keeping her family's surname. Henry had no issue with her switching back. So she did. "A wife should no more take her husband's name than he should hers," she said. "My name is my identity and must not be lost."[9]

WHAT LUCY WOULD DO TODAY: Legal frameworks aren't quite as sexist these days, so taking your spouse's name isn't akin to *totally* losing your identity. Yes, you can be feminist and change your name. But that Stoner gal would probably still keep hers.

money pits

GLASS FLOORS, PINK TAXES, AND GOLDEN SKIRTS

As the world's pro bono workforce, round-the-clock caregivers, and marginalized employees, women start getting short-changed as soon as they're old enough to make a buck. The Babysitter's Club ought to unionize, because boy sitters are paid more and expected to do less unpaid housework and errand-running. When sociologist Yasemin Besen-Cassino looked at how much tweens and teens earn for odd jobs and part-time work, the gender gap emerged at just fourteen and fifteen years old.

"Partly because of continuing, though more subtle, discrimination, a lot of women are hitting a '**glass ceiling**' and finding they can rise no further," magazine editor Gay Bryant wrote in her 1984 book, *The Working Woman Report*. Even though women first identified the invisible workplace barrier, the *Wall Street Journal* made it a household term after publishing a 1986 report on the absence of female Fortune 500 executives, headlined "Breaking the Glass Ceiling."

Since the 1970s, women in the US had shoulder-padded their way into about a third of middle management roles. But corporate brass was more than 98 percent dudes. The invisible barrier was so plain to see, in fact, that the

"I believe that every woman should be a money-producing unit. Needing the money has nothing at all to do with it. But just being able to tell anyone that you have three cents of your own and won't they please mind their own business; to know that you are free and independent and can call your soul your own— that is what economic independence is."

RUTH HALE
feminist socialite, activist, and journalist

White House appointed a Glass Ceiling Commission (of mostly women) to figure it out. In 1996, it disbanded with a pat on the blazer and offered some parting takeaways: Set diversity goals, emphasize meritocracy, and when all else fails, use affirmative action. Despite twenty years of throwing stones at glass ceilings, the global gender wage gap began *widening* in 2016. Hope y'all are stocked up on face oils and snacks, too, because women's income writ large is now more than two hundred years behind men's. And these days, glass ceilings come in all sorts of sexist varieties:

- **Bamboo ceiling:** Gender meets race bias that elevates pay but sinks promotions for Asian women.

- **Celluloid ceiling:** Hollywood has quite the cast of gender gaps behind the camera where most producers (76 percent), editors (83 percent), writers (87 percent), and directors (93 percent) are dudes.

- **Grass ceiling:** The Farmer Jane population has doubled in the past thirty years, but men still oversee 70 percent of the fields.

- **Marble ceiling:** This boulder in front of political office rolls all around the world; women make up less than 7 percent of world leaders.

- **Stained glass ceiling:** Orthodoxy barring women from religious leadership is history's most sacred glass ceiling. Among American congregations, the number of women-led churches didn't budge from 11 percent between 1998 and 2015.

In May 2016, the *Wall Street Journal* analyzed income data among four hundred forty-six major US jobs. According to their number-crunching, men out-earn women in 98.4 percent of them. But good news for gals itching to drive a crane or read utility meters: Those are two of the whopping seven gigs where women are paid more than men, although the differences are slim.[1] Welcome to patriarchy's money pits, y'all.

sexist economics 101

Money is power, and power is male, so what's an unlady to do? Start by banking on you. Evaluate your personal currency; who defines your value and why? Appraise how much your time is worth to you versus how much your minutes count for everyone else—bosses, besties, boy toys, whomever. Is your exchange rate on par with more privileged peers? At the bottom of any money pit is the sexist myth of economic meritocracy; men deserve higher paychecks, financial access, and professional prestige because they work harder than women and children to provide for them. But that's not how the real world works.

WORK
Pink and Blue Collars

FACT:
"WOMEN'S WORK"
IS THE CHEAPEST

26 of the **30** top-paying jobs
are male-dominated

23 of the **30** bottom-paying jobs
are female-dominated

21% lower median pay awaits
the average female- vs.
male-dominated gig

HOME
Stale Breadwinning Standards

FACT:
MOTHERHOOD DOESN'T PAY

Moms earn **74¢** to every **$1**
that dads earn

70% of moms with school-age
kids work

40% of moms are sole
breadwinners

PATRIARCHAL
MONEY PIT$

FACT:
COLLEGE IS CASHING
GALS OUT

65% of US student loans are
taken on by women who earn
56% of the degrees

34% of women repaying college loans
in 2016 couldn't afford basic living costs

30% higher chances of
unemployment await female grads
vs. their male classmates

Bachelor's Nation
SCHOOL

FACT:
GENDER-BLIND JOB LAWS
ARE RARE FINDS

85% of countries enforce laws that
stymie women's job options

34% of economies lack workplace
sexual harassment laws

10% of countries allow husbands
to legally stop their wives from
working outside the home

Big Brother-ed
LAW

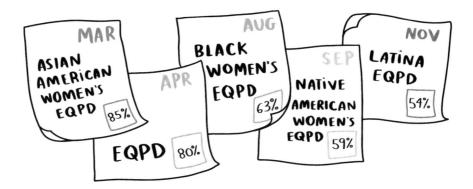

c-u-next-tuesdays

Since its launch in 1996, **Equal Pay Day** has fallen on a Tuesday each April. The occasion marks roughly how much longer someone earning the median gender wage gap of eighty cents to the male dollar would have to hustle to match his annual income. The US National Committee on Pay Equity, which founded the event, also designated Tuesdays to "represent how far into the next work week women must work to earn what men earned the previous week."[2] Breaking down the wage gap math by ethnicity, it becomes a year-long affair.

What's the holdup? **Occupational segregation.** The Brookings Institute think tank spelled it out in 2016: "Compensation patterns in many jobs may still reflect historical patterns when explicitly discriminatory practices partitioned even the most educated women into lower-paying fields like nursing and K–12 teaching."[3] The more everything changes, the more everything stays the same—to the tune of skinnier paychecks.

glass offices

Although glass ceilings get all the attention, the **glass walls** holding them up bring far more women's paychecks down. They create the **horizontal segregation** that splits the labor force into a gender binary like an awkward middle school dance. American gals' top five occupations still revolve around gender-traditional caregiving. Schoolteachers, nurses, administrative assistants, home health aides, and customer service reps are our most common full-time

patriarchy paycheck deductions

In a society where straight, white, cisgender men collectively earn the most money, our wages are garnished according to our not-straight-white-men traits, all of which have zero bearing on job performance. It's time to widen our conversations about how patriarchal politics are endorsed in our paychecks.

- **GENDER:** If gender didn't influence the amount of money we make, then trans employees wouldn't consistently report post-transition pay fluctuations. In one study, trans women's income dropped by a third while trans men saw a small bump.[4]

- **RACE:** Asian and white women are more concentrated in management and professional work, while Latina and black women are more concentrated in lower-paying service occupations. Specifically, Asian American women are at the top, making 85 percent of what white dudes do. Latinas are at the bottom, taking home just 54 percent of a bro's salary.

- **AGE:** The older we get, the more wage gaps compound, since service-industry and hourly work provide little room for negotiation and companies inquire about past incomes.

- **LOCATION:** The sizes of gender wage gaps are all over the map. In the United States, New York has the narrowest gap, with median female income at 89 percent of guys'. Globally, Morocco is the only country where women can expect to make more money than men, but only 27 percent of them work.

- **TAXES:** Gender wage gap deniers sometimes toss out a fiction called the man tax or tax gap, which proposes that since men earn more money overall, they pay more in taxes, which therefore cancels out the gap. However, the nonfiction tax wedge of joint tax filings debunks that premise since, globally, secondary earners are effectively taxed at a 10 percent higher rate compared to primary earners. And who composes the secondary earner slice of the employment pie? Wimmin.

- **SOCIAL SECURITY:** In old age, lower wages translate into lower Social Security, pension, and disability payments as well as other income-based benefits. Multiply that by the fact that women tend to live longer than men, and the potential financial burden weighs even heavier on our shoulders.

- **ABILITY:** Women with visual, cognitive, mobility, or independent living disabilities make just 69 percent of what disabled men do. On top of that, disabled women's unemployment rate is 11 percent, or roughly twice the unemployment rate of able-bodied women.

- **401(K) CONTRIBUTION:** Women are more likely than men to enroll in a 401(k) account—when they qualify. Because women fill a majority of part-time jobs, access to retirement benefits is much harder to come by.

jobs, employing around 10 percent of the female labor market.[5] That figure might sound low until you factor in how women make up two-thirds of the part-time labor force, concentrated in service and retail. But at least those "pink collar" sectors pay gals more equitably, right? If only.

Even in a hot-pink-collar sector like nursing—composed of 90 percent women—male nurses earn an average $5,100 more per year. Likewise, women make up 82 percent of social workers, but the average guy in social work out-earns his female coworkers by more than $7,000 annually. These aren't flukes. Whereas women elbowing their way into male-dominated industries run up against glass ceilings, men who venture into female-dominated jobs ride up **glass escalators**. For dudes, being in the gender minority on the job fast-tracks them up that escalator to faster raises and promotions as compared to their female coworkers.

The unfun's not over yet. If we soar past the glass escalators and shatter the glass ceilings, there's still the **glass cliff** to dodge. This counterproductive pattern, named by a pair of psychologists in 2005, vaults women into leadership during a crisis. Just look for troubled companies that suddenly put women or men of color in charge to pull off massive corporate makeovers. A study of all Fortune 500 CEO switch-ups over a fifteen-year period confirmed that companies are likelier to promote "minority CEOs" when business is tanking. Even though glass cliffs are treacherous, women's failure to scale them triggers an encore kick in our pantaloons. In that Fortune 500 study, when "minority CEOs" couldn't rescue embattled companies, they were usually replaced by white men, a pattern economists dubbed the **savior effect**.

cashing in on gender

In a patriarchy, currency is just as socially constructed as the gender roles that deem finance unfeminine, and **pin money** was the mother of all gender wage gaps. What we think of today as cheapo straight pins were coveted luxuries in medieval England. Hand-forged by their own guilds, pins were such hot items that Parliament limited their sale to the first two days in January. Then like a Black Friday doorbuster crowd, upper-class ladies would flock to the market with the pin money their husbands graciously gave them.

Some prenups of the day guaranteed brides a set sum of pin pennies, and at least a few divorcées successfully sued their ex-husbands for not forking it over, like they might with delinquent alimony today. Over time, as pins became less expensive and shopping more commonplace, the term broadened to mean a housewife's allowance that she could spend as she pleased, no questions asked from her ATM husband.

By the early 1900s, Americans appropriated the pin money euphemism to feminize the wages earned by middle-class women. Faithful to the male breadwinner hierarchy, wives working for pin money kept up the appearance that they didn't *have* to work, deviating from their domestic caretaking roles only long enough to make a little spending money. This earmarked women's money went by all sorts of other names, too, like "egg money," "butter money," and "dole," which underscored both its insignificant sum and the subordination of the recipient.

A 1933 social trends report commissioned by President Herbert Hoover (authored by a dude, it's worth noting), claimed that American women got jobs "as only semi-casuals, seeking pin money." Mary Anderson, the first director of the Women's Bureau of the US Labor Department, begged to differ. "A woman's so-called pin money is often the family coupling pin, the only means of holding the family together and making ends meet."[6]

Until World War II, any money a married woman earned at home from work like sewing, laundering, or pickling produce legally belonged to her husband. Working wives and mothers could only earn supplementary income, and many husbands were control freaks about money, regardless of how much they made. More affluent wives could spend freely on their husbands' credit accounts, but those same husbands often avoided giving their wives so much cash that they could stockpile it without their knowledge.

The tide turned against financial misogyny with help from newly influential home economists, women's organizations, and taste arbiters like Emily Post, who supported wifely allowances. But even today, nearly a century since we began earning in droves and fifty years after enacting laws like the 1965 Equal Pay Act, the pin money mindset—now often called "daycare money" or "vacation money"—continues to bedevil women's employment prospects and paychecks.

9-to-5 nonsense

Gender wage gap naysayers love to insist that men earn more money because women simply choose lower-paying jobs and to work fewer hours. But even if those gross generalizations were true, which they're not, they elide a grueling legal history of restricting women's wage-earning potential. In 1879, for instance, the president of the International Cigar Makers Union told his all-male membership, "We cannot drive the females out of the trade, but we can restrict this daily quota of labor through factory laws."[7]

That brand of sexist strategizing has propagated and institutionalized lasting myths about how women work, such as:

- **Women are defective employees.** Industry devalued women's work and rebranded their domestic skills as biologically determined motherly instincts. In 1908, the US Supreme Court upheld an Oregon law restricting women's work days around mechanical equipment to ten hours to "protect" a woman's "physical structure and a proper discharge of her maternal functions." In 1969, Colgate-Palmolive made an extra chivalrous round of layoffs, canning women working in manual labor roles with the excuse of "protecting our ladies."[8]

- **Women should be afraid of the dark.** Whether or not gals can work the night shift is one of the most pervasive workplace debates around the world. Historically, it's been considered doubly unsafe, threatening women's personal safety and off-the-clock caretaking. However, a quarter of women pulling night shifts prefer the flip-flopped schedule to better accommodate childcare.[9]

- **Women should be protected from booze.** Until the 1970s, women in America's service industry were largely banned from bartending in the name of feminine safety, which couldn't be guaranteed around drunk men. Cocktail waitresses were fine, since they were just serving the drinks—and taking home much less pay than the bro bartenders who mixed them. This paternalistic standard even gave British pub owners the right to refuse to serve female customers.

- **Women are bad with money.** When Congress passed the Equal Credit Opportunity Act in 1974, women could get their own credit cards for the very first time. Today, women still tend to pay a slightly higher interest rate on their credit cards, but they carry slightly less debt on them than men do.

- **Women aren't entrepreneurs.** Until the 1960s when Americans got the Equal Pay Act, the Civil Rights Act, and the Equal Employment Opportunity Commission, it remained impossible in many states for women to keep their names when they got married, own property separate from their husband, or start a business without their husband's legal consent.

Whether you're working for the money or not, patriarchy's paychecks come with more strings attached than Pinocchio.

FIELD ARTIFACT

chutes and glass ceilings

In the 1966 board game *What Shall I Be?: The Exciting Game of Career Girls*, players assumed one of six sterling dream jobs: model, actress, airline hostess, secretary, nurse, and teacher. The challenge? Make it around the board while drawing tokens that present professional obstacles like being overweight, wearing sloppy makeup, or having poor posture. None of those traits had a bearing on snagging a job in manufacturing, which employed the most American women in the 1960s.

Meanwhile, in the boys' version of the game, the career options were states-man, scientist, athlete, doctor, engineer,

and astronaut. It's a safe bet that fictional waist sizes and eyeliner skills didn't factor into their fortunes.

When Parker Brothers brought back *Career Girls* in 1990, job prospects had scarcely improved. Players could now compete for fictional rock star, college student, schoolteacher (not to be confused with unfeminine college professors), fashion designer, "animal doctor" (girls aren't, like, *doctor* doctors, of course), and "supermom," because motherhood is the most important career of all, girls.

the marriage trap

For ages, patriarchy has bought and sold women as commodities, like an ancient wolf of Wall Street. In most male-dominated cultures, before women could legally earn, keep, and inherit their own money, they were just another form of currency that fathers, husbands, brothers, and sons used to secure and expand their own domains. Under **coverture laws**, wives became their husbands' legal possessions upon marriage, and judging by this soundbite from the 1632 *Law's Resolutions of Women's Rights*, they weren't fooling around in the least: "The very goods which a man giveth to his wife are still his own: her chain, her bracelets, her apparel, are all the good-man's goods . . . A wife how gallant soever she be, glistereth but in the riches of her husband, as the moon hath no light but is the sun's."[10]

Even though the laws are long gone, the sentiment has stuck around. When you notice a sudden blip in the environment when you tell an employer you're getting married, it often means that person is thinking, "Oh, god. Next up, *maternity leave*." Worst-case employment scenarios bear out this mindset.

That financial chivalry solidified in early twentieth-century employment policies called **marriage bars**, which became particularly popular in the United States when jobs were scarce, such as during the Depression and between World Wars. They also popped up in Canada, Japan, and Great Britain. Even most pink-collar jobs, such as teaching and nursing, required brides to say "I do" to quitting once they put a ring on it and—if they did manage to keep their job—to not even *think* about clocking in while visibly pregnant. Thanks also to the growing supply of eager workers and the fact that women's jobs were typically segregated into easily replaceable and trainable pools, employers had no qualms about sending Suzy Homemakers back where they belonged (in the kitchen, obvs). Some women even married secretly just to maintain dual-income households.

"I just thought that it was terrible that after all that training, and after getting a job, these women just had to give it all up and be an ordinary housekeeper," said Maureen Cronin more than fifty years after she stood up to Ireland's marriage bar for teachers in the early 1950s.[11] After she got married, Cronin kept working anyway for a year—without pay. Fed up with blatant sexism of the marriage bar system, Cronin volunteered to be a marriage bar test case for the Irish National Teachers' Organization, the country's largest teachers' union.

In the United States, most marriage bars had been formally dissolved by the 1950s. It became harder to turn away educated, capable women, and employers began valuing the maturity and reliability of older, married women workers. But the damage had been done, if not in keeping women out of the workforce altogether, then in relegating them to undervalued "mommy track" roles with little chance of advancement. As long as the patriarchal ecosystem keeps thriving, the pin-money mindset prevails.

 **CLAP BACK WITH FACTS**

bankrupt stereotypes

Sexism plus women's historic lack of access to their own bank accounts and credit cards leaves us with a pirate's chest full of dismissive tropes about how women get and spend their money.

- **TROPHY WIFE:** This term first debuted in Phyllis I. Rosenteur's 1961 book, *The Single Woman*. In it, she defines the "Trophy-Wife" as "the woman who was hard to get because of birth or wealth or beauty—to be kept on exhibition like a mammoth tusk or prime Picasso."[12] Today's trophy wife is all about youth. A 2013 study found that when men on the Forbes 400 list remarry, on average, they go from a spouse seven years younger to a twenty-two-year age gap.[13]

- **GOLD DIGGER:** Borne out of Great Depression–era class anxiety, she began as the streetwise, cunning foil to naïve, spoiled heiresses and trophy wives. She relied on feminine beauty, sex appeal, and an approving male gaze for survival. As white women's employment opportunities broadened, the gold digger lost her sympathetic sheen and devolved into a frequently racialized trope of lazy, conniving women out to take advantage of the men they attract.

- **WELFARE QUEENS:** President Reagan propagated this racist load of garbage during his 1976 campaign. Central to his stump speech was a fictional story about a "welfare queen" who was living high on the hog on government cheese, perpetuating the myth that African American single mothers receiving government assistance are lazy, promiscuous, morally bankrupt fraudsters swindling hardworking taxpayers and perpetuating the "culture of poverty." Welfare-queen dog whistles reverberate today through the impoverished stigma of single motherhood.

off-the-clocked

Those marriage-barred wives didn't sit around twiddling their thumbs. Whereas the home was leisure central for the husband and kids—a place to rest, recharge, and get away from the responsibilities of school and work—it was ground zero for the housewife's labor. In 1925, at least one newspaper was on top of it. The *Manchester Evening News* not only addressed the never-ending nature of housework, advising women to get organized and make to-do lists, but also highlighted how a woman's guilt over putting her feet up could propel her to just keep at her chores instead. In an article that feels pretty much timeless in its examination of a culture glorifying busyness, the newspaper marveled at how "a woman should almost boast of her inability to sit down all day." A decade later, the paper talked to women on the train and discovered that many relished the trip as their only alone time of the day to read, write, or just relax and people-watch.

In the 1960s, '70s, and '80s, second-wave feminism and changing legislation saw new generations of women entering the workforce. By 1989, nearly 75 percent of American women age twenty-five to fifty-four earned income outside the home, compared to only 43 percent in 1960.[14] What these promising numbers hid, however, was that working women were now working double-time.

"These women talked about sleep the way a hungry person talks about food," remarked Arlie Hochschild in her landmark 1989 book, *The Second Shift*. The sociologist coined the term **second shift** to describe the lioness's share of after-hours childcare, housecleaning, and family managing that working moms took on outside the office. By her estimates, those women worked an extra month of twenty-four-hour days of domestic duties each year compared to their male partners.

When the US Bureau of Labor Statistics released updated numbers in 2016, the second shift had dramatically shortened to 102 hours every year. Progress? Absolutely. Equality? Hardly. The gap still speaks to the culturally diminished value of women's time and energy compared to men's. (What *are* men *doing* during those 102 hours?) Especially if we look at this globally, female labor is a basement bargain. Of all the unpaid labor happening around the world, we're doing 75 percent of it.

mommy-tracked

In male-breadwinning, family-wage economies, it's a much wiser financial decision to become a husband and father than a wife and mother. Whereas women have had to fight off restrictions based on their marital and maternal statuses, the more "family man" a fella looks, the better his bottom line. A 2014 study from the University of Massachusetts found that men earn 6 percent more for every child they have, while women make 4 percent less.[15]

According to the US Census, there are only slightly fewer moms working outside the home today compared to working dads. Despite almost numerical parity, bosses tend to perceive working dads as more competent than working moms. When the 2016 World Values Survey asked respondents whether men deserve jobs more than women when economies tank, a lot of folks said yes— especially dudes, go figure. American men are 16 percent likelier than women to agree that gentlemen should get hired first, which is higher than men in even more gender-traditional nations like China (12 percent) and India (10 percent). Whereas gender wage gaps provide quantifiable evidence that something's not right in the paycheck department, this worst-case-scenario question reveals the values beneath the pay discrepancy. After all, this sexist mindset goes, if worst comes to worst, women can keep house and have babies.

Millennial parents aren't thrilled. Working dads and moms are equally likely to say they're having trouble balancing their personal and professional lives, and dads don't lag far behind moms in saying they'd prefer to stay home but need the extra income. Often, gendered expectations clash with new dads' hopes for hanging out with a new baby, too. One of the most common complaints from working dads is supervisors presuming men aren't active contributors to childcare. Even when paternity leave is available, it's rarely equal to maternity leave. Whether explicit or implicit, those expectations for men to serve as responsible, competitive breadwinners mean that just 5 percent of fathers take more than two weeks off after a child's arrival.

Gender roles can sandwich us in tighter than ever before depending on your personal caregiving situation. The term **sandwich generation** was coined in the 1980s to describe people in their fifties and older who are simultaneously caring for both their kids and their aging parents. While more men are stepping up as caregivers for their parents, that role is still largely filled—and often *expected* to be filled—by women. But as always, that pro bono homework costs us. Middle-aged Gen-X women are feeling this especially hard, on the hook for baby boomer parents and Gen-Z kids, and the emotional forecast calls for midlife thunderstorms. Aside from the mental and physical stretch it requires, getting sandwich-tracked can cost women more than $300,000 in lifetime wages and Social Security benefits.

breadwinners and losers

So, is financial equality the solution? When writer Ashley C. Ford casually surveyed 130 millennial girlfriends about who pays for what in their relationships, the breadwinning babes sounded taxed. "The women most frustrated by their breadwinner status never considered it could happen, didn't expect it to last, or can't find a way to do things differently even when they want to," Ford wrote at Refinery29. In short, picking up the couple tab wasn't what these women had signed up for and it didn't pay enough dividends in return. This is a financial arrangement that would make Charlotte Perkins Gilman's feminist heart sing, so why doesn't it feel more like "empowerment"? Bring on the stats!

In 2015, 38 percent of American women married to men earned more than their husbands. And yet findings from both the Council on Contemporary Families and the General Sociological Survey revealed a *Father Knows Best*–style mindset on the rise. Whereas most Gen X and millennial teens thought shared breadwinning and partnered housework were ideal in a marriage, kids who grew up during the Great Recession of the late 2000s have less progressive ideas. In 2014, 58 percent of American high school seniors agreed that male breadwinners and female caregivers were the optimal domestic dynamic. To put a more sexist point on it, the proportion of teens agreeing that "the husband should make all the important decisions" has risen as well.[16]

Of course, statistics don't happen in a vacuum. To understand what those percentages are really telling us, we have to widen our scope. Fortunately, the mashup of money and love brings no shortage of context.

Sociologist Stephanie Coontz noted in the *New York Times* that those unsettling stats among American youth reflect the economic hit felt by male-dominated sectors like construction during the recession, and stress put on families by the lack of institutional support in the form of subsidized childcare, affordable health care, and paid time off. The evidence? Teens growing up in European countries whose governments subsidize those benefits don't share the diminished regard for domestic egalitarianism.

the divorce drain

Women have historically been pretty poorly positioned to handle the finances if they get divorced or their partner dies. Dropping down to one income is challenging enough, but it compounds a lifetime of gendered workplace baggage. Their traditional role as primary caregivers—who might dip out or scale back on careers once kids arrive or their parents get ill—and a persistent wage gap means they likely were bringing home less than a male partner anyway.

Wage gaps pale in comparison to divorce and death cliffs. After a split or being widowed, American women's household incomes fall by about 40 percent, while men in the same situation lose only about 20 percent.[17] Plus, men are more likely than divorced or widowed women to remarry, so chances are, they'll re-pad the nest egg with less disruption.

The financial fallout highlights some crucial changes women can make, regardless of their relationship status.

- **Figure out what you have.** How much cash do you have on hand, and how much are your assets, home, car, and retirement accounts worth? What's your income before and after taxes, and what are your expenses?

- **Know where everything is.** If you're dealing with the trauma of death and divorce, the last thing you want to do is rifle through endless stacks of paper. Organize your files, cards, insurance policies, and other important documents so you know exactly what you have and where it is.

- **Set goals.** Based on income and expenses, determine how much you need to save each month for bills, retirement, emergencies, and other have-tos.

- **Keep your own account.** Regardless of whether you and your partner have a joint account for household expenses, it's smart to keep your own stash. It'll come in handy for both occasional treats and for emergencies. It's not uncommon for women to stay in negative—or outright dangerous—relationships because they don't have the money to leave and start over.

Globally, empowering women with education, financial independence, and the ability to own their own property generally means that if and when they become unhappy in their marriages, they can hit the road.

For example, biological anthropologist Helen Fisher wrote in 2016, "Divorce is common in matrilineal cultures . . . probably because a wife has resources, her children are members of her clan, and her husband has more responsibilities for his sister's offspring than for his own."[18] When spouses are more companions than "vital economic partners," if somebody starts feeling meh, there's not much reason to stick it out.

Empower yourself now with financial education, and you'll be that much better prepared for whatever comes your way.

who cares?

In a pro-natalist culture of mandatory motherhood, who takes care of the kids falls on moms by default. In fact, Finland is the only developed country where dads spend more time with their kids than moms—eight revolutionary minutes each day, to be precise. What's the secret? For starters, high taxes that subsidize prenatal care, childbirth, and a host of other benefits including up to nine weeks of universal, 70-percent-paid paternity leave, which around half of new dads use up entirely. For comparison, the Pew Research Center found that even among large private-sector employers in the United States, just 23 percent offer paid parental leave.[19]

But having the option of generous paternity leave far from guarantees that men will take advantage of it. In fact, the two countries that offer the longest paid paternity leave are struggling to entice men to use it. Both South Korea and

Japan offer a full year of paid leave for fathers, but fewer than 5 percent of men take it because of what psychologists call **pluralistic ignorance**. A 2017 Japanese study published in *Frontiers in Psychology* described this as "a situation in which almost all members of the group privately reject group norms, yet believe virtually all other group members accept them."[20]

Meanwhile, same-sex couples upend expectations when they have kids. There's no traditional gendered script to adhere to, and no one who's automatically assumed to be a better caregiver. In general, they're more likely to split chores and childrearing evenly, taking on the tasks that play to each partner's strengths and interests over automatically sticking with gendered expectations.

Among same-sex couples in the United States, lesbians tend to have more children than gay men, but gay men are likelier than their lesbian counterparts— and just as likely as the straights—to **specialize**, meaning one partner stays home to care for the kids so the other partner can work and make money.[21] Family researchers argue that men in same-sex relationships might not feel as threatened by the link between femininity and caregiving, but there could also be a more obvious force at work: Men earn more than women. It's possible two men and one paycheck would be better off than two women in the same situation.

Regardless, same-sex couples are negotiating more than who stays home. They're tackling some basic—but potentially identity-affirming—issues like . . . what should my kids call me? "Mommy" doesn't work for everyone, especially if you're butch or genderqueer, and while "dad" fits for some, it still comes packaged with masculinity. Polly Pagenheart, who writes the blog *Lesbian Dad*, opted for the cross-cultural caregiver term of endearment *baba* to embrace the role of warm, loving parent without any of the gendered connotations.[22] What works for you, your family, and your kids is ultimately what matters.

Through the lens of same-sex parenting, motherhood and fatherhood gain broader definitions and leave room for all sorts of interests and identities when they're not tied to outdated ideas of what makes a man or a woman. That allows parents to play to their strengths and show their children different facets of their personalities. Maybe more men can embrace caregiving and vulnerability, and fewer women will experience needless guilt for wanting to go back to work.

sisters parenting for themselves

Single and partnered-but-unmarried moms are super common, yet they still raise some eyebrows, particularly if they're poor or women of color with more than one or two kids. But being a single mother in itself doesn't spell doom for children's mental, emotional, or academic well-being. Poor outcomes are more closely tied with issues of income inequality and financial challenges, parenting stress, and family conflict. In other words, it's not the family *structure* that's necessarily affecting the kids; it's the family *dynamic*. Children anywhere fare much better growing up with a single parent than with two parents who can't stop fighting.

Of all single mothers, the least stressed seem to be those who *choose* to go it alone, and the reason is likely linked with money. Birth rates among single women over forty jumped nearly 30 percent from 2007 to 2012. This group tends to be more educated and financially settled, which gives them options when it comes to footing the bill for fertility treatments or adoption, in addition to childcare once they become mothers.

Anecdotally, these women express little ambivalence about having children. Writer Kate Bolick, profiling a group of "choice moms" as she navigated her own mixed feelings on the topic, noted that they were unwavering in their desire for children and felt deeply compelled to make the move to motherhood, partner or no. Health care providers she interviewed said that while most choice moms tend to be white, older, and wealthier than average, the demographics are beginning to shift ever so slightly, possibly reflecting changing attitudes about building the family you want, when you want it.

Wellesley College sociologist Rosanna Hertz uncovered another trend among choice moms: the feeling of being stuck between a career they loved and expectations that they find a man, marry, and *then* have babies. The women Hertz talked to might have picked their own path, but they still struggled with deeply ingrained social messages about family and having it all.

Regardless of their views on feminism, relationships, and gender roles, and whether they're loud-and-proud single moms or reluctant revolutionaries, women who decide to have kids without a partner are redefining family ties bit by bit—and their kids are helping shape the world. "You know, it's interesting," *All the Single Ladies* author Rebecca Traister told Flavorwire. "Obama is the son of a single mother, Bill Clinton is the son of a single mother, Bernie Sanders has a child with a woman he never married. So single parenthood shaped lives of the men who have been our presidents and our candidates for president."

minimum waged

While most single moms call the shots in their households, they're also the likeliest demographic to earn poverty-level wages. In 2008, 20 percent of American single moms were unplugged from the labor market, receiving neither unemployment nor government assistance and making, on average, $535 per month. After the recession in 2011, homes headed by single mothers still comprised 69 percent of households earning less than $10,000.[23]

 **CLAP BACK WITH FACTS**
house balance

The way we communicate about and divvy up household chores has ripple effects on our life satisfaction.

- **ASSUMING ASSUMERS:** Most Americans still think that in hetero couples, wives should handle the bulk of the caregiving and housework while husbands should handle outdoor chores and car maintenance.

- **SPLITTING THE WORK:** Same-sex couples tend not to have hard-and-fast rules about which partner takes on which household tasks. Rather, they tend to be divided along lines of skill, interest, and ability.

- **OUT OF WHACK:** Women in opposite-sex partnerships tend to be the least satisfied with how household and childcare responsibilities shake out. The most satisfied? Men in same-sex relationships.

In other words, raising kids outside of marriage remains more a matter of circumstance than a reproductive choice.

There are also the scores of women and girls around the world who earn far less money in far less promising circumstances to make the things and provide the services that enable upwardly mobile women's professional progress. They're the Uber drivers, dog walkers, geriatric nurses, and nannies who also stitched and steamed upper- and middle-class businesspeople's pantsuits. They're the largely Latina immigrant housekeepers who lobbied Sheryl Sandberg in 2015 to champion their fight for unionization against her alma mater, Harvard University, asking for affordable health care, better working conditions, and more pay. But instead of considering their request, Sandberg put the kibosh on it. "I am not sure that it is logistically or practically possible for me to make individual endorsement decisions on all the specific efforts women and men take across our country," the Facebook COO said in a statement.[24]

But yo, Sheryl! How are *they* supposed to lean in?

professional pyramid scheme

In 2003, Norway became the first country to enforce corporate gender quotas, mandating that women occupy at least 40 percent of public company board seats. It only took four years to hit that target, up from 16 percent, and nations across the European Union followed its lead. But when the National Bureau of Economic Research checked in on Norwegian early adopters a decade later, only the top 5 percent of the highest-earning women in the companies had benefited from a quota-related raise. The other 95 percent of companies' female employees didn't feel a droplet of trickle-down benefits.

Who benefits the most from gender quotas are the companies, not the women they employ. Data consistently link more gender-diverse boardrooms to financial efficiency and higher profits. Satisfying quotas can also lead to a form of tony tokenism called **golden skirts**, which happens when the same belles of the boardroom get tapped for multiple boards, artificially inflating the appearance of leadership diversity.

katharine

Wealthy suffragist, philanthropist, and scientist **KATHARINE DEXTER MCCORMICK** was unusual—and undaunted. When the *Boston Globe* once accused her of being a "suffrage inciter" who exhibited—*horror!*—"unladylike behavior," she didn't mind in the least.[25]

Family-planning and contraception advocate Margaret Sanger was another firecracker. In her early work as a journalist, she'd focused on working-class mothers, whose difficult lives were complicated by children they could barely afford to feed. By 1920, Margaret was the leader of the birth control movement and would go to serious lengths to achieve her vision.

The day she met Margaret, Katharine immediately picked up what Marge was putting down. Testifying at the trial of a man arrested for distributing her birth control pamphlets in 1917 when the era's strict Comstock Laws deemed it illegal, Margaret impressed the brilliant scientist-socialite in the audience. Katharine already believed contraception was key to empowering women. Margaret embodied the possibility for change.

Over lunch in 1921, Katharine and Margaret realized that by funding and promoting birth control research and development, they could change the course of women's lives forever.

Katharine's money, activism, education, and social connections put her at the center of many important circles. Both were unafraid of controversy, and Margaret was a skilled organizer.

Katharine helped Margaret organize and pay for several events, but it's the diaphragm smuggling that really stands out. On the first of many such adventures to help stock Margaret's New York birth control clinic, Katharine went to Switzerland under the guise of enjoying a vacation and instead met with contraceptive manufacturers to purchase crates of diaphragms. With her science degree and wealth, it was easy to convince them she was a physician. She purchased dresses and paid a team of seamstresses to sew the contraceptive contraband into them.

In 1953, the seventy-eight-year-old Katharine found and paid research physicians who could realize Margaret's dream of creating a contraceptive that women could pop like aspirin. By late 1956, though both women suffered ill health, the realization of their dream was in sight. With further testing and, at last, FDA approval, the Pill became available in 1960.

WHAT KATHARINE WOULD DO TODAY: Use her privilege in any way she could to help a friend with a dream empower women to control their own bodies.

Important as they are, women in corporate corner offices aren't reliable bellwethers of female opportunity on the ground floor or even in management. Female managers actually might be more hard-assed toward the women they oversee as what sociologists call a **collective threat response** to both underperforming employees and the professional stereotype threat that women aren't boss material. It's no shade; it's reality. "You can't change the world for women by simply inserting female faces at the top of an unchanged system of social and economic power," Susan Faludi notes in *Backlash: The Undeclared War on American Women*.

Feminism Gets a Job

Ever since the Civil War when American women were first allowed to pursue higher education and clerical work, an individualistic spirit of professional success has saturated the mainstream feminist agenda and public representations of what financial empowerment looks like. The modern marriage of mainstream feminism and finance was consummated in 1898 with suffragist Charlotte Perkins Gilman's seminal *Women and Economics*. In it, Gilman ripped the male breadwinning standard a new one. "[Women] are the only animal species in which the female depends upon the male for food, the only animal in which the sex-relation is also an economic relation," Gilman wrote. The root of female oppression, she reasoned, was economic dependency on men, and it was imperative that women earn their way out of it. And for educated, white women like Gilman, professional careers were the ticket.

But as career-minded suffragists aspired to an upwardly mobile standard established and maintained by white dudes, classism edged in on financial feminism. "Professional ideology also encouraged professional women to see a community of interest between themselves and professional men and a gulf in between themselves and nonprofessional women," writes feminist historian Nancy Cott in *The Grounding of Modern Feminism*. What happened next involved outsourcing the domestic load onto less privileged women. Leading race theorist and UCLA law professor Kimberlé Williams Crenshaw observed how "white feminists were able to gain entry into previously all white male enclaves not through bringing about a fundamental reordering

trickle-down feminist economics

Smashing glass ceilings doesn't rain down raises and respect for the 60 percent of American working girls stuck on the glass floor. That's where traditionally pink-collar, low-paying jobs like retail cashier, housekeeper, office assistant, and customer service rep disproportionately underpay Latina and African American women. In the two-thirds-female food-service industry, for instance, millions of bartenders, hosts, and servers scrape by on the federal *sub*-minimum wage of $2.13 per hour, plus tips, while majority-female retail clerks constantly get their hours cut with little notice.[26] On the glass floor, professional perks like salary negotiation, egg freezing, and paid vacation are fantasies.[27]

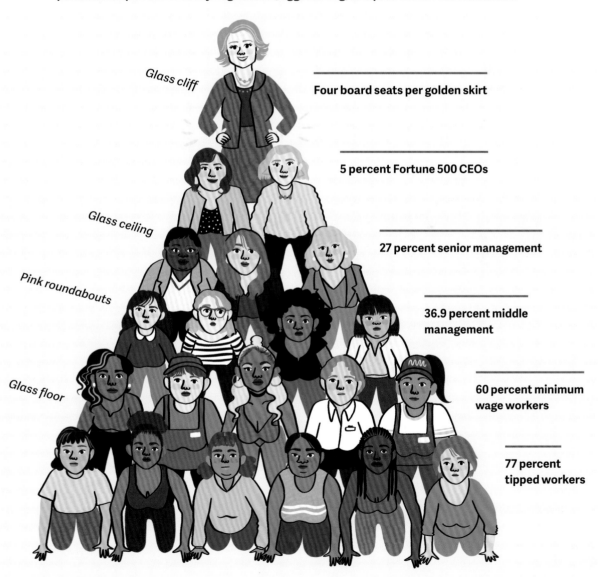

Glass cliff — Four board seats per golden skirt

5 percent Fortune 500 CEOs

Glass ceiling — 27 percent senior management

Pink roundabouts — 36.9 percent middle management

Glass floor — 60 percent minimum wage workers

77 percent tipped workers

of male versus female work, but in large part by shifting their 'female' responsibilities to poor and minority women."

Still today, lower-wage-earning gals are likelier to speak truth to workplace power through organizing and making collective noise instead of one-on-one negotiations. While the gender wage gap isn't budging, women are projected to make up a majority of unionized employees in America by 2023. Why does a wonky stat like that matter? Because on average, the gender wage gap is a narrower nine cents, and women's weekly paychecks are $230 fatter between unionized men and women versus non-unionized workers. Granted, black women's and Latinas' paychecks are lighter than white women's, but they still earn substantially more when organized. Unionizing isn't as sexy as girlbossing, but collective action compounds your influence. Plus, salary transparency, standardized wages, and greater management accountability are baked into the union model.

banks . . . for *her!*

In 1975, a male banking executive told the *New York Times*: "Let's say a young woman came in a branch asking for a $1,000 auto loan. The idea that went through the loan officer's head might have gone something like this: 'She's young, maybe she'll get married soon, then she'll get pregnant and leave her job. Where will our loan be then?'"[28]

Back then, even though married women's income was taxed by the government, banks devalued it on credit applications as a tactic to deny them loans. Single women had an even harder time getting approved for mortgages and loans. And small business loans? If you were single, engaged, newly married, pregnant, divorced, widowed, or just female and breathing, banks would figure out a way to rob you.

Unable to obtain their own lines of credit or take out business loans after getting married, some women decided to take financial matters into their own hands. In 1975, with three million dollars in capital, First Women's Bank opened in Manhattan—the first commercial bank owned and operated by women for women. Betty Friedan opened an account. That same year, the

Times reported, "Women with more sophisticated resources and well-known professional credentials are organizing half a dozen women's banks around the country." Over the next five years, eight more women's banks opened across the United States.

The *Times* also noted that traditionally structured financial institutions like First Women's Bank weren't the only option for sexism-free banking: "Other women—in most cases, less well-established, younger and more closely affiliated with the political 'feminist' movement—have already opened a smattering of much simpler lending institutions. They are credit unions, which need no capitalization and limited capital to organize."[29]

Credit unions began sort of like mutual aid societies for money in communities, pooling resources and financial support in a nonprofit model. Because federal regulations simply required that credit union members share a "common bond," which was traditionally a particular profession or industry, scrappy gals figured that feminism could function as that bond.

With the aid of Gloria Steinem, who championed the feminist credit union model, eighteen had formed by 1976. Organizations like the Feminist Federal Credit Union of Detroit not only provided misogyny-free access to loans but also served as activist recruitment tools; to maintain compliance with federal credit union regulations, they required that members join local feminist groups. And why don't these patriarchy-smashing financial wonderlands still exist? Progress.

By the end of the 1970s, the Equal Credit Opportunity Act had been fully phased in, prohibiting banks from discriminating based on sex, race, and religion. With those sexist barriers to traditional banks removed, women-only banks lost their luster. Not to mention, both women's banks and credit unions suffered from mismanagement largely because of inexperience. First Women's Bank closed in 1989, and while the feminist credit unions held on a bit longer, the last one from that era, the Women's Southwest Financial Credit Union of Dallas, closed in 2012.

Today, equality is mismeasured according to gender wage gaps, female presence in macho jobs, and headcounts of employed moms. But instead of scrambling to bust through glass ceilings, snag corner offices, and get raises already, women need to shift strategies. Women's professional success and breadwinning can still be championed and supported, but as long as it's the primary focus of mainstream and increasingly commercialized feminism, that strategy overlooks the majority of women and girls around the world who can't, won't, and don't pursue college-educated, capitalist dreams of power suits and penthouses.

Corporate feminism has made tremendously positive differences in the workplace. Young women are now proactively coached in salary negotiation. Shonda Rhimes and Amy Poehler taught their disciples the power of saying, "Yes, and." Anne-Marie Slaughter helped drive the nail in the "having it all" coffin with her seminal 2012 *Atlantic* article. Sheryl Sandberg myth-busted work-life balance and got folks to think twice about calling girls "bossy." Although Amy Cuddy's TED–talk-promoted research on **power posing** turned out to be flimsy, it prompted a bigger, beneficial awareness of gender and body language, and arguably begat the anti-manspreading movement. There's zero wrong with teaching women how to pursue a profitable career, as long as it's not at the expense and erasure of others. Manspreaders excepted.

turn down for what

Today, while working-class women are more likely to hold part-time jobs, sometimes several of them, wealthier women are clocking longer hours in full-time jobs with the idea, well-being researchers say, that the time suck is a down payment on plum paychecks and vacation benefits. But exactly when will they find the time to enjoy them? Millennial women in particular have become "work martyrs" for keeping up professional appearances. Scarred by the Great Recession, they don't want to look less committed to their jobs or return from time off to a mountain of unanswered emails.

Work-related unavailability or humblebragging about our packed Google calendars has become a way to broadcast our importance and what a scarce, valuable resource we must be (or, how genuinely inept we are with time management). Researchers refer to it as the "conspicuous consumption of time," meaning weekends at the office are the new mai tais by the pool. It's not a universal view—Europeans generally still view the poolside mai tais as the higher-status marker. But the class distinction isn't so much who works and who doesn't; this brand of busyness is all about the look. Ask yourself:

1. Is your stress spiral a result of uncontrollable circumstances, or can you grab ahold of your schedule and block out time for yourself and your priorities?

2. Do you procrastinate, and does the eventual panic make you feel more motivated to get the job done? Can you rework your schedule to take bites out of that project each day?

3. What favors can you do for your future self to slow the busyness buildup?

bee-ware queen bees

In the 1940s, Ghanaian entrepreneur and marmalade queen Esther Afua Ocloo had a pretty helpful perspective. She pioneered making microloans to women looking to launch and grow small businesses, even if they grabbed some of her market share. With money she'd earned from selling orange juice to the military, Ocloo studied food technology in England. She made a point of learning skills like leatherwork that she could bring home to Ghana and teach other women. Though Ocloo's children fretted that the women she helped were becoming her competition, she relished the bigger picture: Women helping women can change lives. "My main goal is to help my fellow women," she told one interviewer. "If they make better marmalade than me, I deserve the competition."

Unlike Ocloo and her marmalade queens, **Queen Bees** aren't here to make friends. The original Cool Girls (see page 209) of the workplace, they were first identified in a 1974 *Psychology Today* article, though their sting still rings familiar. "The true Queen Bee has made it in the 'man's world' of work, while running a house and family with her left hand," a trio of psychologists wrote. "'If I can do it without a whole movement to help me,' runs her attitude, 'so can all those other women.'"

But as feminists, shouldn't we be unequivocally cheering for women in charge? Actually, no. We should instead dismantle and realign the tokenizing power dynamics that breed Queen Bees. In the process of elbowing their way to leadership, Queen Bees adopt a strategy of disassociating themselves from gal-palling to emphasize how they're, well, not like other girls. They're fierce professionals, not gossipy coworkers who think about their kids all day long.

What's even more incredible is how the wicked female boss and unserious female employee stereotypes coexist. Queen Bees buzz the way they do in order to avoid the other stereotype, while female employees are reluctant to sound alarms about Queen Bees. "Even when workplace bullying becomes severe . . . women are less likely to sue for gender discrimination if their tormentor is another woman," Olga Khazan reported in the *Atlantic* in 2017. "[People] tend to assume that women look out for another."

queen bee symptom checker

A cutting fact often overlooked about glass ceilings: They're nearly impossible for boss babes to break with their likeability intact. And we're not just talking about men giving them a sexist cold shoulder. It's women who have the stronger preference *against* working under another woman, and this probably isn't news to most of us, whether because of personal or anecdotal experience. Avoid slipping into a femmephobia trap by checking yourself for these hive-mind conditions. Buzz, buzz!

- **QUEEN BEE SYNDROME:** Antifeminist women who decide that if they could get to where they are without any supportive sisterhood, then anyone can. Rather than risking fisticuffs with gender discrimination, Queen Bees dodge bias by deemphasizing gal-palness. They *aren't* just one of the gals.

- **FAVORITISM THREAT:** Worry that you'll look biased if you help someone who looks like you.

- **COMPETITIVE THREAT:** Panic that a newcomer who looks like you will steal your thunder.

- **SYSTEM JUSTIFICATION:** Psych concept that long-oppressed groups, struggling to make sense of an unfair world, internalize negative stereotypes.

- **BLACK SHEEP EFFECT:** People are harder on their own tribe members when they deviate from the norm or break the rules.

follow the power

The stakes of financial and economic equity are so real you can feel them. In 2016, Columbia University epidemiologists found that women earning unequal pay for equal work with men were four times likelier to be diagnosed with an anxiety disorder and more than twice as likely to be depressed. That isn't just a case of bad luck, either; researchers isolated the gender wage gap as the common mental health denominator regardless of age, education, occupation, family composition, and other life variables. Likewise, those worrisome rates of anxiety and depression drop when women's incomes rise relative to men's. But even if you're making a fair income, the **role overload**, or **second shift**, of simultaneously managing more of the domestic duties and childcare compounds stress and difficulty sleeping, which in turn makes you more anxious and depressed.

According to **social stress theory**, structural inequality and discrimination drain our mental and physical health, as well as our motivation to kick ass at our jobs. The cure? Overhauling workplaces with paid parental leave, affordable childcare, and flexible work schedules, for sure. But to get it, we've got to get together, talk it out, and speak up.

If we ever want to collectively earn more than pin money, corporate feminism alone won't cut it. We've got tear the whole professional facade down and rebuild.

ladies be shoppin'

Compulsive buying is a common crutch that compensates for identity and mood problems including low self-esteem, anxiety, and depression. Unfortunately, materialism actually *undermines* well-being. So, it's troubling that around 90 percent of adult compulsive buyers are women. We all tend to self-medicate with things we like, and while men tend to view shopping as work, women are way more likely to view it as a gender-appropriate leisure activity. That's not to say men never shop till they drop to feel better. But whereas women, whose compulsive shopping tends to focus on appearance-related items, are dismissed as shopaholics, men who obsessively buy records, cars, and watches are likelier to be branded collectors. The only upshot? Women are far more likely than men to seek help for their shopping addictions.

When you feel the need to spend, take a cold hard look at your motivations—and your bank account. Beauty products and other nonessentials should be paid for out of discretionary income, or what's left over after taxes and essential living expenses are covered. Red flags that you're buying into a harmful shopping habit include experiencing recurrent thoughts about things you want to buy, feeling like you *need* to spend, hiding purchases from loved ones, and constantly wanting to buy more.

There are a few different ways to handle those red flags:

- **Ask yourself what you *really* need.** Is your compulsive shopping making up for feeling frazzled, lonely, or bummed out? Try incorporating more fulfilling practices in your life that bring happiness and meaning, whether that's strengthening relationships, volunteering, or finally picking up that hobby you've been thinking about for years.

- **Shop for someone else, but stick to a budget.** Figure out how much money you can spare, and then ask nonprofits or other causes close to your heart what kind of donations they need.

- **Replace shopping altogether.** Try out other reward-giving activities like exercise and hangouts with friends—just not shopping excursions.

patriarchy taxes from head to toe

In the early 1900s, lady-life pivoted with the rise of dazzling department stores like Selfridges. Suddenly, shopping became a full-blown public event and thus another item that upper-class ladies had to somehow squeeze into their hectic days of needlework and napping. And remember: At the turn of the twentieth century, the Ideal Woman, a lady, was judged by how flatteringly she shone on her husband. Her lovely face? His high status. Her children? His manliness. Her shopping bags? His fat wallet. Somehow, today, ladylike taxes still apply.

SHAMPOO 'N' CONDITIONHER: Women pay **48 percent more** for shampoo and conditioner. At least our hair smells better.

MARKUPS FOR HER: Pink personal care products cost **13 percent more** than blue ones.

BREAST BASKETS: Decent bras easily cost **$50**, but how many do you need? In 2016, Negative Underwear cofounders Marissa Vosper and Lauren Schwab advised *InStyle* readers that a set of four good bras can last one year: 4 x $50 = **$200 per year** on breast cozies.

REAL ESTATE ROYALTIES: Roofs over our she-sheds come with **0.4 percent higher** mortgage rates.

FASHION FINES: Women's clothing costs **8 percent more** than men's, right down to our **3-percent-pricier** socks.

PREGNANCY REPELLENT: When Obamacare stipulated that women have access to copay-free birth control, it saved American women **$1.4 billion** annually.

BABY REPELLENT: On average, first-trimester abortions in the United States cost **$500**, and second-trimester procedures jump to **an average of $1,500**.

PERIODS-DON'T-SUCK-ENOUGH-ALREADY TAX: Around the world, tampons and pads may be subject to a value-added tax, which runs highest in Hungary at **27 percent**. But having no maxi tax doesn't necessarily maxi-mize good times for uteruses, considering that Ireland, which has no tampon tax, has draconian abortion laws.

PREEXISTING CONDITION OF FEMALENESS: $361,200. That's how much a study of 3.5 million insurance medical claims tallied the average lifetime medical costs to be for an average American woman, a third higher than a man's largely due to the combo of pregnancy and a longer life span.

ANXIETY INFLATION: An annual anti-depressant supply averages **$650**. Women are more likely than men to pick up that tab since we're more likely to be depressed, in part due to misogyny and other patriarchal bummers.

SEXUAL ASSAULT SURCHARGE: Rape survivors with private insurance still pay an average of **$950** for the associated medical costs of obtaining a rape kit.

MOTHERLODES OF STUDENT DEBT: Since American women earn a majority of bachelor degrees yet still go forth to earn less than men, we're collectively on the hook for two-thirds, or **$800 billion**, of the nationwide federal student loan debt.

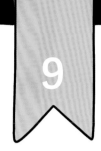

talking points

COMMUNICATING, DEBATING, AND RELATING

Patriarchy has cooked up a buffet of diminutives, slurs, and come-ons for women. Ranging from *sweetheart* to *slut*, these words act as checks and balances for the gender binary in two primary ways. *Baby, sweetie pie, sugar tits,* and the like impose a childlike, delicate femininity that chivalrous sexism loves to objectify on a pedestal. On the flip side, invectives like *whore, bitch,* and *cunt* telegraph an absence of the sugar, spice, and everything nice that patriarchy's fantasy gal exudes. Whether we're *nasty women, feminazis,* or *ball-busters,* the message rings clear: We're willfully and unnaturally misbehaving, and we're monstrously unattractive to the male gaze as a result. Per usual, calling women ugly and undesirable is the most offensive insult patriarchy can fathom. Sick burn, bro.

But as *Mean Girls* taught us, it ain't just bros making those burns. "You've got to stop calling each other sluts and whores," Tina Fey's character implores her female students in the film. "It just makes it okay for guys to call you sluts and whores." Indeed, a 2014 analysis from the UK think tank Demos found that tweets containing *slut, whore,* or *rape* as pejoratives were almost as likely to have come from female-identified Twitter users as male users.

Whether in an expletive-filled tweetstorm or standing in front of a college classroom, women's public communication challenges

"Your time is now, sisters . . . New goals and new priorities, not only for this country, but for all mankind must be set . . . We can do that by confronting people with their humanity and their own inhumanity— confronting them wherever we meet them: in the church, in the classroom, on the floor of the Congress and the state legislatures, in the bars, and on the streets."

SHIRLEY CHISHOLM
first African American presidential candidate in 1972

millennia of ingrained assumptions about our proper place and perceived authority (or lack thereof). It would almost be darkly funny if it didn't still interfere with our progress. Because verbal and social slights are invisible, we buy into the sticks and stones nonsense, telling ourselves that we should suck it up and soldier on. There's an empathy drought when it comes to communication-based attacks, from rage texts to icy body language, and they can torpedo our self-esteem. Not helping matters is the brain, which pays closer attention to negative feedback than positive, explaining why this kind of negging can be so destructive. It becomes the dominant voice in our heads if we let it.

On the flip side, girls are socialized with communication barriers, too. We learn from an early age that angry women are scary, evil stepmonsters, and it's all-around unladylike to lose it. The more we internalize those messages, the more we shove our anger and frustration down until it leaks out as that much-maligned and often women-aligned communication style of passive-aggression.

gossip, anger, and passive-aggression

SARAH STICKNEY ELLIS

Nineteenth-century etiquette author Sarah Stickney Ellis encouraged women to avoid gossiping about their neighbors, calling for discourse that was deeper than trading snarky barbs about someone's clothes or curtains. Giving up "that most contemptible of small-talk," shallow judgments about our peers, frees us to be less worried about the judgments others might pass on *our* frocks and frills.[1] In other words, exercise empathy before running your mouth.

Gossip has long been used as a form of social control; in the earliest days of colonial America, gossiping women constituted a pseudo police force. By talking about social, cultural, and moral transgressors, property-less and powerless women could have a hand in politics and elevate concerns to the community level—to the point where the court might actually intervene.

"Gossiping women acted as mouthpieces of the community," writes Kathleen Brown in her book *Good Wives, Nasty Wenches, and Anxious Patriarchs: Gender, Race, and Power in Colonial Virginia*. Their loose lips "enabled women to become

elizabeth

In August 1906, just sixteen years old and already equipped with a reputation as a skilled debater, anti-capitalist activist **ELIZABETH GURLEY FLYNN** took to a makeshift stage beneath a red flag and demanded the crowd of workers unite and start a revolution. That night was her first of about a dozen arrests. Eight months earlier, the New Yorker had delivered her first public speech before the Harlem Socialist Club titled "What Socialism Will Do for Women."

An unflagging proponent of workers' and women's rights inspired by her equally outspoken and encouraging parents and a voracious reading habit, Elizabeth left high school to continue to agitate for workers' rights full time.

Her public career as an impassioned speaker began in earnest in the 1910s, and by the time she was twenty, she was helping organize major strikes, speaking to huge crowds on city streets, and getting arrested for her civil disobedience—all in an effort to draw attention to the Industrial Workers of the World. Elizabeth channeled her feminist, socialist rage strategically and productively, building bridges to journalists and lawyers who also believed passionately in protecting free speech—allies who might not have shared her vision for a socialist America, but who did believe in her right to stump for it.

In addressing crowds of workers, she didn't speak over people or use language they couldn't understand; she connected with her audience, striving to pull them along with her in solidarity, and she relied on her "youth and loveliness" in her early days of activism to draw further attention to herself and her message.[2]

In later years, her crowds would dwindle as Americans grew fearful and suspicious of Communism, but Elizabeth spent the intervening decades traveling the world, calling for a revolution that would end capitalism, distribute wealth more evenly, and, in freeing women from their financial dependence on men, end gender inequality.

WHAT ELIZABETH WOULD DO TODAY: A loud and loyal activist with an expert instinct for getting her message out, she'd be at the literal and figurative forefront of fights to protect workers and immigrants, pushing her message out on social media, pulling stunts to get noticed, and backing it all up with one hell of a speech.

the voice of moral authority, creating the clamor that pressured individuals to forsake shameful relationships and provoked justices to issue edicts condemning transgressions."[3]

However, townspeople weren't *always* down to listen to all that clamor. In seventeenth-century Virginia, according to Brown, "unruly women" faced the ducking stool, a seesaw that would dunk them underwater until they agreed to behave—i.e., dip out of their unwelcome and unofficial public and political speaking roles.

Let's be clear: Women and men alike can be indirect and passive-aggressive. They just come at it from different angles. At work, for instance, women are more likely to be indirect when telling people what to do (can't be bossy!). Men, however, are more likely to skirt around an issue when they're copping to a mistake (can't be seen as subordinate!).

The bigger difference is with direct, physical aggression, which is a decidedly more masculine behavior. Evolutionary psychologists break it down like so: Whereas our cave-dude ancestors had to compete physically to show status

FIELD ARTIFACT

ye olde silencing tactic

From about the sixteenth to the nineteenth centuries in Europe and America, if dudes in charge decided women's wagging tongues were causing more harm than good in sending rumors up the legal ladder, they might make good on threats to literally silence them. Case in point: the scold's bridle, a horrifying mask used to shut women up, specifically "rude, clamorous" older women judged to be gossips who ran their mouths and bugged their neighbors.[4] This eerily *Handmaid's Tale*-esque torture device came in various versions to punish or threaten religious dissenters, suspected witches, and protesters. Unsurprisingly, the witches got it worst; their bridle featured spikes that would pierce the wearer's tongue and palate.

and win the chance to get a cave-gal pregnant, our physically weaker female ancestors couldn't risk any fisticuffs that might damage their reproductive chances. Instead, Wilma Flintstone and her gal pals relied on **indirect aggression** like ostracizing Betty Rubble and gossiping about her short skirts. Today, though, the way you communicate your anger and aggression probably has far more to do with entrenched gender-norm expectations than what dirty looks Wilma and Betty might've exchanged.

"Men have been encouraged to be more overt with their anger. If [boys] have a conflict on the playground, they act it out with their fists," psychologist and anger researcher Sandra Thomas told the American Psychological Association's *Monitor on Psychology*. "Girls have been encouraged to keep their anger down."

Perceptions of direct aggression's manliness—and women's anger as unappealingly unfeminine—puts us all at a disadvantage. Anger is obviously a normal, gender-free human reaction to injustice, pain, or disrespect, but women have been conditioned to believe that this passive-aggressive power play is an acceptable way to express or experience hostility and conflict. We chew and stew on our anger longer, growing more resentful if we don't deal with the problem head-on. In passively coping and keeping our anger down, as Thomas puts it, we develop a sense of powerlessness that festers and shows up as rumination, depression, and passive-aggressive behaviors.

But it's not as if erupting with rage solves the problem. Thanks to anger's unladylike look, blowing up at someone often feels more like losing control and acting out of character than getting real. And it creates a cycle. When women's anger does boil over as shouting and cursing, Thomas found they often report that their significant others basically rolled their eyes and dismissed what looked like a temporary loss of control or a PMS mood swing. Many women expressed a fear of alienating their partners and profusely apologized for their outbursts rather than work through what set them off.

It's no wonder that women might feel ambivalent about expressing their anger at work, too. While men's angrily expressed opinions have the power to sway listeners, women speaking from a pissed-off place tend to lose influence and appear less credible than their angry male peers. The dichotomy is easy to spot: Just look at how audiences and media respond to political candidates during debates. What great ideas and policies could we be missing out on if we judge a woman as less credible because she's impassioned?

Anger and hurt come packaged together for many women and stem most often from injustice, unfairness, and being denied power and resources. And their anger isn't irrational. On a personal level, women told Thomas they just wanted to be treated with respect and have more equitable divisions of labor at home and at work. The lack of constructively angry role models—and the expectation to instead be selfless and nurturing—is ultimately disempowering.

You can train for productive anger the same way you'd train for a race or performance: through conscious, sustained practice. Experts recommend assertiveness and conflict-resolution training, cognitive behavioral and group therapy, and stress-busting exercise and relaxation techniques like jogging and yoga. The primary goals are to rehabilitate anger's scary image, to ditch gendered notions of self-expression, and to spur self-worth and self-respect so you can ask for what you need. Learning to see anger as an indicator of injustice and a tool for action can empower women to climb over their fears and go after what they want, other people's opinions be damned.

the bitch switch

In 1866, when sculptor Vinnie Ream became the first woman and youngest artist to win a US government commission for a posthumous statue of President Lincoln, Mary Todd Lincoln wrote to a friend trashing Ream for her "forwardness and unladylike persistence."

Women's shameless self-promotion, ambition, and success can threaten other women sometimes even more than men, which brings us to perhaps the most treacherous point in our gendered landscape, the Bitch Switch. Here, all women are catty, high-maintenance shrews, and the most attractive thing you can be is "not like other girls."

We've probably all had our Mary Todd moments. Ever heard good news about a girl you know, and it almost makes the hair on the back of your neck stand up? It just strikes you with bitterness instead of happiness for her, like "good feminists" are supposed to feel?

These sneaky patriarchal instigators are yet another reason why self-honesty and mindfulness are essential for the unladylike journey. In complicated relationship equations, sometimes we are the problem. And that's okay! We just have to be willing to confront it.

let's be frenemies

How well can you pull off a fake smile? Are you able to offer backhanded compliments with a veneer of believability? If not, you need to step up your frenemy game because according to bogus evolutionary psychologists, we're "naturally" evolved to kind of f*cking hate all women who aren't family members. This idea came from primatology studies of chimpanzees, whose males also sit atop their social pyramids, and indeed, unrelated female chimps are tremendously competitive with one another. Until the 1990s, monkey scientists paid little attention to bonobos, assuming them to be simply smaller versions of chimps. But lo and behold, bonobo tribes are female-dominated and, crucially, female-friendly.

It turns out the divisive stereotype that "girls will be girls"—i.e., be catty bitches toward one another—is a whole bunch of monkey business. But its implications are worth remembering the next time we find ourselves bristling at a frenemy's approach. "Now that we have an equally close living relative with a different pattern, it opens up the possibilities for imagining that in our ancestry that females could bond in the absence of kinship, that matriarchies can exist, that females can have the upper hand, that societies can more peacefully run," Angela Saini writes in *Inferior: How Science Got Women Wrong and the New Research That's Rewriting the Story.*

Feminism doesn't mean we have to be besties with every woman always, but all of us can probably do a better job being neutral in our dislike. As in, not turning the fact that you just don't mesh with some folks into undercutting them. But if only getting along were as straightforward as it is in bonobo neighborhoods. We human animals tend to care a lot about what others think of us, especially our girl-peers; from childhood, we also take their criticisms more to heart than those lobbed by boys. This dynamic is an example of how we not only take gender cues from society at large but also from **self-socializing**, or forming our own conclusions about what's the right and wrong way to be you, based on personal experience.

Our little kid brains are no match for all the patriarchal messaging constantly being internalized and externalized all around us, which is why feminist role modeling is a crucial step in the unladylike revolution. Whether we're parents or not, it's on us to demonstrate our egalitarian values as an alternative example for younger kids (and their parents) around us.

FIELD NOTES

friend dating tips

The older we get, the tougher it can be to make new gal pals and keep up with established ones. Studies show that in our late twenties and thirties, women have a harder time staying in touch with old friends. A lot of the problem is simply logistics. Those are the years when we're busiest starting careers, having regrettable hookups, and/or starting families, leaving fewer opportunities to tend our friendships. Oxford University anthropologist Robin Dunbar explains, "You have a limited amount of time, efforts, and emotion that you can invest in your relationship, and women tend to invest very heavily in single individuals." As a result, we're also choosier in the adult friendships we forge—no pressure!

But it's beyond worth the effort to "put yourself out there," as no one ever likes to be told, and go on some platonic dates . . . because that's pretty much exactly what making adult friends is.

- Yes, you can ask a prospective friend out. Having an activity in mind also takes the pressure off the other person having to suggest something.

- Same as with sexy dating, look for someone who makes you laugh.

- Share and be curious, but don't interrogate.

- Be a gentlewoman. Even if it's awkward from the start, pay kindness forward by maintaining a positive attitude—unless you discover she's a closet racist, homophobe, antifeminist monster.

- Don't smother. Healthy friendships aren't meant to be monogamous.

- Don't flake. Always remember: Flake unto others as you would want to be flaked.

femmephobic cool girls

There's a difference between a gal with some guy friends and the Cool Girl Who Isn't Friends with Other Girls. She's the one who swears off same-sex friendships altogether, blaming women as a whole for being too dramatic, catty, or girly. What's up with that? Well, maybe she genuinely enjoys football and beer. Or maybe she just wants to bone the guys (and if so, more power—and condoms—to her).

But if her excuse is that girlfriends are total garbage, she might be taking some not-so-flattering cultural cues about second-rate BFFs. We're all for avoiding interpersonal dramarama, but pump the brakes before assuming that female friendships comprise nothing but cattiness and competition. This is a (wo)manifestation of what's called **internalized misogyny** (see page 25), absorbing centuries of patriarchal messages that we are indeed the weaker sex, more prone to the negative influences of society's ills, and that our relationships are somehow less important than men's.

In a summary of research on friendship, Rannveig Traustadóttir observed, "History does not celebrate female friendships, and there is a longstanding myth that the greatest friendships have been between men." In an essay for the online magazine *The Rumpus*, Emily Rapp spins the more elegant truth that "friendships between women are often the deepest and most profound love stories, but they are often discussed as if they are ancillary, 'bonus' relationships to the truly important ones."

So while it might seem empowering to be "above" lady bestieships, that mindset is also a common patriarchal method used to divide and diminish women. Not so cool after all, girl.

Femmephobia Fix-It Kit

Even if you have girly interests and gal pals aplenty, femmephobia happens because it's a product of the patriarchal ecosystem we're living in. If you start feeling a case of the frenemy, Cool Girl, or stone-cold-bitch-to-other-women coming on, here are some home remedies:

- **Examine your bias.** What do you dislike about the women around you? Question any assumptions you are making based on how they look, act, or dress.

- **Expose your fears.** Are you afraid of being stereotyped in the same way that you stereotype other women? Getting comfortable with your own gender expression and identity will help you be more accepting of others'.

- **Excise your interpersonal anxieties.** Are you worried that asking women to hang out feels like you're hitting on them? Afraid you'll get judged or rejected? Newsflash: People like to be liked! Allow yourself the space to be genuine and earnest, even if making that initial small talk makes you feel like a dork. And if it doesn't work out . . .

- **Open your mind and take the leap.** Recognize that we're all more than what's on the surface. Judging people by their appearance or background is sure to backfire; it just puts walls between you and any potential friends. Be open to differences and learning about other humans. You might learn something about yourself.

- **Accept your differences.** Get comfortable with the idea that not everyone will like you and you won't like every single woman you meet, either. You don't have to force a friendship with someone just because she's a she.

deep-fried voice policing

So, you've finally decided to speak up rather than ball up that anger—or stifle your cool stories, or shrink from leading a political rally, or suppress the idea of hosting a podcast. Congratulations! You're mere seconds away from fielding unsolicited comments about your authority to speak and the way you sound.

The way you *should* sound, of course, is polite, soft, and breathy; devoid of too many opinions or questions; and completely free of curse words and shouting. You know, like a lady who knows her place. "Allowing men stronger means of expression than are open to women further reinforces men's position of strength in the real world," linguist Robin Lakoff wrote in 1973, "for surely we listen with more attention the more strongly and forcefully someone expresses

enraging rage tropes

Sexism is hardly the only layer in the terrible, stale perceptions-of-women's-anger cake. Racist labeling is just another way to dismiss women's emotions, police their speech, and attempt to silence them, rather than validating them and encouraging them to own, understand, and process their anger—or accepting blame if you're the one who pissed them off.

The Angry Black Woman

THE IMAGE: This desexualized, fed-up, loud, argumentative, and nagging stereotype has her roots in the character Sapphire from the 1930s radio show *Amos 'n' Andy*. She reemerged on TV in shows from *Sanford and Son* to *Martin*, and her independence and strength are countered by her perceived hostility and emasculating behavior.

THE FALLOUT: Black women who speak up, push back, or simply don't smile constantly are labeled difficult and angry, absorbing sexist, racist projections that their feelings aren't valid and they're simply overreacting or have a bad attitude. Detractors are quick to label black women who speak up in public—like Representative Maxine Waters or former First Lady Michelle Obama—as angry or flat-out crazy. Assuming a black woman is primed to be angry shifts the blame from people, systems, and circumstances that actually are problematic, placing it squarely on her shoulders for feeling less than stellar about them.

The Spicy Latina Spitfire

THE IMAGE: The trope of the sexy, ditzy, hot-tempered, and tempestuous Latina stems from Mexican actress Lupe Velez's portrayal of Carmelita Lindsey in the series of eight *Mexican Spitfire* films between 1939 and 1944. The spitfire is alive and well in characters like *Modern Family*'s Gloria Delgado-Pritchett, played by Sofía Vergara, a talented businesswoman and actress who plays up the sexy-goofy-woman-with-an-accent act IRL.

THE FALLOUT: Assuming Latinas are little more than ditzy sexpots who might fly off the handle at any moment makes it pretty difficult to take actual, real-life women and their concerns seriously. And treating accents as hilarious, ridiculous, or exotic—rather than a normal aspect of people speaking your language—further objectifies and others them.

The Dragon Lady

THE IMAGE: Her anger is as cold and deadly as the Latina Spitfire's is hot and lively, and she reflects centuries of real-life racist anxieties about Asian women being scheming, seductive manipulators. Americans' imaginations ran wild over biased reports about nineteenth-century Chinese Empress Dowager Tsu Hsi, who was painted as a manipulative, sexually deviant murderer. Emerging from racist "yellow peril" panic, the 1934 comic strip *Terry and the Pirates* ushered in the character of the Dragon Lady, an exotic, mysterious, sexualized, and deeply dangerous counterpart to the male "Oriental Mastermind" trope. Shades of the Dragon Lady show up in a few of actress Lucy Liu's characters like Ling Woo in *Ally McBeal* and O-Ren Ishii in *Kill Bill: Vol. 1*.

THE FALLOUT: If Asian women aren't stereotyped as sexually submissive "Lotus Blossoms" or well-behaved nerds, they're often fetishized and feared as heartless ice queens. The Dragon Lady becomes a one-dimensional caricature rather than a complex human.

opinions, and a speaker unable—for whatever reason—to be forceful in stating his views, is much less likely to be taken seriously."[5]

Across the board, regardless of gender, we still tend to follow the ancient Greeks' example of associating deep voices with authority, trustworthiness, and competence—even, some research indicates, when those voices are coming out of women's mouths. Could that be why women are dropping their vocal

■┣━━━●━▶ FIELD NOTES ◀━●┫━━■

vocal tics and tricks

Complaining about women's voices and manners of speaking is an indirect way to express frustration that they're, you know, talking in public at all. We get dinged for totally normal, often gender-neutral verbal tics like using filler words to get us from one thought to the next, relying on softening language in our work emails, apologizing unnecessarily, and ending our sentences with upspeak.

The motivation? Often, consciously or not, we're working to make ourselves more palatable to classmates, colleagues, and audiences. We soften demands by letting a coworker know we are "just" checking in on that request, despite the fact that the tactic often makes us look more passive-aggressive than laid back. When it comes to our sorries, we tend to perceive more slights than men do, and so we both offer and expect more apologies. **Ritual apologizing** is a conversational tactic girls and women grow up using to smooth things over with our galpals.

And the much maligned upspeak is just another tactic we use to replace tag questions like " . . . right?" or to make sure listeners are following our train of thought. It's also been chalked up to how accustomed women are to getting interrupted. Tired of upspeaking? Own your feelings and your statements. Ending sentences on a down note is a quick way to sound more authoritative and confident.

When those verbal crutches start tripping you up, just take a deep breath and be direct. By slowing down and thinking through what you want to communicate, you can nix some of your "likes" and "ums" if they become distracting. Fill the spaces with breaths or pauses until you've retrained your brain. Ultimately, it's about owning your voice: Be direct, and don't apologize for saying how you feel, voicing an opinion, or taking up space.

register a few notches and veering into vocal fry territory? We humans tend to unconsciously mirror one another's speech patterns, a habit that's usually more pronounced in women as an unconscious community-building tactic. Sure enough, we're not immune to copying the rattling, creaky vocal fry that's become a popular fixture of criticisms lodged at women in particular.

It wasn't so long ago when researchers sounded the alarm that women's vocal fry would decimate their chances in the workplace.[6] People of any age and any gender (but particularly older women) perceive it to be annoying, they warned, and if you *also* dabble in upspeak, everyone will think you sound incompetent, insecure, immature, and a little stupid. Ouch!

What isn't so publicized is that not only is vocal fry common among men and women alike, but college-aged guys actually fry more than their gal pals do: 25 percent of the time for dudes, compared to just 10 percent of the time for women in the study.[7]

So why does it bug people so much when women do it? Aside from just run-of-the-mill sexism, the irritation seems to be linked with how much farther women's voices have to drop than men's in order to fry and that while men fry all over the place, women tend to fry at the ends of sentences. In other words, it might just be more noticeable when women do it. Voices that are drastically atypical for the speaker's perceived sex tend to be judged as less attractive, which jibes with research showing that while women seem like better authority figures when they have deep voices, they're also deemed less attractive than their average-voiced female friends.

On the flip side of that particular pitch-policing conversation? Trans women, for whom speaking in a higher, more traditionally feminine pitch can mean more comfortably occupying their gender identity and therefore more confidently and safely moving through the world. Cis men have thicker vocal folds than cis women thanks to testosterone, and hormone therapy—taking estrogen—won't make them thinner. Trans women who want to change the way they sound have expensive surgical options that address the size of their vocal folds, but less invasive options involve speech therapy that focuses on attributes like airflow, breath, resonance, and intonation.

"Our identities are intimately connected to how we sound," speech-language pathologist Kathe Perez told *The Guardian* in 2015. Perez launched voice-training app Eva in 2013 to address trans and genderqueer folks' concerns about not sounding like the real *them*. Apps like Eva can be invaluable tools for people who can't afford speech therapy or who've attended but want to brush up their vocal skills at home. Perez admits the ongoing practice of changing your voice can be "quite a daunting endeavor," one that can take a year to get the hang of and a lifetime to maintain. "There will never be a point where it's mindless, but there will be a point where it's effortless."[8]

the sound of silencing

Policing women's speech—everything from how they speak to how often they speak—is a pretty familiar concept for anyone who's ever watched television, listened to the radio, or been in public outside their own home. Whether it's criticizing women for vocal fry and upspeak, slamming them for being shrill, or kvetching about them opening their mouths at all, efforts to silence women are decidedly not a new phenomenon. Classicist Mary Beard traces the "first recorded example of a man telling a woman to 'shut up'" to Homer's *Odyssey* when the protagonist's wife, Penelope, requests a song to take her mind off her absent husband, and her bratty son Telemachus manterrupts and shushes her, "for speech will be the business of men."[9]

Just look at the ancient Greeks and their *dis*empowering oratory traditions. As elite, dominant masculinity became inextricably linked with the power of authoritative public speech, the idea that women shouldn't—and *couldn't*— speak assertively or authoritatively in public cemented. It's not that they worried women would trip over their words or speak too softly; they *literally* considered it nigh impossible for women to ditch idle, gossipy chatter. If women did speak up and out, they were shouted down as barking, yapping **androgynes** (literally, "men-women").

The exception? When women communicated women-only concerns or spoke on behalf of others. That sounds pretty familiar: Women commonly get career advice that we'll be more successful in salary and other work-related resource

speaking spectrum

Everything from our intentions to our level of privilege affects how risky speaking up can be.

Sounding stupid

Hurting feelings

Making a mistake

THAT SUCKS

Stepping on toes

Talking over someone

Offending someone

Mistakes happen to all of us when we first start learning and put ourselves out there. Nail a solid apology:

TIMING: Apologize too soon, and you risk ending the discussion before you've both had time to feel your feelings. But wait too long, and the apology might come off as an afterthought.

SINCERITY: Reflect on your own behavior and own up to what you did and whom you affected. Express regret for the specific harm done, and request forgiveness.

ACTION: Show you're sincere by committing to change and following through.

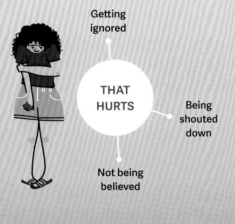

Getting ignored

THAT HURTS

Being shouted down

Not being believed

Think about sexual assault survivors or victims of online trolling and rape threats. Speaking up about their experiences can often leave them dealing with the added trauma of being disbelieved, not taken seriously, or facing retaliation and further harassment.

Getting harassed

Being retaliated against

DANGER ZONE

Being blacklisted and shut out

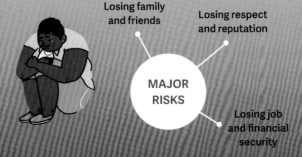

Losing family and friends

Losing respect and reputation

MAJOR RISKS

Losing job and financial security

Class privilege affects how ready and willing some folks are to speak truth to power. Would you be able to recover if speaking up got you fired?

negotiations when we frame our asks in relation to how we serve the greater good of the team, rather than for our own benefit or because we deserve it.

Ancient Greek women were also (as we all still are) discredited based on voice. A man's low pitch communicated courage, whereas women's higher pitch telegraphed vulnerability. This was echoed in myths like that of Cassandra, whose fate dictated she could predict the future, but no one would believe her. Stretching centuries, these prejudices were repeated by American writer Henry James, who in 1906 fretted women would turn language into "the moo of the cow, the bray of the ass, and the bark of the dog."[10] Two decades later in 1926, an American radio station's completely unscientific survey of disgruntled people who'd previously written in to air grievances found that—shockingly—most preferred male voices to female, at a ratio of a hundred to one. The women not only sounded "shrill," the roaring-twenties dudebros said, but they also came off as patronizing with too much personality.[11]

It's a direct line through to today. No matter what our voices actually sound like, we're attacked as shrill, bitchy, angry, nagging, and emotional if we use a public platform to communicate, whether it's to report the news, campaign for office, or push back against abusive online discourse.

You can expect the reaction to your speaking up will be even stronger if you're pointing out inequality and preaching tenets of social justice. Social conservatives often toss out accusations of "political correctness" as a way of slamming change and trying to silence progressives' dissent. For decades, they've attacked vocal college students in particular, but impassioned young people in general, for playing "politics of victimhood." They've dog-whistled to white supremacist sexists in criticizing ethnic or women's studies programs, and they've blasted the "growing intolerance" of liberals.[12]

Really, what haters deride as "PC culture" is in fact a way to make room for marginalized voices, to welcome more people and perspectives to the table, and to pass around the memo that hurtful and hateful language isn't acceptable.

What looks like people pointing fingers and accusing others of taking away their right to be "honest" is a symptom that social change is rolling forward and people who aren't ready for it have gotten a little uncomfortable.

Sounds vaguely encouraging, but knowing the motivations behind attempts to silence you isn't always enough to counter the feeling of *wanting* to withdraw. It's okay—and can be mentally necessary—to step away for a little time out. But staying completely silent in the face of larger injustice—especially if you're in a position of privilege that would allow you to help change things—won't save you from fear and discomfort.

better bonding

Whether with friends, romantic partners, or family, relationships are like plants: When you tend to them, they grow, strengthen, and, if you're lucky, give you snacks and flowers. But those fruit-bearing 'ships aren't going to grow themselves. Regardless of your situation—maybe you haven't seen your bestie in weeks, or you're wishing your bond with your partner were stronger—chances are, taking a hands-off approach to your relationship isn't going to help it flourish.

It's only natural that we want to bond with others. When we get stressed, hormones like cortisol run wild before happy chemicals like oxytocin come play some feel-good slow jams to calm things down. While those slow jams are spinning, you're prompted to snuggle up to your loved ones as a self-soothing behavior and to make sure everyone's okay. This is **tending and befriending**, as psychologists put it. UCLA researchers coined the term as another dimension of the anxiety-inducing, let's-run-from-that-attacker **fight-or-flight** stress response, which is more common among men.[13]

Evolutionary biologists say the tend-and-befriend drive helps form and reinforce bonds with our faves. We say it's just further evidence that it's important to reach out when you're stressed. If your IRL social skills are a little rusty, here are some tips for communicating better and making the most of your time together:

- **Put in some literal face time.** If you opt for the warm glow of your screen over the one from your friend's happy face, you're hardly alone. Watching television is literally Americans' number-one leisure activity, and we spend an average of three hours a day doing it. A distant second? Socializing with friends, which clocked in at roughly forty minutes a day (and, no, smoking a solo bowl while you watch Abbi and Ilana get high on TV does not count as socializing).[14] As helpful as social media and texting can be for keeping tabs on each other, getting together is good for your brain. Even a light touch from a loved one can spark a rush of endorphins, something that's tough to replicate through your touchscreen.

- **Commit to contact.** Some researchers optimistically call long-distance friendships "flexible," rather than fragile, meaning that while your geographically close pals might share more literal closeness and IRL moments with you, the added effort required to stay in touch with a long-distance friend means the bond won't break.[15] Good news for the 89 percent of American college students who report having a long-distance bestie.[16] If you have a long-distance friend, commit to a regular phone date, instant-message catch-up, or pen-pal exchange. Way back in 2004, 82 percent of college students emailed their BFF at least once a week.[17] At this point, that might have evolved into using drones to drop care packages, but either way, it's an important practice we could all stand to adopt.

- **Try new things.** Self-expansion is on fire in the early stages of a relationship as you learn and try new things together. Consistently pursuing that thrill a few years in is a way to continue bonding and growing together.

- **Be a good listener.** Active empathic listening is more than jargon; it's a vitally important communication skill that can serve our 'ships well. Put yourself in the other person's shoes as they talk. Note their body language, facial expressions, and tone of voice. Ask questions and engage like a human person. You're not going to learn much about someone else by doing all the talking—communication is a two-way street.

- **Be intentional in the moment.** Everyone speaks different love languages (even friends) and has different definitions of quality time, but committing to someone means committing to pursuing that quality time as often as you can. For women who live with their partners, spending dedicated couple time at least once a week is linked with a significant boost in relationship happiness. Being intentional about showing your partner love, affection, and undivided attention puts you in the moment and helps communication, commitment, and even sexual intimacy blossom.

The more adept you are at strengthening bonds, effectively communicating, and actively listening, the better equipped you'll be to build sustaining relationships and, eventually, coalitions. Your mental health—and future activism—depends on it.

invest in friendpreneurship

Remember Sarah Stickney Ellis from page 202? She penned many a guide in the 1800s for women's roles as daughters, wives, and mothers, but she placed their egalitarian friendships at the center. She emphasized that it was ridiculous to risk those friendships by competing to the point where it "cast a shade upon their intercourse with each other."[18] Preach.

Jealousy—whether based on love, looks, or success—is a natural part of any relationship, especially if you're not feeling so secure in yourself. This doesn't leave much room to be a great ally. A constant undercurrent of unfair comparison and unhealthy competition can leave you feeling at odds with your pals and peers.

But if we believe what we see on basic-cable high-school dramas and reality television, jealousy is the fuel for inevitable lady-competition fire, the root of the inescapable trope that women are too catty to be anything more than frenemies. Sounds exhausting. What are we even competing for? This isn't *The Bachelor* or *Project Runway*; this is real life, and we really *are* here to make friends. It's much more beneficial, sanity-preserving, and patriarchy-smashing to celebrate others' successes, rather than trying to top them or tear them down.

A fabulous side effect of being confident in yourself and claiming your unladylikeness is gaining the mental and emotional space to be a cheerleader for your fellow humans when they kick

ass, and a linebacker-sized shoulder to cry on when their lives are in disarray. Cheering people on means you get to learn from them, not to mention flex that empathy muscle by putting their needs, wants, and wins ahead of your own from time to time. Channel your confidence into your connections; don't be too shy to team up with a crew of badasses, all of whom are successful, passionate, engaged, and brilliant in their own unique ways.

 One such rad lady is journalist and podcaster Ann Friedman, who coined the perfect term for the squad-building concept: **Shine Theory**. Friedman came up with a solution for any insta-insecurity: "When you meet a woman who is intimidatingly witty, stylish, beautiful, and professionally accomplished, *befriend her*," she advised in *New York* magazine's "The Cut" in 2013. "Surrounding yourself with the best people doesn't make you look worse by comparison. It makes you better."

Friedman said she learned the importance of befriending powerful ladies from *her* power bestie and *Call Your Girlfriend* podcast cohost, Aminatou Sow: "I don't shine if you don't shine."

boundary building

Positive, constructive communication is the best way to address conflict across all of our relationships—and ideally head it off at the pass. If something makes you uncomfortable, stand up for yourself. Gently but firmly draw a line and let people know what you won't tolerate. Boundaries are a sign of self-respect. When people abide by them, they're showing you respect, too.

But being assertive, setting boundaries, and saying no can be tricky for women, since we are socialized to be people-pleasers and are judged for subverting expectations. This is especially true for women who might be lower on the social, relationship, economic, or workplace totem poles than the person pushing them. We're simply not socialized to tell folks to back off or to ask for what we want and need—especially if what we need is a little space.

If you feel you're not getting your needs met, or are giving up important parts of yourself in a relationship, there's a real danger that the unhealthy connection can spiral into bitterness and resentment. Ask yourself why you're accepting a subordinate, passive role in your own life and relationship. Is it safer to let someone steamroll you than to speak up and face a potentially angry or upset reaction? And if you suspect that you're on the other side of that dynamic, ask yourself why you want that friend or partner to think and act a certain way, or value certain things, when they're supposedly someone you care about. Do you really value them if you're trying to control and mold them into someone else?

FIELD ARTIFACT

friendship braid-celets

One fashion statement folks wholeheartedly embraced during the Georgian and Victorian eras was jewelry made with their loved ones' hair, the most popular way both to be reminded of your pal and to *show* that you were constantly thinking of her.

Hairy jewelry had symbolized a range of emotions, from mourning to affection, but by the sappy 1840s, it was mostly a fashion statement. In *Love Entwined: The Curious History of Hairwork in America*, author Helen Sheumaker cites an 1844 women's magazine's assertion that "sentimental bracelets, composed of hair

. . . are now considered indispensable." You simply weren't a properly sentimental middle-class gal without some hair-inlaid rings or brooches!

Hair bracelets, for instance, often featured a silky braid attached on either end to clasps that might also sport pearls or jewels. In 1858, a writer drooled over one such bracelet, declaring, "hair jewelry may be said to have arrived at perfection." Unfortunately (or not?) the late nineteenth century rise in germ theory and changing hygiene practices, not to mention shifting fashions, meant women grew out of their hair-jewelry phase.

it's okay to peace out

Not every relationship is shiny and salvageable, though. As our lives, priorities, and politics change, it's common to outgrow relationships and see old connections unravel. You're not the same person at thirty-five that you were at twelve, and while holding onto old bonds is a precious privilege, sometimes—thanks to new jobs, new cities, and new hobbies—it just doesn't happen. People evolve, and if your priorities no longer line up, it's okay to peacefully drift. And while some of your relationships will naturally run their course, in the interest of your health and well-being, you might want to follow the example of Matilda Joslyn Gage and hurry others along.

Gage, an American suffragist and abolitionist, certainly had no time to waste on bad company. An author, historian, speaker, and advocate for Native American rights, she cofounded the National Woman Suffrage Association in 1869 with BFFs Susan B. Anthony and Elizabeth Cady Stanton. Alongside her fellow busy buds in the 1880s, she coedited the first three volumes of *History of Woman Suffrage*. But when Anthony and Stanton proved to be more racist than radical, Gage took her inclusive, anti-Church, patriarchy-smashing stance elsewhere. To her, the vote was but one stop on a path to greater equality, and cutting ties with women like Anthony and Stanton, who would rather join with conservative, pro-Christian-state temperance activists than with black Americans—was a sacrifice she was willing to make.

ELIZABETH CADY STANTON

There's a lot of emotional space reclamation in shedding toxic people from your life, people who've perhaps taken advantage of you or taken you for granted; people who've overwhelmed you with negativity; maybe even garbage humans who've tried to hurt you outright. In prioritizing your own self-worth and emotional needs over those of oppressive or soul-sucking frenemies, you're choosing to exercise your agency and your right to build the mentally healthy life you deserve.

Maybe this knowledge bomb will help you recover: On the flip side of all the heart- and brain-healthy benefits of fabulous friendships and loving partnerships, toxic bonds have been shown to be equally toxic to our bodies. People with negativity-filled close relationships are at a higher risk for heart disease and cardiac arrest. All those negative emotions spark an explosion of unhealthy chemical and hormonal reactions in your body, stressing you out and putting wear and tear on your whole system.[19] So break up with that bad bud before she gives you a heart attack!

If you do decide to dip out, take along a few tips and tricks:

- **Come clean.** Whether you're feeling fed up with a friend or with a partner, try honesty first. Without pointing fingers or blowing your top, explain how you feel and why you feel that way. Cop to being unsure about a shared future. Being upfront gives the other person a chance to address your feelings, clear up any miscommunication, and get on the same page.

- **Be clear.** If you've decided it's definitely done and you're going to break up face-to-face or phone-to-phone, keep things brief, respectful, and honest. Don't yell or belittle. With sensitivity, explain how you feel and that you've made up your mind so there's little room for misinterpretation and an hours-long sobfest. Don't say you'll keep in touch or check in if you don't intend to do so.

- **Fade out.** Slow fading has gotten a bad rap in romantic relationships— for good reason. It can be a dick move to leave someone wondering what happened if they've already gotten invested. But when it comes to acquaintances, not-so-good friends, and not-worth-a-second-date folks, it's okay to fade away rather than fake it. People get busy.

- **Ghost if you have to.** Getting out of a toxic, negative, or outright abusive situation sometimes requires you to peace out without notice and put your cell and social on lockdown for safety and sanity.

Learning to accept that you're better off without some people and that you don't have to please everyone—nor do you have to take their crap or enable their harmful behavior—is a massive mental and cardiac relief, not to mention a sign of maturity and self-assurance. Go spend time with people who get you!

marching orders

RESIST, PERSIST, AND RAISE HELL

The election of Donald Trump in November 2016 prompted women across the United States—and the world—to look for ways to take collective action. What started as a white Hawaiian woman's Facebook event page calling for a march in Washington, D.C., turned into a massive event helmed by seasoned organizers, most of whom were women of color. Along the way, conflict erupted over inclusivity, representation, and intention: *Why were so few women of color involved on the front end? Why were white women getting so defensive about that question? Would participants take the fight home once the big event ended?* But ultimately, millions of women and allies participated in the Washington event and staged sister marches in thirty-two countries across the globe.[1]

The day proved to be both catharsis and catalyst for countless participants, many of whom, from grandmothers to toddlers and every age in between, had little to no previous activist or marching experience. It also proved to be an excellent opportunity to listen to more seasoned activists, particularly women of color and other marginalized people who'd been sounding alarm bells long before anyone put on a pussy hat.

While sign-toting demonstrators flooded streets around the world, political pundits were already asking: What's next?

"We've got to think that we have choices. We can produce something different. Maybe it won't change your life for all time. Maybe it won't change society for all time. But each of us can choose to do something different, because we recognize that for our own humanity we have to."

GRACE LEE BOGGS
human rights advocate and author

A few things are for sure: If we want to distance ourselves from our divided past and establish lasting momentum, we're going to have to leave habits of class-exclusive activism behind, use our privilege powers for good, and work together.

class acts

Historically, full-time patriarchy smashing has been a classy business. Unladylike trailblazers like New Zealand's Kate Sheppard refused to accept the sexist status quo and decided to do something about it—and keep on doing something about it until folks paid attention. Stepping out for her convictions in the late nineteenth century when ladylike domesticity reigned, Sheppard articulated and published her women's equality ideals through pamphlets, which were basically old school zines; she lobbied Parliament to permit women's participation; and generally made a lot of men nervous. Then, after more than twenty years of rabble-rousing, Sheppard celebrated Kiwi gals becoming the first in the world to win female suffrage in 1893.

Well-heeled, headstrong women got a shapely leg up in getting their points across through access to privileges like fancy family ties, wealth, education, and free time. These are the gold-plated economics of trailblazing. In the early 1900s, for instance, it would've been way harder for rad Chinese suffragist Kang Tongbi to spearhead an anti-foot-binding campaign if her father hadn't been someone important in the imperial government who shared his daughter's passion for social reform. Like her fellow turn-of-the-century New Women, Tongbi's chance to attend college, travel, and choose her life's path further shaped her feminist politics.

A few decades earlier, after the Civil War and into the thick of the industrial revolution, American society was rapidly changing, but women still didn't have the vote, and black people faced a criminal justice system that wanted to keep them locked away. So how were they supposed to effect change?

Why, just get well-to-do women together, of course! Spreading from New York across the country, the Progressive Era women's club movement, though largely racially segregated, allowed women the chance to exchange ideas and come up with action plans for social and political reform.

Led by Mary Church Terrell under the slogan "Lifting as We Climb," the National Association of Colored Women (NACW) sought to combat the stereotypes and discrimination black Americans faced in the late nineteenth century. Without a doubt, respectability was one of their weapons, but it alone couldn't combat how black children were treated in the justice system. An organization that drew together two hundred state- and local-level women's clubs from around the country, NACW funneled its members' drive into reform of the country's shoddy juvenile justice system. NACW advocated at every level of government to keep children safe and away from crime, and their Illinois delegations played key roles in pushing for the establishment of juvenile courts.

MARY CHURCH TERRELL

Even today, money and status afford upper-crust gals more time, access, and purchased bot followers on Instagram to buck norms and champion causes that might be impossible for regular Janes with little or no resources to spare. That said, many a movement also has been led and strengthened by the women of color and working-class women who bear the brunt of sexist and racist politics and policies, movements that sometimes were then steamrollered when wealthier—or dudelier—folks showed up on the activist scene.

In an interview for the Civil Rights History Project in 2011, activist Gwendolyn Zoharah Simmons recounted her experiences as a field director for the Student Nonviolent Coordinating Committee's (SNCC) Mississippi Freedom Summer Project in 1964. Simmons described struggling to be taken seriously as a female director and to access the same kinds of resources her male colleagues received. Fellow SNCC activist Lonnie C. King echoed Simmons's sentiments, relating his surprise when Nashville, Tennessee, civil rights leader Diane Nash was "leapfrogged," as he put it, by less qualified men for bigger positions.

In pushing women aside—both in real time and in our history books—we absorb the idea that women took no major risks, played no major roles, and dreamed up no major plans. Without looking beneath the enforced respectability that many radical women in the abolition, suffrage, and civil rights movements grappled with, it might appear that if they made a difference, it was a merely an accidental sidenote. Just look at the bus boycotts.

"It was a rebellion of maids, a rebellion of working-class women, who were tired of boarding the buses in Montgomery, the public space, and being assaulted and called out-of-there-names and abused by white bus drivers," said Ruby Nell Sales, another former SNCC activist interviewed for the Civil Rights History Project. "And that's why that movement could hold so long. If it had just been merely a protest about riding the bus, it might have shattered. But it went to the very heart of black womanhood, and black women played a major role in sustaining that movement."

FIELD NOTES

activist packing list

Activism has many facets and faces, countless motivations and methods. No matter what direction you take, draw inspiration from the women who have come before you and pack a few essential tools:

- **AMAZING ALLIES:** When you identify problems and spot a chance to fix them, making change happen can feel like a demoralizing uphill slog if you're by yourself with limited power and no keys to the old-boys' club. So why not turn to like-minded allies and create a supportive network of your own to help lift others as you climb and intimidate the hell out of people standing in the way of progress?

- **ABUSE AWARENESS:** Simmons put her foot down about sexual harassment in the SNCC ranks, but you won't always have leaders or allies who can protect you. Plus, it's not as if you won't face abuse or ill treatment from counterprotesters,

police, and random strangers on the internet. Steel yourself and develop an action—or reaction—plan.

- **AMBITION AND RESOURCEFULNESS:** Being doubted, underestimated, and overlooked means that you'll need to not only find support from fellow activists around you, but also develop and tap into a well of ambition within you to persist and accomplish your goals.

- **ASSERTIVENESS:** Whether you're stepping into a leadership role or falling in line with other worker bees, if you're getting loud and proud about a cause, you'll likely need to shed any polite, shrinking violet tendencies and get comfortable pressing on despite being told no.

Figuring out how to embrace ambition, find and build a supportive coalition, and maintain your momentum will allow you to launch into action.

own your feminist ambition

We all know the ABCs of how women's ambition is perceived: It's Aggressive, Bossy, and Cold. We're overreacting if we see a change that needs making, and we're greedy, domineering, and selfish if we want to lead the effort. Astronomer Caroline Herschel—born in 1750 and the first woman to discover a comet—rolled her eyes at the gendering of gumption. "And was there ever a woman without vanity? Or a man either? Only with this difference, that among gentlemen the commodity is generally styled ambition."[2] Sick burn, Hersch.

CAROLINE HERSCHEL

How can we get down off the tightrope of bitchiness versus drive and accept our own ambitions?

- **Funnel your feminist rage.** Once you ditch settling for passivity, dig out your tools of self-awareness and self-worth, then zero in on your passions. What ignites your excitement or pisses you off? What systems do you want to work to change? Look around for role models and examples. Who is where you'd like to be, doing what you want to be doing?

- **Pick your battles.** It's not that you can't tackle all types of injustice, but you can't take it all on at once. While the temptation might be to stretch yourself across causes and commitments—donating here, volunteering there, marching to who knows where—you'll likely be a more effective activist and advocate if you focus your time, energy, and money in one or a few specific areas where you can help make an impact. Otherwise, you could wind up feeling overwhelmed, unheard, and ineffective.

- **Prioritize your goals.** When you have multiple goals competing for your time and attention—you want to volunteer, start your own nonprofit, launch a zine, and squeeze in some travel with your boo—you're bound to feel a little harried. The perception that your goals interfere with one another turbo-charges stress and anxiety. This heightened anxiety, in turn, makes you feel as though you have less time, which stresses you out even more.

When you're simultaneously motivated and half-terrified to do a bunch of things at once, it kicks up **goal-conflict anxiety**. That high energy can also make you impatient. You feel you have less time to accomplish your task, so you wind up trying to process information and make decisions more quickly—all of which can backfire if you slip up in your rush to push through as quickly as possible.

Researchers back two methods of countering the conflicting-goal anxiety spiral: (1) breathe, and (2) get excited. More specifically, practice deep breathing to slow your heart rate and recenter yourself, then work to mentally reframe your anxiety as excitement for the possibilities that lie ahead. Our brains are programmed to spot danger and focus on the negative, but consciously working to frame your anxieties in the positive light of opportunity will fuel your ambition.

Don't be too proud to get scrappy, either. Twice divorced with seven kids, Mexican American labor leader Dolores Huerta relied on a caregiving network of friends and family to babysit while she birthed a migrant farmworker movement. When Dolores found her way to grassroots organizing in the 1950s, ladylike activism involved registering voters, teaching citizenship and naturalization classes, and taking care of the meeting prep. But Huerta wanted to make more of a difference, whether her single motherhood affronted folks or not; besides, she had bigger foes to face.

Alongside Cesar Chavez, Huerta co-founded what ultimately became the United Farm Workers of America, and in 1965, they launched La Huelga, the struggle, a grape-pickers' strike and national grape boycott that won farmworkers fairer pay and better working conditions. For her efforts, Huerta was arrested more than twenty times, and in 1988, she was hospitalized after a brutal police beating during a protest. But guess what? The kids were all right.

Like Huerta, all your activist tasks can turn into a tumbleweed if you try to stick to a strict, inflexible daily to-do list. Plan your mission out like this instead:

- **Check the weather.** Accept and embrace the tangle of feelings you might be dealing with that have kept you from stepping up. You might feel overwhelmed, anxious, uncertain, and even hopeless about finding the "best" way to get involved. There's no such thing as best. Find what fits.

- **Take inventory.** List all the sh*t you're good at and enjoy doing, and then all the sh*t you're not so great at, in addition to your limitations and non-negotiables.

- **Map out the need.** Research specific organizations and causes that need support. What kind of contributions are they looking for? Match your inventoried skills, abilities, and passions with what's needed.

- **Look for mile markers.** Seeking out the incremental, smaller goals you can achieve—and celebrate!—along the way will give you a better view of how the rest of your priorities can integrate into your larger plan of action. Breaking it down keeps you from getting overwhelmed and burning out.

- **Pick the right path.** You can then determine what daily, weekly, and monthly tasks you must shed or shore up to make your dream a reality.

- **Lighten your load.** To maximize your time and minimize distractions, group all the smaller, annoying, have-to tasks into manageable chunks on the edges of your day that you can sweep aside all at once. This frees up the brain space that would otherwise be bugging you in the background and distracting you from your primary task. Eventually your small-tasks-to-the-back strategy becomes habit, and you'll think about it even less.

Giving yourself uninterrupted time and space to concentrate will let you wring that much more out of your creativity, ambition, and intellect. World domination is just around the corner.

mind the message

While you're busy practicing taking up as much space as possible, consider how you can tailor your message to your audience without compromising your meaning or intention. Start with understanding your audience and considering what will resonate with their priorities and perspectives. Ideally, you shouldn't have to soften or tweak your language; the message should be grasped and appreciated for its merits. But realistically, it can be crucial to communicate in a way that can be heard by your intended audience. As for how to make that communication magic happen, neuroscience offers a compelling lead.

Neurolinguist George Lakoff specializes in how our brains unconsciously process social and political speech. "If the language activates certain neural circuits, every time a neural circuit is activated it gets stronger," Lakoff told *On the Media,* offering as an example Donald Trump's depressingly effective election catchphrases. "The more you repeat it, the stronger it gets, in whoever hears it."[3]

To more effectively boombox a political cause à la feminism, Lakoff recommends leading with a "positive alternative" or truth of what an equitably renovated society would look like, establishing your values in the process. This probably works at professional networking events as well, transforming you into a confident, walking resumé. Otherwise, teeing off with what's *not* hunky-dory further normalizes the status quo in our unconscious brains whether we're hearing or speaking it.

On a personal level, this means that if you want to influentially exercise your feminism, *you* are all you need to start. Finally, we have some agency around here! We pay so much attention to *who* is doing feminism, when it would be more effective to focus on the *what* of our collective goals of social justice and compassionate humaning. Instead of being feminists who react to culture, let's proactively and preemptively showcase our feminisms as tangible, positive alternatives to the disingenuous and discriminatory subtexts of faux empowerment. Not only does really, truly challenging our own ideas sharpen our truth, but it also fosters points of solidarity. That combo of self-reflection and support is essential to successfully dropkick surrounding patriarchal bullsh*t.

saying it with style

Florynce "Flo" Kennedy was a lawyer, Black Power activist, and second-wave feminist force of nature. In 1974, when People magazine described her as "the biggest, loudest and indisputably, the rudest mouth on the battleground," Flo took it as a compliment.

That was a year after she'd led a "pee-in" at Harvard (with fake urine) to protest the lack of women's bathrooms on campus. The female students had sought her out and requested her help because they knew Flo could get their message across.[4] You may have heard one of her most famous—and misappropriated— zingers: "If men could get pregnant, abortion would be a sacrament."

She also put her wardrobe to work for the cause. Rarely seen without her signature cowboy hat, pink sunglasses, and red nails, Flo dressed as loudly and irreverently as she championed racial and gender equality. Her public image flouted rules courting respectability as a woman of color; she gave zero f*cks how she was judged. In 1968, when Flo served as legal adviser to Valerie Solanas, the legit misandrist who shot Andy Warhol, the judge threatened to kick her out for wearing pants. "Well, your honor," Flo volleyed back, "you are there in a dress."

Almost twenty years prior, talking back won Flo a spot in law school. When Columbia Law School initially denied her admission on the basis of race, it reversed course after Flo threatened a public lawsuit. After college, her law degree and politics converged—her colorful career highlights include co-founding the National Organization for Women, representing Billie Holiday against souped-up drug charges, and attempting to sue the Catholic Church for tax evasion to protest their vocal abortion opposition.

"Make noise. Cause trouble," Flo advised. "You may not win right away, but you'll sure have a lot more fun."

online call-out culture

What's more likely to get someone to listen? Calling them and their ideas a sh*t sandwich with extra stupid mayo? Or calmly pointing out why their words are harmful? If somebody's pressed your buttons and said ignorant things, keeping your cool can be awfully difficult. With a single retweet, it's so deliciously easy to make sure countless strangers note your disapproval and pile on.

Shame is a pretty basic, human-nature way to try to keep folks in line, but online "shame-storming," as *Bloomberg* writer Megan McArdle put it in 2015, removes any shred of social context from the conversation. In erasing empathy and allowing outrage to rapidly spiral, shame-storming weaponizes communication against strangers and can lead to real-life consequences ranging from losing jobs and having to move to grappling with PTSD. As journalist Jon Ronson put it in his 2015 book *So You've Been Publicly Shamed*, "When we find ourselves shaming people in a manner that echoes their transgression, that should set off alarm bells."

Calling jerks out has its place—and we've already established that women's anger is normal and justified—but is rushing to judgment and yelling at people on the internet really the most effective method?

Before you stoke an online shame storm, ask yourself:

- Do I understand what this person meant, and is it any of my business?

- Am I helping, or will my involvement complicate things for the people involved?

- Do the people on whose behalf I'm pissed off actually have the situation under control?

- Is this important enough to prompt me to take a stand?

- If so, can I counter the perceived jerkishness in a more productive way, like donating to Planned Parenthood if they're talking smack about reproductive rights, or to Girls Who Code if someone's trolling a woman in the tech space?

And if you do jump into the fray, remember to let calm prevail. Ask questions, consider the answers, and thoughtfully respond. The internet is often a terrible place full of people who are ready to get really angry really fast. You don't owe anyone your time and energy, and no one owes you theirs, so it's okay to jump back out. Plus, leading an internet mob—as opposed to striking up an actual discourse or just ignoring it—doesn't make you a hero; it simply makes you someone who tweets a lot. When we get defensive, we're more likely to misinterpret and get resentful. Instead, pause, take a breath, and remember: Happiness and kindness—and butting out—are infinitely healthier and more rewarding than self-righteousness.

calling in: changing minds or wasting time?

Okay, so we're well aware that the internet can be a hellscape sometimes. But what if your IRL interactions aren't much better?

Let's say your Aunt Martha and her friends have been watching some Fox News and reading some alt-right fearmongering blogs. They post their fears to Facebook and Twitter, talk about them on their lunch breaks, and wind up reinforcing one another's limited worldviews—to the point where, when Aunt Martha walks through the door for Thanksgiving, she's guns a-blazin' with some racist or transphobic bullsh*t.

Take a deep breath. Calling people out face-to-face isn't as easy as the whole online shame-storming thing, but you might be able to speak up without either one of you setting the centerpiece on fire. Here's what you need to know before you engage.

- **What doesn't work:** Trying to confront Aunt Martha with studies or articles that clash with her worldviews might push her further into the cozy embrace of her closely held beliefs. Has saying, "Well, actually . . . " ever worked for anyone? She's just going to go back to her bad-news friends and get a feel-good rush when they validate her. The more validated she feels, the less successful your attempts to change her mind by reasoning with her will be.

- **The loophole:** People start to question their beliefs if and when they realize they don't fully understand the ins and outs of their positions or those positions' implications.

- **The strategy:** Ditch the moralizing, the pleading, the insults, and the smugness. Instead, employ empathy, honesty, and curiosity. State how you feel. Ask Aunt Martha not just why she believes what she does, but how the ideas and policies she supports actually function and affect people. Follow up with "Why?" a few more times. Together, think through the implications of those beliefs. Light bulbs might not go off right away, but it's a more promising start than having a shouting match.

- **The dodging maneuver:** Beware **whataboutism**, a tactic meant to deflect criticism and derail from the topic at hand by insinuating that the other person's a hypocrite. Let your auntie know you see what she means, but that bringing up Hillary Clinton's emails isn't helpful to the topic at hand.

- **When to hang it up:** Things getting heated or a little off track isn't necessarily a sign to step on the brake, but the conversation has clearly derailed when the insults and personal attacks start flying. Tell Auntie you'll have to agree to disagree for now, and maybe you can reconnect when you've both cooled down.

Remember: You can't always change people's minds. What you *can* control is how you react, communicate, and treat others.

coalition construction

Building a strong, diverse coalition in the name of revolution and activism isn't quite the same as building a friend group. Sure, it involves the same willingness to actively listen and learn about yourself and others, but it also requires an openness to getting a little uncomfortable and working with people across multiple identities—people you might have little in common with beyond a handful of world-changing goals.

"Coalition work is not work done in your home. Coalition work must be done in the streets. And it is some of the most dangerous work you can do. And you shouldn't look for comfort," singer, composer, and activist Bernice Johnson Reagon told a crowd in 1981. "Some people will come to a coalition and they rate the success of the coalition on whether or not they feel good when they get there. They're not looking for a coalition; they're looking for a home! . . . In a coalition, you have to give, and it is different from your home."[5]

And that coalition will only get so far with homogenous perspectives from people who all look, think, and act alike. Starting out with a supportive network of people just like you can be empowering and healing, giving you a nurturing home base of support from which to grow. But ultimately, as Reagon argued, "that's nationalism."

"At a certain stage nationalism is crucial to a people if you are going to ever impact as a group in your own interest," she said. "Nationalism at another point becomes reactionary because it is totally inadequate for surviving in the world with many peoples."

It's true that our chosen groups and labels can make us inflexible, dogmatic, and closed off to anything that challenges our identity. But those labels can also have a magical effect, inspiring solidarity and self-definition. They can even be springboards for political action.

In 1977, a group of black women in Washington, D.C., were fed up with the National Women's Conference action plan. The two-hundred-page document contained only a few paragraphs specifically addressing women who weren't white, so the group set to work creating a substitute. With their "Black Women's Agenda," the group traveled to the Houston conference only to realize other minority women wanted to be included in the effort and felt doubly overlooked.

Out of those discussions and negotiations, a new political identity took shape: **women of color**. Speaking in 2011, reproductive justice activist and organizer Loretta Ross said the term holds a "solidarity definition, a commitment to work in collaboration with other oppressed women of color who have been 'minoritized.'"[6]

The label was a way to look beyond the biological. "When you choose to work with other people who are minoritized by oppression," Ross said, "You've lifted yourself out of that basic identity into another political being and another political space."

reach out and be a better ally

Consider the current frameworks of government, capitalism, and white-supremacist, heterosexist patriarchy and how these power structures support, oppress, and otherwise collide with individuals' agency, abilities, and goals. Be prepared to push back and speak up, even—and especially—if those institutions have benefited you in the past. Seek out different voices so you're not trapped in a perspective-reinforcing echo chamber that minimizes others' points of view. And try Google or a good book before asking marginalized folks to educate you on *their* oppression. For help overcoming the fear of rejection and misunderstanding to connect with someone who seems different, let's look to Japanese American activist Yuri Kochiyama, who launched a life of advocacy, allyship, and agitation after her release from a World War II internment camp.

1. Listen and Critique

Yuri was an apolitical twenty-one-year-old when she and her family were sent to an internment camp in 1942 after the Japanese bombing of Pearl Harbor. Having been mostly sheltered from outright racism in her suburban hometown, Yuri felt her eyes open as she listened to the stories of older internees. Even still, "It didn't make me political," Yuri said, "because I didn't understand the politics of why these things were happening."[7] That awakening was in the mail, though.

Yuri's political consciousness shifted into protest once she moved to Harlem in the 1960s and began to follow the civil rights movement. In 1963, Yuri spotted Malcolm X in a courthouse and reached out to him—literally. He accepted her handshake and her desire to talk about segregation, inviting her to his office. He was critical to her continued political awakening, inviting her to attend meetings at his Organization of Afro-American Unity. Through their friendship, Yuri began to understand widespread systemic racism and question her own less radical approach to injustice.

2. Ask How You Can Help

Before you step over or go around the people you're trying to help, find out whether your intentions are in line with the goals of people who are affected and already doing the work.

As Yuri listened to her elders in the internment camp, her skills as an organizer blossomed. Inspired by their stories, she launched a letter-writing campaign to support Japanese American troops who were in the difficult position of serving a country that now deeply distrusted them.

Fast-forward to New York in the 1960s, and Yuri maintained her methods. She and her husband established a group to help ostracized Japanese- and Korean American soldiers find recreation and housing. And she invited local activists, political speakers, and freedom riders to her Harlem home and fought alongside neighbors for better schools in the community.

3. Stand Up to Bullies

Whether you simply refuse to participate in bullsh*t behavior or actively tell jerks to stop their abuse, don't stand for cruelty, discrimination, or prejudice that worsens oppression. It's never your job to change someone's mind, but you can be straightforward from a personal standpoint: Express your discomfort, request an end to the comments, and let your behavior reflect your beliefs.

When it came to standing up for marginalized folks' rights, Yuri was willing to walk the walk. In 1963, she was among a slew of people arrested in Brooklyn for protesting discriminatory hiring practices of construction crews that refused to hire black and Puerto Rican workers.

4. Support the Movement

Being an ally is about helping others and dismantling oppression, so it's critical to put the well-being of the movement at the forefront.

In the wake of Malcolm X's assassination in 1965, more activists were arrested and suppressed. Yuri penned letters to political prisoners, helped organize their legal defense, maintained detailed records on who was imprisoned, and authored articles for civil rights publications. Arguing that "political prisoners are the heartbeat of the struggle," Yuri made it her mission to support them.

Through the rest of the 1960s and '70s, she mentored emerging Asian American activists, protested the Vietnam War and nuclear proliferation, and demanded reparations for Japanese American internees.

Yuri was irrepressible. Once her activist fire was lit as a young woman, she spent the rest of her life lighting the way for others, a process that involved hashing out her differences with and learning from an ally like Malcolm X. She was able to take on big-picture battles for civil rights without making the fight about herself, and she joined coalitions not to take control, but to give to the movement all she could. What can you bring to the table that adds to the conversation without silencing others?

And how can you keep going once you're there?

 CLAP BACK WITH FACTS

getting involved

It's a privilege to have the time and ability to voluntarily serve your community and stand up for what you believe in.

- **LABELS MATTER.** A 2017 study of American Millennials found a reticence to describe themselves as "activists," a term associated with active, public campaigning. They were more likely to call themselves "supporters" of a cause. Regardless, dudes were more likely to call themselves activists than women were.[8] Figures.

- **WOMEN LIKE HELPING.** If you're looking for a way to make a difference, the first two ideas that usually pop up are donating some money or volunteering some time. It turns out that women do both more often than men, and we're also more likely to say helping other people makes us happier than helping ourselves.[9]

- **INVOLVEMENT EMPOWERS.** Volunteering reduces feelings of hopelessness, and working for the collective good through neighborhood activism helps people feel a stronger sense of control over their lives. All of these factors bolster mental health.

- **MONEY AND MEDIA TALK.** Organized, targeted boycotts of corporations à la #GrabYourWallet are effective when they grab major media attention. Once news of a consumer boycott against one of *Fortune* magazine's "Most Admired" companies hits the media—and stays there for a while, which is key—the targeted company's stock price tends to fall almost 1 percent per day. Restoring their reputation matters, and about a quarter end up making some concession.[10]

maintain momentum

Whenever you experience inevitable adversity, pain, or loss, how do you move on and start over with grit, grace, and panache, rather than getting mired in fear, bitterness, and regret? This question is especially poignant when thinking about the hard work of activism, where the road can be long and the gains incremental.

Psychologist Edith Chen coined the term **shift and persist** to describe the coping strategy of hardy people who recognize and accept stress as a learning opportunity and who press forward through adversity.[11] Being mentally and emotionally nimble enough to roll with the punches and find a deeper meaning is key to resilience, as are confidence and control. Not just thinking but *believing* you're in the driver's seat—and that if you fail, you'll be able to learn from it—influences your ability to get back up and move on. And that's crucial to making sure you can sustain that persistence for the long haul.

Rather than staying deflated and helpless, throwing up your hands, and assuming all is lost, you can counteract some of your pessimistic reflexes by asking yourself a few questions.

- What can I control, and how can I minimize the damage right now?

- How can I work with others to make change now and over the long haul?

- What positive impact can I have right now, and what can I learn from this mess going forward?

Forgiveness—of others and of yourself—can have a pretty huge positive impact. The active process of working through your pain and forgiving can help unburden you of any heavy resentment, anger, and rumination you've been toting around. The benefits go beyond the spiritual or metaphorical, though; you just might feel physically lighter and more powerful. In one study, people who forgave perceived hills to be less steep and were able to jump higher during a fitness test.[12]

While you're doing all that forgiveness-induced high-jumping, take a minute to be grateful for the other measurable physical perks. Practicing forgiveness has been linked to lower cholesterol, blood pressure, anxiety, depression, and stress, not to mention lower levels of physical pain, a reduced risk of heart attack, and better sleep.

Being trapped in negativity can leave you feeling powerless, and ruminating also increases aggression and clouds your ability to clearly consider the incident. Choosing to forgive might seem overwhelming or even impossible for people who've just been hurt because it involves taking a long, hard look at the offender, the offense, and your own imperfect self. Let's break it down by reviewing some basic steps for moving on:

- **Recognize and reflect.** You can't do the work until you know there's work to do. Acknowledge the injustice, examine how it affected you, and give yourself time to process your emotions. You might feel angry, ashamed, or guilty, particularly if the incident comes with social stigma and victim blaming. Early on, there might be social, religious, or gender-based pressure to forgive, but forgiveness can't begin until you release your anger and desire for revenge.

- **Be kind to yourself.** People low on the well-being scale tend to be quick to blame themselves for negative experiences. Have compassion for yourself. Whatever abuse, pain, and shame you've suffered at the hands of another person is not your fault. Self-condemnation reflects self-loathing and a desire for punishment, but you do not deserve to be treated poorly. Accepting that you cannot control other people, and therefore cannot control their harmful actions, will start setting you free to learn to forgive yourself. Ultimately, practicing compassion for yourself strengthens your ability to be kinder and more generous in general.

- **Empathize and understand.** The last thing you might want to do is put yourself in the shoes of someone who hurt you, but empathizing with—not excusing—them can breed compassion and understanding. Testing this out on college students showed that those who focused on the ideas of unconditional love and empathy toward an offender had a steep decline in blood pressure and heart rate.[13]

- **Choose to move forward.** When you're ready, you can decide to forgive once you realize that holding on to the pain and negativity is doing more harm than good. But the motivation to forgive can't stop at "It's the nice thing to do," or "I'm better than she is if I forgive." Truly relinquishing your pain to direct positive feelings toward the offender takes a commitment—but in doing so, you'll make more room for gratitude, enjoying the present, and reclaiming your power and confidence.

It's okay to grieve over a loss or setback, but feeling sorry for yourself won't help you move forward. Don't fear the pivot. Make the conscious decision to pick yourself up and go on.

shirley

Under the 1968 campaign slogan "Unbought and Unbossed," SHIRLEY CHISHOLM—only the second black woman elected to the New York state legislature—earned 67 percent of the vote on her way to becoming the first black woman in Congress. A teacher and day care director-turned-legislator, Shirley was cold-shouldered in Washington but beloved by women activists and feminists. The summer after her historic election, Rosa Parks introduced Shirley at the Women's Political Action Committee, admiringly calling her a "pepper pot," or feisty woman.[14]

As the race for the 1972 presidential election heated up, Shirley decided to push history along. "I ran because most people thought the country was not ready for a black candidate, not ready for a woman candidate," she said. "Someday—it was time in 1972 to make that someday come."[15]

On the campaign trail, Shirley endured assassination attempts, filed a lawsuit to participate in debates, rebuffed calls to drop out and make room for white opponents, and listened to Missouri Representative Bill Clay publicly question her sanity. Fully aware of her "double handicap" as a black woman, she saw her black male colleagues turn their backs over fears she'd bring her women's-lib nonsense on the campaign trail, and watched her feminist allies support male candidates, white or black, over her. Lacking support, Shirley had to step aside.

She fought, and she lost. She shifted, and still, she persisted.

Shirley returned to Congress a massively popular figure: A 1974 Gallup poll named her one of the top ten most-admired women, ahead of Coretta Scott King and Jackie O. She continued to serve for many years, eventually becoming the first black woman to serve on the powerful House Rules Committee. In 1982, she left Congress on her own terms, deciding not to seek reelection. Even then, she cofounded the National Political Congress of Black Women, stumped for Jesse Jackson's 1984 and 1988 presidential campaigns, and taught at Mount Holyoke before eventually retiring.

In her autobiography, Shirley wrote: "That I am a national figure because I was the first person in 192 years to be at once a congressman, black, and a woman proves, I would think, that our society is not yet either just or free."[16]

WHAT SHIRLEY WOULD DO TO TODAY: The unstoppable force would pound the pavement as a census taker, just as she did in 1970, to ensure the people of her neighborhood felt secure standing up and being counted amid a politically charged time.

step up and act out

Your unladylike mission, and one you're most definitely choosing to accept, is to take all the skills you've been practicing—your self-worth and self-care, allyship and awareness, anger and ambition—and strengthen them with action.

Stepping up and speaking out against injustice is often a privilege and a risk. Not everyone can spare the energy or resources it takes to fight back. And for sure, it's easier to do nothing, to ignore, or to wait for others to steer. But with the relationships you've been fortifying and the bridges you've been building, you can find a self-affirming place in the larger feminist collective. The unladylike, unexpected route is one of action—it's one of hellraising and confrontation, of owning our messy realities and responsibilities and choosing to do something.

Plus, it's a good-for-you cycle. Volunteering, for instance, is correlated with better mental health and trust. Membership in a movement fosters a sense of collective identity, pushing participants to continue fighting for change. The longer activists spend dedicating their time and energy to a cause, the more the movement roots itself in them as an intrinsic value and facet of their identity. This propels them to continue not only educating themselves, but bolstering the belief that they can—and have to—make a difference.

Get It Together

Even more delightful than any personal, internal benefits? Teaming up to take a hammer to the status quo. Women in groups never cease to confuse and scare the patriarchy, whether we're going to the bathroom together or marching for our rights. We're inevitably side-eyed as if we're witches casting spells to destroy their crops and leave them impotent. Maybe we are, maybe we aren't; the thing about women getting together is that we're so good at it, and just like witches in a coven, we gain strength from our collaboration.

The magic of rallies, protests, marches, strikes, and sit-ins lies not only in the optics of signs and crowds, but in the power of raising our voices with other impassioned people so those in power are forced to listen. Take some notes from women who know how to get angry, get organized, and claim their space.

WALK OUT

Building on the momentum of the 2017 Women's Marches, the #MeToo movement, and the continuing push against a rising global tide of nationalism, activists came into 2018 ready for a fight and unwilling to accept the same old sh*t.

On March 8, International Women's Day, more than 5 million women in Spain ditched their jobs, chores, and shopping to call for an end to sexist oppression, violence, unfair working conditions, and unequal pay. Whether walking out for a few hours or taking the entire day off, the striking women had the support of unions, politicians, and public figures. Shouting, "if we stop, the world stops," hundreds of thousands of Spanish women marched through streets in cities across the country, venus symbols painted on their cheeks.

Their rabblerousing echoes that of their Icelandic sisters. After the United Nations declared 1975 to be International Women's Year, representatives from some of Iceland's biggest women's groups got together to figure out how to mark the milestone. Members of the radical Red Stockings group pushed the idea of a strike: Women would leave their homes and jobs, their husbands and children, to protest unfair pay and highlight through their absence just how much their work contributed to society. The group agreed, settling on the name "Women's Day Off." On October 24, 1975, 90 percent of the country's women went on strike. A crowd of twenty-five thousand women gathered, forcing several businesses to close. The strike paid off: In 1976, the country barred workplace and school gender discrimination, and in 1980, citizens elected their first female president, Vígdís Finnbogadóttir.[17]

find your path

Depending on your creativity, mobility, and how much time and money you have to spare, there are countless ways to build community and make a difference.

Time

- Raise awareness online.
- Pitch your story to news outlets.
- Call your lawmakers, but keep it concise.
- Write letters, postcards, and emails to friends, family, community leaders, and lawmakers.
- Volunteer from home. Maybe you can build websites, enter data, or help with research.
- Strategize events, marches, and rallies.
- Keep learning as issues evolve.

Time and Money

- Create banners and posters for marchers.
- Rent vans and buy food to help transport and feed protesters.
- Bail protesters out of jail if they get arrested during an event.
- Start a nonprofit of your own.
- Launch a fund or scholarship.

Money

- Donate money to your cause. Organizations love when you commit to making a monthly donation, even if it's small.
- Take out ads on behalf of your cause in print, online, or on TV.

Mobility and Time

- Canvass your neighborhood. Wear comfy shoes and prep for rejection.
- Lobby your legislators in person.
- Volunteer in person.

Your Pick!

Ask yourself: What would an unladylike activist do?

Mobility and Money

- Drop off personal items like tampons, socks, and underwear to shelters.
- Vote with your dollars by supporting progressive- and women-owned businesses.

Mobility

Fold education, activism, or small degrees of change into your daily routine, whether it's carpooling, reading up on local government, or something else that could fit into a lunch break.

You don't even have to be a fully grown adult to change the national conversation, though. Six days after Spanish women walked off the job in 2018, kids across the US walked out of school to call for gun control and mark a month since a shooter had killed seventeen students at Marjory Stoneman Douglas High School in Parkland, Florida. In a single month, fed up with complacency, powered by social media savvy, and led by badasses like Emma Gonzáles—a bisexual, Cuban American 18-year-old with a shaved head—Florida teens and their allies accomplished what no adults had managed to do: squarely keep the country's focus on gun laws and even get corporations to sever ties with the National Rifle Association.

SPREAD THE WORD

No massive Twitter following? No problem. Turn to your galpal network for help instead.

When Philadelphia craft shop owner Phile Chionesu wanted to bring thousands of black women together for an empowering rally, she didn't have any high-powered connections or experienced promoters at her side. And yet, largely through underground organizing and word of mouth, and with help from a group of fellow Philly women, she successfully planned, promoted, and launched the 1997 Million Woman March, bringing hundreds of thousands together to encourage unity and community involvement.

Nearly seventy years earlier, Igbo women in Nigeria fed up with the burdens of British colonial rule and taxation took to the streets. Their November 1929 protest, which the women called a "war" and the Brits dismissed as a "riot," was sparked by an elderly woman named Nwanyeruwa who turned to her network of badass lady friends with her frustrations.[18] Together, they helped spread the word throughout the region by passing along palm leaves signaling it was time for action. Their efforts paid off: More than ten thousand women gathered outside a government building for days, some of them in traditional warrior dress with face paint. Eventually, word spread even farther, and women across two provinces joined in protesting sexist, racist laws. The mass protests successfully sparked changes in how the region was governed and taxed, putting more power back in the people's hands.

FIND YOUR FIT

Squeezing thousands of likeminded folks into a single space on short notice isn't always the best or easiest tactic. Sometimes our activist missions require a little attention-grabbing creativity. Ever heard of a protest *quinceañera*?

In July 2017, amid the heat of a Texas summer, a small group of teen girls gathered at the state Capitol decked out in confection-like gowns normally reserved for a *quinceañera*, or a fifteenth-birthday celebration. Music was playing, but it wasn't a party; the fifteen girls were there to protest anti-immigrant legislation referred to as the "show me your papers" law and meet

FIELD NOTES

our sisters' steps

There's a lot to learn from our predecessors, as well as folks working for change right now.

- **GOOGLE IT FIRST.** Take a cue from the 2017 Women's March and do your due diligence before you greenlight an event or a hashtag. Make sure you're not swiping some other movement's name or undermining work people in the space are already doing.

- **GET THE WORD OUT.** Whether by passing palm leaves or posting to social media, get your plans into other women's hands ASAP.

- **HAVE A CLEAR GOAL.** It's not that your march needs a tagline, but being able to communicate a clear message about why you're taking action will get more people engaged and on the same page, and it

will ultimately be what helps sustain and grow the movement beyond the march.

- **BE INCLUSIVE AND EMPATHETIC.** Think beyond your own experience of the world and look for ways to include passionate participants across a spectrum of ethnicities, religions, abilities, genders, and economic realities.

- **ATTRACT ATTENTION.** Politeness won't win you any attention, and keeping to yourself won't make the news, so don't be scared to get loud—literally, and with some creative clothing choices.

- **KEEP THE ENERGY ALIVE.** Marches and rallies might be a reaction, but they're not the end of the action. Bring your energy, lessons, and goals home to push for change in your own backyard and beyond.

with lawmakers to express their concerns. While the girls weren't able to stop the law, they found their voice and made a bold statement.

Speaking of voices, you could always try singing your discontent. On August 9, 1956, anti-apartheid leaders including Albertina Sisulu and Lilian Ngoyi led a historic protest of South Africa's racist pass laws, which dictated where black citizens could travel. Twenty thousand women from all over the country, many with children in tow, marched to the government buildings in Pretoria to lay their petitions outside the prime minister's doors. Then the entire crowd fell silent. After thirty minutes, the women began to sing the hymn "Nkosi sikelel' iAfrika" ("Lord Bless Africa") and the protest song "Wathint' Abafazi, Wathint' Imbokodo"—in English, "You strike a woman, you strike a rock!"—before dispersing. Pass laws would not be repealed until 1986, but Women's Day is celebrated annually in South Africa on August 9.

Going up against government officials was business as usual for Native American activist Janet McCloud. Along with members of her family and community in Washington state, McCloud was regularly harassed, threatened, and arrested in the 1960s for fishing in waters that, while technically on tribal land, weren't protected as such. Inspired by sit-ins, McCloud organized a string of "fish-ins" that earned her international attention and pissed off local game wardens. In October 1965, during a fish-in led mostly by women, state agents in speedboats rushed the protesters, rammed their boats, and threw several folks, including McCloud, in jail. Nine years later, the continued pressure paid off: In 1974, a judge upheld a nineteenth-century treaty, allowing fourteen tribes fishing access to the contested waters.

Join the Club

From grassroots to global influence, the value that unstoppable activists including these powerful women share is **collectivism**, a belief in our interdependence as part of a community. Caring for the collective means not hanging up our hats when we've gotten ours or shrugging when our privilege protects us from policies that hurt others. It means remembering our unladylike lessons and understanding that "nobody's free until everybody's free," as Fannie Lou Hamer said, and that it's on us to "lift as we climb," just like Mary Church Terrell and her club-women sisters did.

In short, to make a sustainable *movement*—rather than a move that benefits us alone—it's imperative that collectivism inform our feminism and our politics. That perspective demands we fight for universal health care, paid family leave, affordable education, common-sense gun control, and higher minimum wages, not just because each activist would benefit from a safer environment, but because *everyone* would, regardless of our rank on the social or economic ladder. A collectivist approach gives us all space to pursue our best lives.

Activism is a visible manifestation of an unladylike life. It's a sign you're not content to accept the status quo. It's evidence you're willing to break out of your comfort zone and fight for a force that's bigger than you alone. And however you contribute, it's your moral, ethical, and unladylike responsibility to step up and do something.

What do you believe in? What do you stand for? Get unladylike and find out.

ACKNOWLEDGMENTS

From C and C

This book would not have happened—or it would have taken much, much, *much* longer to materialize—without the support, guidance, enthusiasm, and gentle prodding of a handful of amazing people.

Our agent, Monica Odom, reached out to two scattered podcasters in 2014, and over the past couple of years (whoa, has it been that long?), whether acting as Business Monica or Confidante Monica, she has shown us endless patience, support, and love. She's brilliant and adorable, fierce and loving, and we're so lucky to have her.

We adore our illustrator, Tyler Feder, for being an incredibly loving, giving, vulnerable, and hilarious copilot, always open to new ideas—including creating a book with two strangers from the internet.

The tearful Slack conversation with those two ladies the day after the 2016 election was an excellent and so-necessary way to get out of bed and recommit to this book's importance.

Shout-outs also to our legal and financial dream team of John Seay, Helen Ngo, and Ava Rhodes. Y'all have helped steer us into entrepreneurship like the bunch of business badasses that you are. Thank you for helping us stand up for ourselves.

We've been constantly in awe of our Ten Speed Press team—editor Kaitlin Ketchum and designer Betsy Stromberg—for their hard work and enthusiastic pursuit of and belief in this project. Oh, and for keeping us in line and under word count. (Caroline is especially grateful for the word-count help.) Thanks also to Kristin Casemore, Natalie Mulford, Dan Myers, Kristi Hein, and Julie Mazur.

We're grateful to our families, friends, and partners, too, not only for their support and encouragement, but also for their understanding when they wouldn't see or hear from us for days on end. We've both missed dinners, drinks, shows, birthdays, and other get-togethers while locked away researching and writing. Thank you for continuing to love us and invite us places. Please keep doing that.

As feminist nerds with a love of history and an unquenchable thirst for women's wisdom, we're indebted to all of the women we've learned so much from in researching for this book—both the ones we've profiled and the ones who've remained in the background of the stories and advice we share.

And some of our deepest thanks—truly, gratitude that's so intense it's almost impossible to express—goes to the loyal folks who've listened to us and followed us since our days hosting *Stuff Mom Never Told You*. Thank you, thank you, thank you for staying with us all these years, for sharing your stories, hopes, and fears, and for continuing to ask about our progress. Your enthusiasm, curiosity, and trust have kept us motivated, and your emails have made us laugh and cry. In reaching out, you've propelled us forward. This book is for all women looking to find their way, but it's especially for you.

 ## From Cristen

When I think about everything that brought me to *Unladylike*, I see my mom teaching me to read and ferrying me back and forth every week to our neighborhood bookmobile. I hear my dad in the kitchen telling me that if I can read, I can do anything. I think of Bill, Noelle, Matthew, and Anna, who indulged my tween poetry phase, laughed at my jokes, and let me be my truest, strangest self.

I remember running into my eleventh-grade English teacher, Mrs. Leary, not long after graduating high school. She was the type of hardass teacher who doled out compliments so selectively you knew they were genuine. She also played favorites, and I wasn't one of them. But years later when I saw her again, she took my arm with conviction and told me to bet on myself. It took another ten years or so, but I'm finally getting brave enough to do it.

To my lifers. To the core four. To my lady boos. I wouldn't be here without y'all. That goes double for my work wife, life coach, and feminist coconspirator, Caroline Ervin. I'm so glad we got drinks at that sporting pub a lifetime ago!

Finally, my favorite feminist and husband, Chris, thank you. Thank you for showing me unending encouragement, love, and patience. Thank you for driving across London while I frantically typed on my iPad. Thank you for listening whenever I felt hopeless. Thank you for encouraging me to quit my job and do the thing already. Thank you for making our life together.

 ## From Caroline

First of all, I couldn't have done this without the love of my parents and my person. Thank you for the space and the encouragement,for being a sounding board, for getting me out of the house sometimes, for not letting me fall *completely* apart, and for distracting me with *Mario Kart*. I owe you *so many* hugs and dinners. Your love and patience have meant everything to me.

I wouldn't be where I am without my English teachers at the Walker School, and without the mentorship and respect I received from Doug Wine and James Folker, two dudes who dragged me into newspapers and therefore accidentally helped me find a semi-productive way to channel my anxiety.

And Ellen Cornwell and Elizabeth Letts—you probably have no idea what our front-porch book chats meant to me, but I have to tell you that they truly meant the world. Your encouragement—and, in Elizabeth's case, shared enthusiasm over obscure feminist history—was a touchstone to which I returned throughout the process. (Ellen, I'll write that family history book one of these days.)

Finally, I have to thank my work wife, my friend of more than a decade, and the person who challenges and inspires me and makes me ugly-laugh every time we're together: Cristen Conger. You have led me on a truly unexpected, life-changing adventure, and I will be forever grateful.

Cristen Conger and Caroline Ervin are the Atlanta-based, journalistically trained, research-addicted hosts of the podcast *Unladylike* and the cofounders of Unladylike Media, where they produce inclusive digital media.

As creators and former cohosts of *Stuff Mom Never Told You*, iTunes' first (or close to it) educational women's podcast, the pair has spent the better part of a decade contextualizing constructs, debunking body myths, sourcing cultural stereotypes, and overusing *heteronormative* in casual conversation. They're fun.

Cristen Conger

Cristen Conger is a writer, podcaster, and professional womansplainer. Her personal inspiration traces back to childhood and the dual impact of her mom teaching her how to read and her dad once telling her, "If you can read, you can do anything." She's been on a mission to prove him right ever since.

An Athens, Georgia, native, Cristen graduated from The University of Georgia Grady College of Journalism in 2006, though not before meeting her future work wife, Caroline Ervin, at the *Red & Black* campus newspaper. Before starting Unladylike Media, Cristen was a senior staff writer and host at HowStuffWorks.com, where she created and cohosted the *Stuff Mom Never Told You* podcast and YouTube channel. Offline, Cristen has spoken to audiences large and small, including SXSW Interactive, the Carter Center, Creative Mornings, and MailChimp. In whatever free time she has left, Cristen takes way too many pics of her dog, practices yoga, and guilt-binges *Real Housewives*.

To learn more about Cristen and her digital media portfolio, sashay away to her personal website, cristenconger.com.

Caroline Ervin

Caroline Ervin is a feminist investigator working to uncover the hidden histories of women who've changed the world. A 2006 graduate of the University of Georgia's Grady College of Journalism, she employs her word-nerd background in her digital media approach to educating audiences about history, health, politics, and pop culture through a gendered lens.

In her role as a public speaker, Caroline has addressed issues ranging from sexism and STEM jobs to social media and body image as part of the SXSW Interactive festival, the Clemson University Women's Leadership Conference, the Carter Center's diversity-awareness sessions, and Vanderbilt University's Eating Disorders Awareness Week. A highlight remains enlightening a fundraiser crowd about the power and beauty of the clitoris.

When she has time for a break, you can find her relaxing over some genealogy research with a gin and tonic. She should probably go outside more often.

Connect with Caroline at carolineervin.co and on Twitter @thecarolineerv.

Tyler Feder

Tyler Feder finger-painted the invitations to her first birthday party and hasn't stopped creating since. A Northwestern University graduate and calligrapher's daughter, Tyler draws playful illustrations that focus on intersectional feminism and mental health.

Since taking the plunge and posting her artwork online, Tyler has had the pleasure of illustrating for Netflix, Comedy Central, and ESPN. Her artwork has been featured by the Huffington Post, Glamour, and (most importantly) Mindy Kaling's Instagram account. After the 2016 US election, Tyler drew free portraits of over a hundred marginalized people and compiled them into a print that raises money for the ACLU.

When she's not busy illustrating, Tyler enjoys jigsaw puzzles, milky coffee, and never leaving the house.

You can keep up with her on Instagram @tylerfeder and support her work at roaringsoftly.com.

NOTES

INTRODUCTION

1. Lisa B. Thompson, *Beyond the Black Lady: Sexuality and the New African American Middle Class* (Champaign, IL: University of Illinois Press, 2009).

2. Kimberle Crenshaw, "Demarginalizing the Intersection of Race and Sex: A Black Feminist Critique of Antidiscrimination Doctrine, Feminist Theory and Antiracist Politics," *University of Chicago Legal Forum*, no. 1 (1989): Article 8.

3. Joshua Rothman, "The Origins of 'Privilege'," *New Yorker*, May 12, 2014, http://www.newyorker.com/books/page-turner/the-origins-of-privilege.

CHAPTER 1

1. Jaime Grant et al., *Injustice at Every Turn: A Report of the National Transgender Discrimination Survey* (Washington: National Center for Transgender Equality and National Gay and Lesbian Task Force, 2011).

2. Torben Iversen and Frances Rosenbluth, *Women, Work, and Politics: The Political Economy of Gender Inequality* (New Haven: Yale University Press, 2010).

3. Lisa Wade and Myra Marx Ferree, *Gender: Ideas, Interactions, Institutions* (New York: W. W. Norton, 2014).

4. Elizabeth Sweet, "How Did Toys Get Stereotyped by Sex?" *New York Times* (December 22, 2014): https://www.nytimes.com/roomfordebate/2014/12/22/why-should-toys-come-in-pink-and-blue/how-did-toys-get-stereotyped-by-sex.

5. Anne Harrington, "The Fall of the Schizophrenogenic Mother," *The Lancet* 379, no. 9823 (April 7, 2012): 1292–1293. http://www.thelancet.com/journals/lancet/article/PIIS0140-6736(12)60546-7/fulltext.

6. Moya Bailey, "More on the Origin of Misogynoir," http://moyazb.tumblr.com/post/84048113369/more-on-the-origin-of-misogynoir.

7. Gene Demby, "What We Know (and Don't Know) About 'Missing White Women Syndrome'," NPR, April 13, 2017, https://www.npr.org/sections/codeswitch/2017/04/13/523769303/what-we-know-and-dont-know-about-missing-white-women-syndrome.

8. Serena Mayeri, "Pauli Murray and the Twentieth-Century Quest for Legal and Social Equality," *Indiana Journal of Law and Social Equity* 2, no. 1 (2014): 80–90. https://www.repository.law.indiana.edu/cgi/viewcontent.cgi?referer=https://www.google.com/&httpsredir=1&article=1014&context=ijlse.

9. Kathryn Schulz, "The Many Lives of Pauli Murray," *New Yorker*, April 17, 2017, https://www.newyorker.com/magazine/2017/04/17/the-many-lives-of-pauli-murray.

10. British Psychological Society (BPS), "Men, Not Ladies, First: We're Still Sexist in Writing," *Science Daily* (March 12, 2010): www.sciencedaily.com/releases/2010/03/100311092431.htm.

11. Maya Singer, "Gigi Hadid and Zayn Malik Are Part of a New Generation Who Don't See Fashion as Gendered," *Vogue*, July 13, 2017, https://www.vogue.com/article/gigi-hadid-zayn-malik-august-2017-vogue-cover-breaking-gender-codes.

12. Jo Paoletti, *Pink and Blue: Telling the Boys from the Girls in America*. (Bloomington, IN: Indiana University Press, 2012).

13. Paoletti, *Pink and Blue*.

14. Julia Serano, *Whipping Girl: A Transsexual Woman on Sexism and the Scapegoating of Femininity* (Cambridge, MA: Da Capo Press, 2016).

CHAPTER 2

1. Victoria Colliver, "Endometriosis Sufferers Long Blamed," *SF Gate*, October 30, 2012, http://www.sfgate.com/health/article/Endometriosis-sufferers-long-blamed-3994639.php.

2. Kate, Seear, *The Makings of a Modern Epidemic: Endometriosis, Gender and Politics* (New York: Routledge, 2016).

3. Dina Gusovsky, "Women Suffering in Silence: The Endometriosis Crisis," CNBC, May 19, 2016, https://www.cnbc.com/2016/05/19/this-neglected-disease-is-a-hidden-drain-on-womens-success.html.

4. S. Simoens et al., "The Burden of Endometriosis: Costs and Quality of Life of Women with Endometriosis and Treated in Referral Centres," *Human Reproduction* 27, no. 5 (September, 2012): 1292–1299.

5. Ellen B. Gold, "The Timing of the Age at Which Natural Menopause Occurs," *Obstetrics and Gynecology Clinics of North America* 38, no. 3 (September, 2011): 424–440. https://www.ncbi.nlm.nih.gov/pmc/articles/PMC3285482.

6. Olga Karapanou and Anastasios Papadimitrou, "Determinants of Menarche," *Reproductive Biology and Endocrinology* 8 (September, 2010):115. https://www.ncbi.nlm.nih.gov/pmc/articles/PMC2958977.

7. Michelle Polak, "Menstruation," in *Girl Culture: An Encyclopedia*, Volume 1, ed. Claudia Mitchell and Jacqueline Reid-Walsh (Westport, CT: Greenwood Press, 2007).

8. Markham Heid, "You Asked: What Does My Period Say about Me?" *TIME*, November 16, 2016, http://time.com/4571769/period-blood-menstrual.

9. James Hamblin, "PMS and the Wandering Womb," *The Atlantic*, October 16, 2002, https://www.theatlantic.com/health/archive/2012/10/pms-and-the-wandering-womb/263398.

10. Suyin Haynes, "How an Indian Comic Book is Teaching Girls about Their Periods," *TIME*, December 12, 2016, http://time.com/4590678/menstrupedia-aditi-gupta-taboo-india/.

11. Danielle Preiss, "Law in Nepal Sets Penalties for Forcing Woman into a Menstrual Shed," NPR, August 10, 2017, https://www.npr.org/sections/goatsandsoda/2017/08/10/542585664/law-in-nepal-sets-penalties-for-forcing-a-woman-into-a-menstrual-shed.

12. Alicia Fortinberry, "The Surgeon Who Said Women are Unfit for Highest Office Now Slices Up Some of His Colleagues," *People*, August 2, 1976, http://people.com/archive/the-surgeon-who-said-women-are-unfit-for-highest-office-now-slices-up-some-of-his-colleagues-vol-6-no-5/.

13. Anna Brown, "The Data on Women Leaders," Pew Research Center, March 17, 2017, http://www.pewsocialtrends.org/2017/03/17/the-data-on-women-leaders.

14. "Women Mayors in U.S. Cities 2017," Center for American Women in Politics, September 2017, http://www.cawp.rutgers.edu/levels_of_office/women-mayors-us-cities-2017.

15. Alana Semuels, "When Women Run Companies," *The Atlantic*, December 27, 2016, https://www.theatlantic.com/business/archive/2016/12/female-bosses-in-the-workplace/506690.

16. Leora Tananbaum, *Catfight: Women and Competition* (New York: Seven Stories Press, 2002).

17. Leslie Ashburn-Nardo, "Parenthood as a Moral Imperative? Moral Outrage and the Stigmatization of Voluntarily Childfree Women and Men," *Sex Roles* 76, no. 5-6 (March 2016): 393–401. doi: 10.1007/s11199-016-0606-1.

18. "Female Age-Related Fertility Decline," The American College of Obstetricians and Gynecologists, no. 589 (March 2014): 719–721. https://www.acog.org/Resources-And-Publications/Committee-Opinions/Committee-on-Gynecologic-Practice/Female-Age-Related-Fertility-Decline.

19. Andrea Tone, *Devices and Desires: A History of Contraceptives in America* (New York: Macmillan, 2002).

20. Rose Eveleth, "Lysol's Vintage Ads Subtly Pushed Women to Use Its Disinfectant as Birth Control," *Smithsonian*, September 30, 2013, https://www.smithsonianmag.com/smart-news/lysols-vintage-ads-subtly-pushed-women-to-use-its-disinfectant-as-birth-control-218734.

CHAPTER 3

1. Lisa Hix, "From Boy Geniuses to Mad Scientists: How Americans Got So Weird about Science," *Collectors Weekly*, August 4, 2017, https://www.collectorsweekly.com/articles/how-americans-got-so-weird-about-science.

2. Kuheli Dutt et al., "Gender Differences in Recommendation Letters for Postdoctoral Fellowships in Geoscience," *Nature Geoscience* 9 (2016): 805–808.

3. Amanda Hess, "How the Myth of Artistic Genius Excuses the Abuse of Women," *New York Times*, November 10, 2017, https://www.nytimes.com/2017/11/10/arts/sexual-harassment-art-hollywood.html.

4. Gina Rippon et al., "Recommendations for Sex/Gender Neuroimaging Research: Key Principles and Implications for Research Design, Analysis, and Interpretation," *Frontiers in Human Neuroscience* 8 (2014): 650. doi: 10.3389/fnhum.2014.00650.

5. Alison Piepmeier, *Girl Zines: Making Media, Doing Feminism* (New York: NYU Press, 2009).

6. Julie Holland, "Medicating Women's Feelings," *New York Times*, February 28, 2015, https://www.nytimes.com/2015/03/01/opinion/sunday/medicating-womens-feelings.html.

7. "Understanding the Stress Response," Harvard Health Publishing, last updated May 1, 2018, http://www.health.harvard.edu/staying-healthy/understanding-the-stress-response.

8. Audre Lorde, *I Am Your Sister: Collected and Unpublished Writings of Audre Lorde*, eds. R. P. Byrd, J. B. Cole, and B. Guy-Sheftall (Oxford, UK: Oxford University Press, 2009).

CHAPTER 4

1. Kake Young, Jane Fisher, and Maggie Kirkman, "Women's Experiences of Endometriosis: A Systematic Review and Synthesis of Qualitative Research," *Journal of Family Planning and Reproductive Health Care* 41 (2015): 225–234. doi: 10.1136/jfprhc-2013-100853.

2. National Institutes of Health, "How Many People are Affected or at Risk for PCOS?" U.S. Department of Health and Human Services, January 31, 2017. https://www.nichd.nih.gov/health/topics/pcos/conditioninfo/risk.

3. WomensHealth.gov, "Chronic fatigue syndrome." Office of Women's Health, December 20, 2017. https://www.womenshealth.gov/a-z-topics/chronic-fatigue-syndrome.

4. Thomas Gerschick, "Toward a Theory of Disability and Gender," *Signs*: Journal of Women in Culture and Society 25, no. 4 (2000): 1263–1268. https://www.journals.uchicago.edu/doi/abs/10.1086/495558.

5. Catherine Driscoll, *Girls: Feminine Adolescence in Popular Culture and Cultural Theory* (New York: Coumbia University Press, 2002).

6. M.G. Lord, *Forever Barbie: The Unauthorized Biography of a Real Doll* (New York: Walker and Company, 2004).

7. Amanda Hess, "Leave Barbie Alone! She's Not the Skinniest Doll on the Block," *Slate*, February 5, 2014, http://www.slate.com/blogs/xx_factor/2014/02/05/barbie_s_not_the_skinniest_doll_on_the_block_measuring_barbie_bratz_monster.html.

8. Viren Swami and Martin J. Tovée, "Resource Security Impacts Men's Female Breast Size Preferences," *PLOS One* 8, no. 3 (March 6, 2013). http://doi.org/10.1371/journal.pone.0057623.

9. Gudrun Doll-Tepper, Katrin Koenan, and Richard Bailey, *Sport, Education and Social Policy: The State of the Social Sciences of Sport* (London and New York: Routledge, 2016).

10. J. Scurr et al., "The Influence of the Breast on Sport and Exercise Participation in School Girls in the United Kingdom," *Journal of Adolescent Health* 58, no 2 (February 2016): 167–73.

11. J. Scurr et al., "The Influence of the Breast on Sport and Exercise," 167–73.

12. Boston Women's Health Collective, *The New Our Bodies, Ourselves: A Book by and for Women* (New York: Simon & Schuster, 1996).

13. Ana L. Flores-Mireles et al., "Urinary Tract Infections: Epidemiology, Mechanisms of Infection and Treatment Options," *Nature Reviews Microbiology* 13, no. 5 (2015): 269–284. doi:10.1038/nrmicro3432.

CHAPTER 5

1. Jada Yuan and Aaron Wong, "The First Black Trans Model had Her Face on a Box of Clairol," *New York Magazine*, December, 14, 2017, https://www.thecut.com/2015/12/tracey-africa-transgender-model-c-v-r.html.

2. Vivian Diller, *Face It: What Women Really Feel as Their Looks Change* (Carlsbad, CA: Hay House, 2011).

3. Noliwe Rooks, *Ladies' Pages: African American Women's Magazines and the Culture That Made Them* (New Brunswick, NJ: Rutgers University Press, 2004).

4. Evelyn Glenn, *Shades of Difference: Why Skin Color Matters* (Redwood City, CA: Stanford University Press, 2009).

5. William M Liu, *Social Class and Classism in the Helping Professions: Research, Theory, and Practice* (Los Angeles: Sage, 2011).

6. Glenn, *Shades of Difference*.

7. Erin Shinners, "Effects of the 'What is Beautiful is Good' Stereotype on Perceived Trustworthiness," *University of Wisconsin LaCrosse Journal of Undergraduate Research* 12 (2009). http://citeseerx.ist.psu.edu/viewdoc/download?doi=10.1.1.500.8086&rep=rep1&type=pdf.

8. Richard Russell, "A Sex Difference in Facial Contrast and its Exaggeration by Cosmetics," *Perception* 38, no. 8 (Janurary 2009): 1211–1219. http://journals.sagepub.com/doi/10.1068/p6331.

9. Catherine Saint Louis, "Up the Career Ladder, Lipstick in Hand," *New York Times*, October 12, 2011, https://www.nytimes.com/2011/10/13/fashion/makeup-makes-women-appear-more-competent-study.html.

10. Arabelle Sicardi, "A Bridge Between Love and Lipstick." *BuzzFeed*, January 21, 2015, https://www.buzzfeed.com/arabellesicardi/queer-beauty.

11. Elline Lipkin, *Girls' Studies* (Berkeley, CA: Seal Press, 2009).

12. Sally K. Ride, interview by Rebecca Wright for NASA Johnson Space Center Oral History Project, October 22, 2002. https://www.jsc.nasa.gov/history/oral_histories/RideSK/RideSK_10-22-02.htm.

13. Carol S. Dweck, "Carol Dweck Revisits the 'Growth Mindset'," *Education Week*, September 23, 2015. https://www.edweek.org/ew/articles/2015/09/23/carol-dweck-revisits-the-growth-mindset.html.

14. United States Department of Labor Bureau of Labor Statistics, "Average Hours Per Day Spent in Selected Activities by Sex and Day," August 10, 2017, https://www.bls.gov/charts/american-time-use/activity-by-sex.htm.

15. Alex L. Jones and R. S. S. Kramer, "Facial Cosmetics and Attractiveness: Comparing the Effect Sizes of Professionally-Applied Cosmetics and Identity." *PLoS ONE* 11, no. 10 (October 2016). http://journals.plos.org/plosone/article?id=10.1371/journal.pone.0164218.

16. Julie Creswell, "Young and in Love . . . With Lipstick and Eyeliner," *New York Times*, November 22, 2017, https://www.nytimes.com/2017/11/22/business/millennials-cosmetics-boom.html.

17. Helena Pike, "At the Gym, Selfie-Ready Makeup," *Business of Fashion*, March 15, 2017. https://www.businessoffashion.com/articles/intelligence/at-the-gym-selfie-ready-makeup.

18. Kyle Buchanan, "Leading Men Age, but Their Love Interests Don't," *Vulture*, April 18, 2013, http://www.vulture.com/2013/04/leading-men-age-but-their-love-interests-dont.html.

CHAPTER 6

1. Barbara Frederickson and Tomi-Anne Roberts, "Objectification Theory: Toward Understanding Women's Lived Experiences and Mental Health Risks," *Psychology of Women Quarterly* 21 (June 1997): 173–206.

2. Michael Housman and Dylan Minor, "Toxic Workers" (working paper 16-057, Harvard Business School, Cabridge, MA, 2015). http://www.hbs.edu/faculty/Publication%20Files/16-057_d45c0b4f-fa19-49de-8f1b-4b12fe054fea.pdf.

3. Colin McNairn, *Sports Talk: How It Has Penetrated Our Everyday Language* (Victoria, BC: Friesen Press, 2017).

4. Thomas Keith, *Masculinities in Contemporary American Culture: An Intersectional Approach to the Complexities and Challenges of Male Identity* (New York: Routledge, 2017).

5. Beth Quinn, "Sexual Harassment and Masculinity: The Power and Meaning of 'Girl Watching'," *Gender and Society* 16, no. 3 (June 2002): 386–402.

6. Amelia Tait, "Spitting out the Red Pill: Former Misogynists Reveal How They were Radicalized Online," *New Statesman*, February 28, 2017, https://www.newstatesman.com/science-tech/internet/2017/02/reddit-the-red-pill-interview-how-misogyny-spreads-online.

7. World Policy Analysis Center, "Preventing Gender-Based Workplace Discrimination and Sexual Harassment: New Data on 193 Countries," (UCLA Fielding School of Public Health, 2017): https://www.worldpolicycenter.org/sites/default/files/WORLD%20Discrimination%20at%20Work%20Report.pdf.

8.   Courtney Connley, "University of Virginia Professor: 'Men Benefit Professionally from Sexual Harassment'," CNBC, November 3, 2017, https://www.cnbc.com/2017/11/03/u-va-professor-men-benefit-professionally-from-sexual-harassment.html.

9.   Jan Wynen, "Sexual Harassment: The Nexus Between Gender and Workplace Quthority: Evidence from the Australian Public Service," *Australian Journal of Public Administration* 75, no. 3 (July 2016): 345–358.

10. Laura Thompson, "'I Can be Your Tinder Nightmare': Harassment and Misogyny in the Online Sexual Marketplace," *Feminism & Psychology* 28, no. 1 (2018): 69–89. http://journals.sagepub.com/doi/abs/10.1177/0959353517720226.

11. Kelly Cue Davis et al., "A Qualitative Examination of Men's Condom Use Attitudes and Resistance: 'It's Just Part of the Game'," *Archives of Sexual Behavior* 43, no. 3 (August 2013): 631–43. doi: 10.1007/s10508-013-0150-9.

12. Stephanie A Sanders, Brandon J. Hill, Richard A. Crosby, and Erick Janssen, "Correlates of Condom-Associated Erection Problems in Young, Heterosexual Men: Condom Fit, Self-Efficacy, Perceptions, and Motivations," *AIDS and Behavior* 18, no. 1 (2014): 128–134. https://www.ncbi.nlm.nih.gov/pmc/articles/PMC3701748/.

13. Evita March and Danielle L. Wagstaff, "Sending Nudes: Sex, Self-Rated Mate Value, and Trait Machiavellianism Predict Sending Unsolicited Explicit Images," *Frontiers in Psychology* 8, no. 2210 (2017). https://www.ncbi.nlm.nih.gov/pmc/articles/PMC5741673/.

14. *Meritor Savings Bank v. Vinson*, 477 U.S. 57 (1986).

15. Enid Nemy, "Women Begin to Speak out Against Sexual Harassment at Work," *New York Times*, August 19, 1975, http://www.nytimes.com/1975/08/19/archives/women-begin-to-speak-out-against-sexual-harassment-at-work.html.

16. Nemy, "Women Begin to Speak out Against Sexual Harassment at Work."

17. Roper Center for Public Opinion Research, "Americans' Response to the Nomination of Clarence Thomas," November/December 1991, https://ropercenter.cornell.edu/public-perspective/ppscan/31/31012.pdf.

18. Ricardo Lopez, "Anita Hill on Sexual Harassment: 'Today, More People Would Believe My Story,'" *Variety*, December 8, 2017, http://variety.com/2017/biz/news/anita-hill-uta-sexual-harassment-1202634689.

19. Helen Brown, *Sex and the Office* (New York: Open Road Media, 2012).

20. C. Feldblum and V. A. Lipnic, *"Select Task Force on the Study of Harassment in the Workplace,"* U.S. Equal Employment Opportunity Commission, June 20, 2016, https://www.eeoc.gov/eeoc/task_force/harassment/upload/report.pdf.

21. Leah Beckmann ed., "It's Impossible to Prevent Someone from Eyefucking You," *Matter*, October 6, 2014, https://medium.com/matter/its-impossible-to-prevent-someone-from-eyefucking-you-a1cd688392b2.

22. Michelle Hamilton, "Running While Female," *Runner's World*, February, 2017, https://www.runnersworld.com/running-while-female.

23. Sarah Jacoby, "As Many as 10 Million People May Have Been Victims of Revenge Porn," Refinery29, December 15, 2016, http://www.refinery29.com/2016/12/133141/revenge-porn-statistics-survey.

24. Shira Tarrant, *The Pornography Industry: What Everyone Needs to Know* (New York and Oxford, UK: Oxford University Press, 2016).

25. Debby Herbenick et al., "Sexual diversity in the United States: Results from a Nationally Representative Probability Sample of Adult Women and Men," *PLoS ONE* 12, no. 7 (July 20, 2017): https://doi.org/10.1371/journal.pone.0181198.

26. Shayna D. Cunningham, Deanna L. Kerrigan, Jacky M. Jennings, and Jonathan M. Ellen, "Relationships Between Perceived STD-Related Stigma, STD-related Shame and STD Screening Among a Household Sample of Adolescents," *Perspectives of Sexual and Reproductive Health* 41, no. 4 (2009): 225–230. https://www.ncbi.nlm.nih.gov/pmc/articles/PMC4334654/.

CHAPTER 7

1. Sarah Overbaugh Hallenbeck, "Writing the Bicycle: Women, Rhetoric, and Technology in Late Nineteenth-Century America," (PhD dissertation, University of North Carolina at Chapel Hill, 2009): https://cdr.lib.unc.edu/indexablecontent/uuid:c39fde6d-c00d-4928-8082-6f9d1e0184ab.

2. D. Herbenick et al., "Sexual Diversity in the United States: Result from a Nationally Representative Probability Sample of Adult Women and Men" *PLOS One* 12, no. 7 (2017): e0181198. https://doi.org/10.1371/journal.pone.0181198.https://doi.org/10.1371/journal.pone.0181198.

3. B. Engel, *Loving Him without Losing You: How to Stop Disappearing and Start Being Yourself* (New York: John Wiley & Sons, 2000).

4. Flora Grant, "Purdue Libraries Land New Rare Items for Amelia Earhart Collection," *Perdue News*, May 2, 2002, https://news.uns.purdue.edu/html4ever/020502.Earhart.donation.html.

5. Sophie Coulombeau, "Why Should Women Change Their Names on Getting Married?" *BBC News Magazine*, November 1, 2014. http://www.bbc.com/news/magazine-29804450.

6. Coulombeau, "Why Should Women Change Their Names on Getting Married?".

7. Claire Cain Miller and Derek Willis, "Maiden Names, on the Rise Again," *New York Times*, June 27, 2015. https://www.nytimes.com/2015/06/28/upshot/maiden-names-on-the-rise-again.html?_r=0.

8. K. Lawson, "Half of Americans Think Women Should Be Required by Law to Take Husband's Name," *Broadly*, January 27, 2017, https://broadly.vice.com/en_us/article/half-of-americans-think-women-should-be-required-by-law-to-take-husbands-name.

9. S. McMillen, *Lucy Stone: An Unapologetic Life* (Oxford: Oxford University Press, 2015).

CHAPTER 8

1. Paul Overberg and Janet Adamy, "What's Your Pay Gap?" *Wall Street Journal*, May 17, 2016, http://graphics.wsj.com/gender-pay-gap/.

2. Shira Tarlo, "What Is Equal Pay Day? Here's Everything You Need to Know," *NBC News*, April 4, 2017, https://www.nbcnews.com/news/us-news/what-equal-pay-day-here-s-everything-you-need-know-n741391.

3. Richard V Reeves and Nathan Joo "Occupational hazard? The Future of the Gender Pay Gap" Brookings Institution, March 7, 2016, https://www.brookings.edu/blog/social-mobility-memos/2016/03/07/occupational-hazard-the-future-of-the-gender-pay-gap.

4. K. Schilt and M. Wiswall, "Before and After: Gender Transitions, Human Capital, and Workplace Experiences," *The B.E. Journal of Economic Analysis & Policy* 8, no. 1, article 39 (2008): http://citeseerx.ist.psu.edu/viewdoc/download?doi=10.1.1.175.6759&rep=rep1&type=pdf.

5. Women's Bureau, "25 Most Common Occupations for Women," U.S. Department of Labor, August 10, 2017, https://www.dol.gov/wb/stats/most_common_occupations_for_women.htm#chart1.

6. J. Traflet, "Gendered Dollars: Pin Money, Mad Money, and Changing Notions of a Woman's Proper Place," *Essays in Economic and Business History* 26, no. 1 (2008): 189–202.

7. J. Warren, *Women, Money, and the Law: Nineteenth-Century Fiction, Gender, and the Courts* (Iowa City: University of Iowa Press, 2009).

8. Suzanne McGee and Heidi Moore, "Women's Rights and Their Money: A Timeline from Cleopatra to Lilly Ledbetter," *The Guardian*, August 11, 2014, https://www.theguardian.com/money/us-money-blog/2014/aug/11/women-rights-money-timeline-history.

9. Claire Cain Miller, "The 24/7 Work Culture's Toll on Families and Gender Equality," *New York Times*, May 28, 2017, https://www.nytimes.com/2015/05/31/upshot/the-24-7-work-cultures-toll-on-families-and-gender-equality.html?_r=0.

10. Meg Lota Brown and Kari Boyd McBride, *Women's Roles in the Renaissance* (Santa Barbara, CA: Greenwood, 2005).

11. Maureen Cronin, "Opinion: 'In the 1950s, I fought the Marriage Ban and Continued Teaching with No Pay'," *TheJournal.ie*, September 9, 2014, http://www.thejournal.ie/readme/marriage-ban-teachers-into-union-1950s-1661077-Sep2014.

12. Ben Zimmer, "Decades of Scorn for 'Trophy' Wives," *The Wall Street Journal*, May 16, 2014, https://www.wsj.com/articles/the-trophy-wife-from-ancient-greece-to-a-song-by-future-1400284908.

13. T. Pollet et al., "The Folden Years: Men from the Forbes 400 Have Much Younger Wives When Remarrying than the General U.S. Population," *Letters on Evolutionary Behavioral Science* 4, no.1 (2013): 5–8.

14. "Women in the Labor Force," U.S. Department of Labor Women's Bureau. (Accessed March 19, 2018): https://www.dol.gov/wb/stats/NEWSTATS/facts/women_lf.htm#four.

15. Claire Cain Miller, "The Motherhood Penalty vs. the Fatherhood Bonus," *New York Times*, September 6, 2014, https://www.nytimes.com/2014/09/07/upshot/a-child-helps-your-career-if-youre-a-man.html.

16. Stephanie Coontz, "Do Millennial Men Want Stay-at-Home Wives?" *New York Times*, March 31, 2017, https://www.nytimes.com/2017/03/31/opinion/sunday/do-millennial-men-want-stay-at-home-wives.html.

17. Stacy Rapacon, "Why Women Should Rethink Their Finances After Divorce," U.S. News & World Report, August 14, 2017, https://money.usnews.com/money/personal-finance/family-finance/articles/2017-08-14/why-women-should-rethink-their-finances-after-divorce.

18. Helen Fisher, *Anatomy of Love: A Natural History of Mating, Marriage, and Why We Stray* (New York: W. W. Norton & Company, 2016).

19. Drew Desilver, "Access to Paid Family Leave Varies Widely Across Employers, Industries," *Fact Tank* (blog), Pew Research Center, March 23, 2017. http://www.pewresearch.org/fact-tank/2017/03/23/access-to-paid-family-leave-varies-widely-across-employers-industries.

20. Isabella Steger, "Researchers Have Figured out Why Almost No Men Take Paternity Leave in a Country that Offers 12 Months of It" *Quartz*, September 22, 2017, https://qz.com/1084591/despite-japans-generous-paternity-leave-only-2-3-of-men-take-it-because-they-think-their-peers-would-disapprove.

21. Leanne Roncolato and Michael E. Martell, "Modern Families: Bargaining and Time-Use in Same-Sex Households." (Paper presented at the annual meeting of the American Economic Association, Chicago, IL, January 2017): https://www.aeaweb.org/conference/2017/preliminary/1740?page=4&per-page=50.

22. Abby Dorsey, "The New Lesbian Dad," *The Advocate*, April 8, 2013, https://www.advocate.com/print-issue/current-issue/2013/04/08/new-lesbian-dad.

23. Becky Ahlberg, "U.S. Single Parent Households," My Safe Harbor. (Accessed January 29, 2018): http://lib.post.ca.gov/Publications/Building%20a%20Career%20Pipeline%20Documents/Safe_Harbor.pdf.

24. Sarah Leonard and Rebecca Rojer, "Housekeepers Versus Harvard: Feminism for the Age of Trump," *The Nation*, March, 2017.

25. A. Fields, *Katharine Dexter McCormick: Pioneer for Women's Rights* (Westport, CT: Praeger, 2003).

26. Kathryn Casteel, "The Minimum Wage Movement Is Leaving Tipped Workers Behind." *FiveThirtyEight*, February 7, 2017, https://fivethirtyeight.com/features/the-minimum-wage-movement-is-leaving-tipped-workers-behind/.

27. U.S. Bureau of Labor Statistics, "Employee Benefits in the United States—March 2017," https://www.bls.gov/news.release/pdf/ebs2.pdf.

28. Anne Colamosca, "Financing by Women, for Them," *New York Times*, February 9, 1975, https://timesmachine.nytimes.com/timesmachine/1975/02/09/76819037.html.

29. Colamosca, "Financing by Women, for Them."

CHAPTER 9

1. S. Ellis, *The Select Works of Mrs. Ellis: Comprising the Women of England, Wives of England, Daughters of England, Poetry of Life, &c., Designed to Promote the Cultivation of the Domestic Virtues* (New York: J. & H. G. Langley, 1843).

2. L. Vapnek, *Elizabeth Gurley Flynn: Modern American Revolutionary* (Boulder, CO: Westview Press, 2015).

3. K. Brown, *Good Wives, Nasty Wenches, and Anxious Patriarchs: Gender, Race, and Power in Colonial Virginia* (Chapel Hill: University of North Carolina Press, 1996).

4. "Scold's bridle, Germany, 1550–1800," Brought to Life, Science Museum, http://broughttolife.sciencemuseum.org.uk/broughttolife/objects/display?id=5343.

5. Robin Lakoff, "Language and Woman's Place," *Language in Society* 2, no. 1 (1973):45–80 (accessed February 3, 2018) https://web.stanford.edu/class/linguist156/Lakoff_1973.pdf.

6. R. Anderson et al., "Vocal Fry May Undermine the Success of Young Women in the Labor Market," *PLOS One* 9, no.5 (2014): e97506. https://doi.org/10.1371/journal.pone.0097506.

7. Markham Heid, "You Asked: What Is Vocal Fry?" *TIME*, November 2, 2017, http://time.com/5006345/what-is-vocal-fry.

8. Ruth Spencer, "Eva: Transgender Voice-Training App Helps Women and Men Talk the Talk," *The Guardian*, June 2, 2015, https://www.theguardian.com/society/2015/jun/02/eva-transgender-voice-training-app.

9. Mary Beard, "The Public Voice of Women," *London Review of Books* 36, no. 6 (2014): 11–14.

10. Beard, "The Public Voice of Women," 11–14.

11. D. Halper, *Invisible Stars: A Social History of Women in American Broadcasting* (New York: Routledge, 2014).

12. Moira Weigel, "Political Correctness: How the Right Invented a Phantom Enemy," *The Guardian*, November 30, 2016, https://www.theguardian.com/us-news/2016/nov/30/political-correctness-how-the-right-invented-phantom-enemy-donald-trump.

13. K. McGonigal, *The Upside of Stress: Why Stress Is Good for You, and How to Get Good at It* (New York: Random House, 2015).

14. "American Time Use Survey Summary," U. S. Department of Labor Bureau of Labor Statistics, June 27, 2017, http://www.bls.gov/news.release/atus.nr0.htm.

15. V. Policarpo, "'The Real Deal': Managing Intimacy within Friendship at a Distance." *Qualitative Sociology Review* 12, no. 2 (2016): 22–42.

16. A. Johnson et al., "Relational Closeness: Comparing Undergraduate College Students' Geographically Close and Long-distance Friendships," *Personal Relationships* 16 (2009): 631–646.

17. Johnson, "Relational Closeness," 631–646.

18. Sarah Ellis, *The Select Works of Mrs. Ellis* (New York: J. & H.G. Langley, 1845).

19. R. De Vogli et al., "Negative Aspects of Close Relationships and Heart Disease," *Archives of Internal Medicine* 167, no. 18 (2007): 1951–1957. http://archinte.jamanetwork.com/article.aspx?articleid=413183.

CHAPTER 10

1. Heidi M. Przybyla and Fredreka Schouten, "At 2.6 Million Strong, Women's Marches Crush Expectations," *USA Today*, January 22, 2017, https://www.usatoday.com/story/news/politics/2017/01/21/womens-march-aims-start-movement-trump-inauguration/96864158.

2. C. Brock, *The Comet Sweeper: Caroline Herschel's Astronomical Ambition* (London: Icon Books, 2007).

3. *On the Media*, "How Talking About Trump Makes Him Normal in Your Brain," WNYC, December 2, 2016, https://www.wnyc.org/story/george-lakoff?tab=transcript.

4. Eric Grundhauser, "The Great Harvard Pee-In of 1973," *Atlas Obscura*, December 23, 2016, https://www.atlasobscura.com/articles/the-great-harvard-peein-of-1973.

5. B. J. Reagon, "Coalition Politics: Turning the Century," *Home Girls: A Black Feminist Anthology*, ed. B. Smith (New York: Kitchen Table: Women of Color Press, 1983).

6. Lisa Wade, "Loretta Ross on the Phrase 'Women of Color'," (blog), *The Society Pages*, March 26, 2011, https://thesocietypages.org/socimages/2011/03/26/loreta-ross-on-the-phrase-women-of-color.

7. D. Fujino, *Heartbeat of Struggle: The Revolutionary Life of Yuri Kochiyama* (Minneapolis: University of Minnesota Press 2005).

8. Mitch Lipka, "Are Women More Generous Than Men?" *Money*, December 1, 2015, http://time.com/money/4130729/women-more-generous-than-men.

9. "Phase 2: The Power of Voice: A New Era of Cause Activation & Social Issue Adoption," The 2017 Millennial Impact Report, http://www.themillennialimpact.com/sites/default/files/reports/Phase2Report_MIR2017_091917_0.pdf.

10. Brayden King, "The Tactical Disruptiveness of Social Movements: Sources of Market and Mediated Disruption in Corporate Boycotts," *Social Problems* 58, no. 4 (2011): 491–517. doi: 10.1525/sp.2011.58.4.491.

11. K. McGonigal, *The Upside of Stress: Why Stress Is Good for You, and How to Get Good at It* (New York: Avery, 2016).

12. X. Zheng et al., "The Unburdening Effects of Eorgiveness: Effects on Slant Perception and Jumping Height," *Social Psychological and Personality Science* 6, no. 4 (2014): 431–38.

13. J. North, "The 'Ideal' of Forgiveness" *Exploring Forgiveness*, eds. R. D. Enright and J. North (Madison: University of Wisconsin Press, 1998).

14. B. Winslow, *Shirley Chisholm: Catalyst for Change* (New York: Avalon Publishing, 2013).

15. Rajini Vaidyanathan, "Before Hillary Clinton, There Was Shirley Chisholm," *BBC News Magazine*, January 26, 2016, http://www.bbc.com/news/magazine-35057641.

16. S. Chisholm, *Unbossed and Unbought* (Boston: Houghton Mifflin, 2010).

17. Kirstie Brewer, "The Day Iceland's Women Went on Strike," *BBC News Magazine*, October 23, 2015, http://www.bbc.com/news/magazine-34602822.

18. "Igbo Women Campaign for Rights (The Women's War) in Nigeria, 1929," Global Nonviolent Action Database, July 15, 2011, https://nvdatabase.swarthmore.edu/content/igbo-women-campaign-rights-womens-war- nigeria-1929.

INDEX

r

race
  anger and, 211
  education and, 65–66,
    69–70
  feminism and, 30–31,
    34–35
  gender wage gap and,
    170, 173, 191, 192
  intersectionality
    and, 9
  ladyhood and, 1–2
  misogyny and, 25
  reproductive justice
    and, 57–59
  stereotypes about,
    66–67, 71–73
Rainey, Gertrude "Ma," 156
rape
  acquaintance, 147
  date, 147
  prevalence of, 142
  spousal, 147
  Title IX and, 145–46
rape acceptance
    myth, 144
rape crisis centers, 147
rape crisis hotlines, 147
rape culture, 142–43, 146
rape kits, 147
rape shield laws, 147
Reagan, Ronald, 32, 179
Reagon, Bernice
    Johnson, 237
Ream, Vinnie, 206
red dress effect, 129
Red Stockings, 246
relationships
  abusive, 140–42, 159
  bonding and, 217–19
  boundaries and, 220–21
  crafting, 157, 164–65
  ending, 159, 222–23
  individuality and,
    163–65
  settling and, 156–57
  See also partners

religious leadership,
    glass ceiling for, 170
reproductive justice,
    57–59
retirement benefits, 173
Rhimes, Shonda, 194
Ride, Sally, 119
Rihanna, 80
Rodin, Judith, 46
role overload, 197
Romans, Sarah, 43–44
Ronson, Jon, 234
Roosevelt, Eleanor, 26
Rosenteur, Phyllis I., 179
Ross, Diana, 112
Ross, Loretta, 57, 238
Rubin, Gayle, 16
rumination, 77

s

Sagan, Carl, 62
Saini, Angela, 207
Sales, Ruby Nell, 228
Sandberg, Sheryl, 188, 194
Sanders, Bernie, 187
sandwich generation,
    181–82
SANEs (sexual
    assault nurse
    examiners), 147
Sanger, Margaret,
    56, 189
savior effect, 174
Schiaparelli, Elsa, 29
Schlafly, Phyllis, 32
Schwab, Lauren, 199
Schweik, Susan M., 110
scold's bridle, 204
second shift, 180, 197
Seear, Kate, 39
self-care, 84–86
self-socializing, 208
self-worth, 11, 84
Selter, Susanna
    Madora, 27
settling, 157

sex
  healing and, 148
  painful, 148
  See also
    masturbation;
    orgasms;
    relationships;
    sexuality; virginity
sex determinism, 99
sexism
  examples of, 27, 46
  neuro-, 64
  Supreme Court
    decisions and, 130
sex objects, 125–26
sexual assault, 144,
    145–46, 199.
    See also rape
sexual attraction,
    153–56, 158
sexual fluidity, 153–56
sexual harassment, 95,
    127, 133–40, 143,
    171, 228
sexuality
  intersectionality
    and, 9
  spectrum of, 10
shame-storming,
    234–35
shampoo, 199
Sheppard, Kate, 226
Sheumaker, Helen, 221
shift and persist, 241–42
Shine Theory, 220
The Shirelles, 112
shopping
  compulsive, 197–98
  sexism and, 199
Sicardi, Arabelle, 116
silencing, 204, 214,
    216–17
Simmons, Gwendolyn
    Zoharah, 227
single mothers
  children's well-being
    and, 186
  by choice, 186

family ties redefined
    by, 187
  income of, 187–88
  stereotypes about, 179
single women, 157–58,
    160, 162–63
Sisulu, Albertina, 250
skinned-knee effect, 70
Slaughter, Anne-Marie,
    194
slut-shaming, 149
small penis
    syndrome, 100
smashes, 154–55
smegma, 103
Smith, Bessie, 156
social media
  misogyny and, 25
  shame-storming and,
    234–35
Social Security, 46,
    173, 182
social stress theory, 197
Solanas, Valerie, 233
Solinger, Rickie, 57
Sontag, Susan, 105
South Asian
    feminisms, 34
Sow, Aminatou, 220
speaking
  risks of, 215
  verbal tics, 212
  voice pitch and, 210,
    212–14
  See also language;
    silencing
specializing, 185
spectatoring, 148
spinsters, 157
sports, 95, 96, 145
spousal rape, 147
Stanton, Elizabeth Cady,
    167, 222
Steinem, Gloria, 15, 193
Stenberg, Amandla, 15
sterilization, 57–59
Stevens, Nettie, 99
Stone, Lucy, 167

Published in the United States by Ten Speed Press, an imprint of the
Crown Publishing Group, a division of Penguin Random House LLC, New York.
www.crownpublishing.com
www.tenspeed.com

Ten Speed Press and the Ten Speed Press colophon are registered trademarks
of Penguin Random House LLC.

Library of Congress Cataloging-in-Publication Data
  Names: Conger, Cristen, author. | Ervin, Caroline, author.
   Title: Unladylike : a field guide to smashing the patriarchy and claiming
      your space / Cristen Conger and Caroline Ervin ; illustrated by Tyler Feder.
   Description: California : Ten Speed Press, [2018] | Includes bibliographical
      references and index.
   Identifiers: LCCN 2018006581
   Subjects: LCSH: Feminism. | Sexism. | Self-esteem in women.
   Classification: LCC HQ1155 .C66 2018 | DDC 305.42—dc23
   LC record available at https://lccn.loc.gov/2018006581

Hardcover ISBN: 978-0-399-58045-1
eBook ISBN: 978-0-399-58046-8

Printed in China

Design by Betsy Stromberg

10 9 8 7 6 5 4 3 2 1

First Edition